Mystery & Tradition

Catholicism for Today's Spiritual Seekers

Joseph Stoutzenberger

Praise for *Mystery & Tradition*

"Stoutzenberger can show the wisdom and beauty of Catholicism with no implied criticism of those who are on a different path. The walls that keep Muslims and Jews, religiously affiliated and "Nones," Catholics and other Christians, and ancient and modern thinkers neatly sorted and separated into non-overlapping circles crumble into the common soil from which they arose: the human search for meaning and purpose."

—**Ann Marie Bahr, PhD, Professor Emerita of Religion, South Dakota State University**

"Written in an engaging style, *Mystery & Tradition* invites the reader into the world of Catholic doctrine, spirituality, liturgy, and prayer. This is a very helpful book for those seeking to know Catholicism in its breadth and depth."

—**Sr. Ilia Delio, OSF, Josephine C. Connelly Endowed Chair in Theology, Villanova University**

"*Mystery & Tradition* is one of those rare finds that is an invaluable help in our ministry as spiritual directors. It is written in an engaging, conversational style, which allows the scholarly and deeply insightful content to be easily accessible. Moreover, each chapter includes questions to ponder and a chapter review. We find that very helpful in our role as facilitators leading small group discussions, and it would also be useful for teachers in classroom settings."

—**Michael and Kathleen Dolan, Spiritual Directors and Associates at Daylesford Abbey, Paoli, PA**

"As an educator, I am excited by all the opportunities *Mystery & Tradition* can provide to the classroom. It is thought-provoking and provides its readers with a compelling case for Catholicism and the church's place in the world today. This book made me proud to be Catholic."

—**Jenai Grigg, PhD, Professor of Sociology and Assistant Dean of General Education, Holy Family University**

"*Mystery & Tradition* is an easy read but reflects solid scholarship as well as insights from a variety of writers, theologians, and saints. Stoutzenberger doesn't avoid controversial topics but addresses them fairly and thoughtfully, inviting readers to do the same. In some ways it is a modern catechism; but unlike most, the questions come after the explanations of Catholic thought and practice. Parish catechumenate teams preparing converts in the Rite of Christian Initiation of Adults would find this to be a valuable resource. It offers ample opportunities for discussion and reflection about timely topics."

—**Glenn Kuhnel, Former Director of Liturgy and Interfaith and Ecumenical Affairs, Diocese of St. Augustine, FL; Author of *The Slaughter of Innocents: A Morality Play***

"While I have been a Catholic all 75 years of my life and have master's degrees in religious education and divinity, I found *Mystery & Tradition* to be informative, authentic, and enriching to my own faith journey. It challenged me to rethink some matters and reexamine what I have always believed. Don't miss this golden opportunity to deepen your own faith journey."

—**Rev. Terry M. Odien, Former President of the National Conference of Diocesan Directors of Religious Education and former Vicar for Clergy, Diocese of Camden, NJ**

"*Mystery & Tradition* deals with real issues such as the decline of religious faith and practice in the USA today and political, cultural, and theological contexts throughout church history. The author evidences neither a conservative nor liberal stance; he simply presents with unusual balance the wisdom and truth of a contemporary Catholic worldview."

—**Father Vincent O'Malley, Priest, Educator, Author**

"Stoutzenberger's book is a lucid and comprehensive presentation of the history of the Catholic Church, an overview of its central tenets, and an examination of its place in the modern world. With clear, accessible prose, he addresses such issues as the Catholic relationship with the Bible, an overview of the gospels and sacraments, the often misunderstood role of Mary in the Church, and the doctrine of the Communion of Saints."

—**Edwin Romond, Poet and Teacher, Author of *Man at the Railing***

"Where can we find hope and meaning in today's world? *Mystery & Tradition* is a gift for our time. The Catholicism Stoutzenberger explains so well offers a vision of how the human community needs to be and a path forward that Catholics and non-Catholics alike would do well to consider. His examples and quotes, as well as his own insights, give readers a sure foundation for following that path."

—**Father Joseph Tedesco, OCSO, Superior of Mepkin Abbey Trappist Monastery, Moncks Corner, SC**

iPub Cloud International

Poughkeepsie, NY 12603

iPubCloud.org

Copyright © 2023 Joseph M. Stoutzenberger

All rights reserved. This book or any portion thereof

may not be reproduced or used in any manner whatsoever

without the express written permission of the publisher

except for the use of brief quotations in a book review.

Library of Congress Control Number: 2023916654

ISBN: 978-1-948575-66-9 (paperback)

ISBN: 978-1-948575-65-2 (ebook)

For Aidan

"All religion begins in wonder."

—A. Heschel

Contents

Preface 1
   A Note on Reading the Text 3
Chapter 1 Religion and Faith 7
   I. Religion 7
   II. Catholic Faith 16
Chapter 2 The Existence of God 29
   I. Origins of Belief in God 29
   II. Can We "Know" God Exists? 34
   III. Atheism: The Denial of God 36
   IV. Imaging God 42
Chapter 3 Scripture: A Gift from God in Word and Story 53
   I. Modern Science and the Bible 53
   II. Catholicism and the Bible 63
   III. The Contents of the Old Testament 68
Chapter 4 The Gospels: The Good News of Christ 79
   I. The Makeup of the New Testament 80
   II. The Four Gospels 87
Chapter 5 Jesus: Word of God Made Flesh 103
   I. The Jesus of History 104
   II. Key Christian Beliefs about Jesus 111
   III. Teachings of Jesus 121
Chapter 6 The Church: Carrying on the Message of Jesus..133
   I. The Church as the People of God 134
   II. The History of the Church 141
   III. Mary's Role in the Church 151
   IV. Saints in a Catholic Worldview 155
Chapter 7 The Catholic Sacramental Worldview 167
   I. Seeing the World as Holy 167
   II. Symbol and Ritual 175
   III. Jesus, the Church, and the Sacraments 180

 IV. Sacramentals: The Richness of Catholic Spirituality 186

Chapter 8 The Sacraments of Initiation 191
 I. Baptism: Initiation into New Life 192
 II. Confirmation: Mission and Witness 201
 III. Eucharist: Christ's Sacrifice Made Present 204

Chapter 9 The Sacraments of Healing and Service 215
 I. Sacraments of Healing 215
 II. Sacraments of Service to the Community 221

Chapter 10 Prayer and Devotions: Catholic Spiritual Practices 235
 I. Pray Always 235
 II. Prayer and the Cycles of Life 241
 III. Catholic Spiritual Practices 247

Chapter 11 Foundations of Catholic Morality 259
 I. Morality and the Message of Jesus 260
 II. Three Foundations of Catholic Morality: Scripture, Natural Law, and Tradition 270
 III. Conscience: Making Moral Judgments 283

Chapter 12 Personal and Social Dimensions of Morality 293
 I. Morality as Right and Wrong Behavior 293
 II. Virtue and Character 300
 III. Modern Catholic Social Teaching 303

Chapter 13 Catholicism Today 315
 I. Pope Francis, Model of Catholicism Today 315
 II. Clergy Abuse and Misuse of Power 324
 III. What Does Catholicism Offer Today? 332

Acknowledgements 345
About the Author 346

Preface

Two Catholic priests were walking through their Philadelphia neighborhood where one of their churches was being torn down to make way for a condominium complex. They asked each other if the tearing down of this one church building was symbolic of where the entire Catholic Church in America was heading. Should Catholicism be demolished, or is there something worth salvaging in it? What might be lost? Would a rich and fruitful source of hope, beauty, and meaning be lost if Catholicism were reduced to ashes? This book explores the makeup of Catholicism and holds onto the belief that there is much in it that is worth saving. However, the Catholicism worth saving cannot be a prepackaged, unchanging, unquestioned Catholicism that does not engage with where people are today. It must be the living, growing, self-critical reality that has, in truth, existed over time and continues to be expressed in the lives of Catholics everywhere.

Though we may not realize it, we are on a spiritual quest. Like other religions, Catholicism invites us to explore, ponder, and analyze "big picture" questions that have plagued human beings from time immemorial. Those questions can be unsettling and frightening. What an awesome privilege and responsibility—and, yes, a burden—it is to probe the meaning of life and to try to figure out what to do about it. Catholicism has a two-thousand-year history of looking into profound questions. What kinds of questions does Catholicism address that we also would do well to consider? To begin with, how about the following:

Is there more to life than what I am usually aware of?
Does anyone or anything give me hope?
Does the message "God is love" mean anything? What does the concept of "God" even mean?
Is there wisdom in ancient scriptures and truths worth pondering in what is handed down by those who came before me?
What do I value, and why do I value it?
Should I care about people I don't know?

How should I decide what the right thing to do is?
Beyond my family, are there people I feel connected to?
Are there symbols and rituals that speak to me powerfully?
Are there traditions I hold onto that give meaning to my life?
Why is there so much suffering and hatred in the world? Aren't we all in this together?
What world am I helping to create that I want to bequeath to my children and grandchildren?

These and more questions are addressed in different chapters of this book. It proposes that Catholicism offers insight into the very questions you might ask yourself in moments of pondering and reflection when you step back from the daily business of life and the distractions that occupy your thinking most of the time. The Catholic worldview is a time-honored lens through which to explore important questions facing all of us, and it is not always what commonplace impressions make it out to be. If you want to learn about where we are as a human community and how we got here, you would do well to include Catholicism as an important part of your study.

This book itself is a "stepping back" in its approach to Catholicism. It provides an overview of Catholic beliefs, practices, and traditions that also seeks to explain the unique worldview that underlies Catholicism—that is, what is behind what Catholics believe and do. Along with basic information, it also seeks to give a *feel* for the religion. Seeing the book's title, Catholics might say, "I know all about that already." Non-Catholics might say, "Why should I care about what Catholicism teaches?" This book has something to offer both audiences. If you are on a quest to understand what life is all about, you can use the discussion of topics to help in your quest wherever you find yourself along that journey. Interspersed throughout the book are questions for reflection and discussion based on information presented in the body of the text. Hopefully, they provide food for thought that can prove fruitful in identifying your own take on the topics.

As an introductory overview, the book does not exhaust the richness of Catholic tradition or its unique worldview. It seeks to explain concepts without relying too heavily on theological terms and language. It is intended to be a conversation—or at least a stimulus for conversation. You will find quotes from various sources that draw on themes in the text as well as concrete examples that illustrate the concepts under discussion. Many of the quotes come from Catholic sources, the Bible and church documents, but many come from non-Catholic sources to mine wisdom from multiple traditions. These inserts provide additional starting points for reflection on the themes addressed in the body of the text. The text does not presume that the reader is Catholic or familiar with Catholicism. It does invite you to think about, analyze, and even question the information presented. As you are reading and your own questions emerge, if nothing else, consider Rilke's counsel and apply it to your study of Catholicism: "Try to love the questions themselves, like locked rooms and like books that are written in a foreign tongue."

A Note on Reading the Text

Before you begin reading, here are some references found frequently in the text.

The Bible consists of two parts, what Christians typically call the Old Testament (OT) and the New Testament (NT). What Christians call the Old Testament is the Jewish Bible, written almost entirely in Hebrew. Because Jews, Christians, and Muslims have different names for the collection of writings in the Jewish Bible/Christian Old Testament, scholars use the term "Hebrew Bible" to refer to this set of writings. The New Testament consists of writings from soon after the time of Jesus; its focus is Jesus, and it was written entirely in Greek. There are many English translations of the Bible. This text uses the New Revised Standard Version (NRSV) translation. The books of the Bible are divided into chapters and verses. If you see a quote followed by a name and numbers, it refers to a particular book and the chapter and verse of that book. For example, John 3:16 means that the passage is from the Gospel according to John, chapter 3, verse 16. This book uses "Old Testament" and "New Testament" for the two sections of the Bible recognized by Christians.

Vatican Council II. The world's Catholic bishops met in Rome over the course of three years, from 1962 to 1965. The council examined Catholic teaching and practice and produced several documents that have guided the church ever since. The entire collection of documents can be found on the Vatican website (www.vatican.va) under "The Documents of Vatican Council II."

Catechism of the Catholic Church (referred to throughout the text as the *Catechism*). In 1985, a gathering of bishops decided that it would be valuable to produce a summary of Catholic teaching—a catechism—as a reference for church leaders and teachers directly, and all Catholics indirectly. The previous official catechism was published after the Council of Trent, which took place from 1545 to 1563. The new catechism was translated into English in 1992. The entire *Catechism* is posted on the website of the United States Conference of Catholic Bishops (www.usccb.org). Both the documents of Vatican Council II and the *Catechism* are divided into numbered sections for easy reference.

Quotes in the text from church documents and other sources at times use "man" or "men" in the generic sense to refer to "men and women." Rather than change the language in quotes to comply with today's usage, the text keeps the terminology as it is found in the translation of scripture and church documents used.

The abbreviation "St." is used for a person officially recognized as a saint by the church.

In the middle of the sixth century, a Christian monk named Dionysius Exiguus was given the task of creating a calendar consistent with what was known at the time about months and years. He set the birth of Jesus as he understood it to have happened as the beginning of a new age and called it AD, *Anno Domini*, "in the year of the Lord." The years before that he labeled AC, for *Ante Christum* (in Latin, "before Christ"). An English scholar named Bede changed that to BC for the English "before Christ." For over half a century now scholars have recognized that those designations have a Christian orientation and may indicate a lack of sensitivity to non-Christians. However, the calendar with this designation has been in use for fifteen hundred years and is standard around the world. Replacing it would be cumbersome, and what would take its place as a starting point? The creation of the world, as in Jewish tradition? The founding of the city of Rome, as in the pre-Christian Latin tradition? The founding of the city of Medina as a formal community of Muslims, as in Islam? A suggestion came out of these discussions among scholars: Keep the calendar intact but change the designation "AD" to "CE," for Common Era—that is, the "commonly accepted era," and change "BC" to "BCE," for "Before the Common Era." This book follows the Common Era system.

An Incarnational and Sacramental Perspective. The terms "incarnation" and "sacrament" are key to appreciating a Catholic worldview. These concepts refer to a perspective on the human condition and reality itself that is uniquely Catholic. Explanations and illustrations of these concepts run throughout the book.

Chapter 1
Religion and Faith

Catholicism is a religion with a history. Its starting point is the person of Jesus. To understand Catholicism, we must explore what religion is and its role in human existence. Religion takes people into depths of experience that evade easy explanations and that are hidden behind what we typically are aware of as we go about our daily business. All religions require faith. Catholicism is rooted in a two-thousand-year-old faith in Jesus. This chapter looks at the concepts of religion and faith to help us understand Catholicism and its view of ultimate reality and the meaning of human life.

> Therefore, the human spirit must be cultivated in such a way that there results a growth in its ability to wonder, to understand, to contemplate, to make personal judgments, and to develop a religious, moral, and social sense.
>
> Vatican Council II, "The Church in the Modern World," #59

I. Religion

Have you ever pondered the "bigger questions" and "profound mysteries" of life? What are those questions, and what brought on those questions?

To whom do you go for help and guidance in making sense of them?

Are there sources of wisdom from the past that shed light on these questions? Sacred writings or revered teachers that you have gained wisdom from?

Is there a larger community that supports you in your pursuit of insights into these questions?

What gives you hope?

Jesus, Christianity, and Catholicism

Jesus, the Good News

> The good news of Jesus Christ, the Son of God.
>
> Mark 1:1

What are the basics of the Catholic faith? You might think that "Catholic faith" refers to a set of basic beliefs, such as those listed in what are known as the ***Apostles' Creed*** and the ***Nicene Creed***, both of which are treasured by Catholics and other Christians alike. However, the creeds were not written and promulgated until centuries after the beginning of Christianity. Something more basic that planted the seed of the Christian movement preceded the creeds: Jesus is good news! In the beginning was an experience. The experience, no more easily articulated than falling in love is, was a sense that my life matters, there is cause for hope, I am not alone, someone cares, we're all connected. In the midst of the uncertainties of life, there is meaning. An early account of this experience, known as the Gospel according to Mark, called it "good news," which is the meaning of the word gospel. The good news sprang from encounters with a man known to history as Jesus, who came to be recognized as a fellow human being—yes, but also as more than human. He himself was the good news, a doorway into that mystery of life in which all of us find ourselves. What he said and did and meant transformed the world. He walked the earth briefly but left friends and followers to spread the good news, as best they could, not just in words but also in deeds.

A sixth-century image of Christ in St. Catherine's monastery on Mt. Sinai in Egypt

More and more people found good news in their own encounters with Jesus—who came to be known as the Christ—even though they had not met him in the flesh. Christian communities told stories, prayed together, celebrated together, and carried on the work of Jesus. They kept the good news alive; it was too precious to let die. Right from the start they also had their disagreements, as any human community would. In different places there came to be different ways of talking about Jesus, different styles of worship, different ways of interpreting the message. Through it all, the basic message remained: Jesus Christ is good news because he is the Son of God, the long-awaited Messiah-king anticipated by Jews of the time, one who experienced death itself and conquered it, and the savior of the world. "The world," life itself, can be an agonizing experience, filled with pain and grief and sorrow. Jesus pointed to a deeper reality. He himself experienced the agony but was the embodiment of hope because he embodied a love that surpassed all human understanding from a source that was beyond human comprehension.

What Does "Christian" Mean?

The various communities dedicated to Jesus became known as "followers of the Way" and then simply as "Christians." Some leaders of those communities reminded everyone of their unity despite their diversity and talked about their faith being in the "catholic" church. ***Catholic*** means universal or whole. This is a faith that is not identified with one local community as opposed to others; true faith is found throughout the whole—like yeast in bread, an image Jesus himself used. Therefore, the opposite of "catholic" in its original meaning is narrow-mindedness or short-sightedness, separating oneself from others. The designation "Catholic" was synonymous with "Christian" until some major divisions occurred. In the eleventh century, a split occurred between the churches of the eastern part of the Roman Empire, centered in the capital city of Constantinople, and the church in the west, centered in the old capital of Rome. In the east, the Christian churches that rejected union with the pope took the name ***Orthodox***; only a few in the east remained in union with the western church and continued to call themselves *Catholic*. Another separation occurred in the western church in the sixteenth century. By the middle of that century *Catholic* was a term to identify a church community distinct from other Christians in Western Europe, who became known as ***Protestants***.

What Does "Catholic" Mean?

For better or for worse, "Catholic" today is used to designate an identity separate from other Christian groups: Catholic, as opposed to Orthodox; Catholic, as opposed to Protestant. Lately there has even been a well-intentioned further distinction: "I'm not Catholic (or Baptist or Lutheran or Presbyterian, etc.), but Christian." The last designation—"I'm Christian"—is an attempt to leap over the past two thousand years of history and focus solely on one's personal relationship with Jesus. That's not the Catholic understanding of what it means to be Christian. Universality did not wash away diversity, even from the very beginning of the Christian movement. For instance, a man named Simon, renamed Peter by Jesus himself, came to the startling realization that people didn't have to become Jewish to join the Christian community. His realization, brought forth by the missionary St. Paul and agreed upon by the elders of the community, opened the door to diversity, and as a result some Christians ate pork, as was customary in their culture but something Jesus most assuredly never did. Greek soon took over as the language of choice in this more diversified community—again, not the language commonly spoken by Jesus—or the first apostles, for that matter. Jewish Christians and Gentile (non-Jewish) Christians both shared the same good news but brought distinctly different perspectives to it. Followers of the Way down in Egypt, up in Ephesus, and over in Rome blended Christianity with their own cultures in ways that Christians back in Jerusalem were not expecting. The good news of Jesus has a history, and it has a home within communities of flesh-and-blood people. It is not a static reality untouched by human hands.

Of course, a Catholic worldview shares much in common with other Christian groups, with other religions, and even with well-meaning people who seek the truth without identifying with any religion. The recognition that the good news of Jesus is for everyone, even if they are not Catholic, has had a choppy history, emphasized at some times and in some places more than in others. Since the Second Vatican Council in the 1960s, the official Catholic position is that all people of goodwill can work together for the common good, as discussed in chapter 13. Pope Francis expressed this view in a 2017 homily: "The Lord has redeemed all of us, all of us, with the Blood of Christ: all of us, not just Catholics. Everyone! 'Father, the atheists?' Even the atheists. Everyone! ... We must meet one another doing good. 'But I don't believe, Father. I am an atheist!' But do good: We will meet one another there."

What associations immediately come to mind when you think about Christianity today?
What associations come to mind when you think about Catholicism today?
Do those associations express good news for you? Explain.

All nations form but one community. This is so because all stem from the same stock, which God created to people the entire earth, and also because all share a common destiny, namely God.

Catechism, #842

Religion: Doorway to Mystery

Religion doesn't exist; only religions do. That being said, all religions attempt to achieve a similar purpose. They recognize that we exist in a sea of mystery, like fish in water. At times, there are breakthroughs into our awareness of that mystery, cracks in the wall that let a sliver of light into the darkness of our consciousness. Religions attest to that breakthrough and try to make sense of it. The great twentieth-century rabbi Abraham Heschel tells us that all religion begins in wonder. He often used a more bracing term: ***radical amazement***. One must pause and wonder to let the light shine through. What a dull existence it would be if there were no room for amazement! What is truly amazing is to glimpse that which is holy, the sacred. In his book *Radical Judaism*, a student of Heschel's named Rabbi Arthur Green says this about an experience of the holy: "The 'sacred' refers to an inward, mysterious sense of awesome presence, a reality deeper than the kind we ordinarily experience." To attain that sense, we need to break through the "mask of ordinariness." Moments of astonishment, Green tells us, are for him the starting point of his religious life.

Mystery. Wonder. Amazement. Astonishment. Are these words you associate with the pursuit of truth? Surely, they are words we would associate with science. Galileo pondered the mystery of the movement of the sun and the earth, which led him to break through the "mask" of ordinary perception that the sun revolves around the earth. It's safe to say that every scientific discovery began in wonder. Religions probe even deeper into the mystery we find ourselves in. American mystic Howard Thurman quotes sociologist Russell Gordon Smith to remind us that wonder should not end at the door to the chemistry lab:

> The scientific mood does not imply that other moods are fatuous or futile; it does not hold that truths it enables men to discover are the only truths. ... [The scientist] knows too well that behind the symbols of mathematics and the formulae of chemistry and physics and the rigid generalizations of psychology and social sciences lie the unexplained mysteries of twilight and music, of autumn nights fringed with silver, of human fortitude and idealism. (*The Mood of Christmas and Other Celebrations*, p. 4)

There's a human quality to the mysteries that science can't explain. Thurman and his sociologist friend point out that those mysteries, hard if not impossible to grasp, are who we are and what the ground of our being is. They deserve our attention and should be approached with wonder and awe. They are what we might call holy, since they pertain to the wholeness of reality. The fact that our minds cannot fully comprehend this all-encompassing mystery is no reason to dismiss it. Actually, isn't the opposite true? The *Catechism* (#237) reminds us of the "hiddenness" of mystery but also that God leaves "traces" of what the essential mystery is. A word for this quality of mystery is ***ineffable***, which describes something that is too great to be expressed or described in words. The search for understanding mystery and insightful ways to talk about it is the quest of a lifetime, a religious quest. Our religion is our response to the mystery of life.

Religious Questions

Theologian Hans Küng lists questions that religions address: "Where do we come from and where do we go? Why do what we do? Why is the world as it is? Why are we here? What then is the ultimate reason and meaning of all reality?" He then asks:

> Is there something which sustains us in all this, which never permits us to despair? Something stable in all change, something unconditioned and absolute in the relativizing experienced

everywhere? And what is the character of this ultimate reality? Good or evil? Indifferent or friendly to human beings? Incomprehensible, without any qualities, or perhaps even greater than all that can be conceived? It is that utterly reasonable and yet more than reasonable reliance on an ultimate great mystery in our life which demands trust, requires a commitment, and which at the same time makes it possible both to stand still and to go forward. (*Reforming the Church Today*, p. 131)

What is clear from Hans Küng's list of questions is that any examination of life that does not include the spiritual is only partial. Traditionally, religions have been the conduit for exploring these ultimate questions and seeking some window into ultimate mystery. Nowadays, science is also looking into such questions, hopefully in partnership with and not in dismissal of insights from religions.

Explain the message in the Hans Küng quote. What is your response to his message?

The State of Religion Today

The Pew Research Center regularly polls to find the percentage of Americans who identify with a religion or attend religious services. The headline on their website for a number of years now reads, "US decline of Christianity continues at a rapid pace." Americans who self-identify as Christian declined from 74 percent to 65 percent over the decade of the twenty-teens. Americans who self-identify as atheists, agnostics, or "nothing in particular" have risen to 26 percent, giving rise to a new designation for people with no particular religious affiliation: *nones*. Americans who say they attend religious services only a few times a year have increased to 54 percent, while 45 percent attend services at least once a month, which is down 10 percent over the decade. Other religions aren't faring any better than Catholicism, and it's hard to imagine that this downward trend will reverse anytime soon. Still, a lot of Americans do consider themselves religious, much more so than in other Western countries. So-called atheists are still looked upon as outliers by many Americans. For instance, unlike in many other countries, it's hard to imagine a self-described atheist being elected president of the United States. On the other hand, Ron Reagan, the son of President Ronald Reagan, has actually done commercials on cable television sponsored by the Freedom from Religion Foundation espousing the values of atheism.

It is inaccurate to lump all nones together. Some people who grew up in a religious household and no longer practice are simply indifferent to religion. Others are antagonistic to religion and think the world would be better off without any form of it. Since the number of nones is growing steadily, a question is, what is to become of those fundamental questions about the mystery of life posed by Hans Küng and others, questions that only religions seem to ask? Canadian philosopher Charles Taylor calls the current trend toward dismissing religion *progressive disenchantment*. He observes that we have moved "from a society where belief in God is unchallenged and indeed, unproblematic, to one in which it is understood to be one option among others and frequently not the easiest to embrace." Another way he poses the question is this: Why is it so much harder to believe in God today than it was five hundred years ago? We might add, Why is it harder to believe today than it was even seventy years ago? Timothy Egan describes the problem this way in *A Pilgrimage to Eternity*: "We are spiritual beings. But for many of us malnutrition of the soul is a plague of modern life." Huston Smith uses the term "amnesia" to describe the dominant modern spirit—spiritual amnesia.

Some nones don't concern themselves with questions about ultimate reality. Others are what Taylor calls "seekers." That is, they are searching for insights into the great mysteries of life but eschew traditional religions and conventional terms such as *god*, *heaven*, *hell*, and *sin*. Seekers might describe themselves as "spiritual, but not religious." They might look to alternative sources of truth, such as Buddhism, which they may interpret to be "religionless religion" (an interpretation that seems inaccurate if you actually go to most Buddhist temples). They might dismiss Christians as actually being the nonseekers since they perceive Christians as uncritically holding onto beliefs that are unfounded in science, experience, or common sense. Shouldn't nonreligious people and religious people alike, including Christians, be seekers, open to new understandings and interpretations of truth?

In Mark's Gospel, Jesus encounters a man whose son is sick. The man pleads for Jesus to help his son. Jesus tells him that all things are possible for one who believes. "Immediately the father of the child cries out, 'I believe; help my unbelief!'" (9:24). Perhaps this expresses a perspective on the profound mysteries of life that Christians can share with nones who are seekers. When faced with the challenges that call into question the very meaning of life, both cry out. They don't just think about things in a dispassionate manner. The cry is a plea for wisdom, some insight into the purpose of life and our place in the grand scheme of existence. It is a pursuit that engages their entire being: mind and heart, soul and guts. The father's response to Jesus reminds us of how inadequate we are when faced with mystery. Ultimate truth always seems to be just over the horizon or fluttering among the shadows in a dense forest. We can say, "I believe," but that pronouncement is always followed by "Help my unbelief." Belief and unbelief are not the polar opposites they appear to be. When belief becomes absolute certitude, it is no longer belief. Even Christians can relate, at least at times, to the sentiments expressed in the opening lines of that most Catholic of poems, Dante's *Divine Comedy*: "Midway upon the journey of our life / I found myself within a dark forest, / For the straightforward path had been lost."

> This search for God demands of man every effort of intellect, a sound will, "an upright heart," as well as the witness of others who teach him to seek God.
>
> *Catechism*, #30

> Are you, or do you know, a none when it comes to religion? How would you describe their understanding of religion and the questions posed by religions?
>
> Do you agree with Charles Taylor that it is harder to believe in God today than it was two generations ago? If so, why is that? Talk to an older person about what they believe about the great mystery of life.
>
> Can you relate to a young girl's experience as described in this exchange between her and a hookah-smoking caterpillar sitting on a mushroom? What role can religion play, given the precarious nature of human existence?

"Who are *you*?" said the Caterpillar.

> Alice replied, rather shyly: "I—I hardly know, sir, just at present—at least I know who I *was* when I got up this morning, but I think I must have been changed several times since then."
>
> "What do you mean by that?" said the Caterpillar sternly. "Explain yourself!"
>
> "I can't explain *myself*, I'm afraid, sir," said Alice, "because I'm not myself, you see. … I can't understand it myself to begin with and being so many different sizes in a day is very confusing."
>
> <div align="right">Lewis Carroll, <i>Alice in Wonderland</i></div>

Catholicism proposes that in the midst of uncertainty and the ever-present pull of unbelief there is the person of Jesus, who lived the human experience and gave his life to demonstrate that there is meaning and purpose to life and grounds for hope. That proposition brings us to the question of faith, specifically Catholic faith.

II. Catholic Faith

Catholics tend not to use the term "the Catholic religion." Instead, they talk about "Catholic faith" or even "*the* Catholic faith." Thomas H. Groome of Boston College points out that there are multiple dimensions to faith as Catholics understand it. Each dimension blends with the others. Here are four elements of faith that help clarify how the term is understood and lived by Catholics.

Heart: Faith as Basic Trust

> It is only with the heart that one can see rightly; what is essential is invisible to the eye.
>
> Antoine de Saint-Exupery

Shortly before his death, the noted psychologist Carl Jung was interviewed on British television. Jung delved more deeply into the spiritual dimensions of the human psyche than any of his contemporary psychologists, so the interviewer naturally asked him, "After all of your study into the human soul, do you still believe in God?"

Jung chuckled at first and then replied, "I don't believe in God. … I know there's God."

How could a person of science such as Jung make such an unequivocal statement? The *Catechism* also talks about "the certitude of faith." Jung and the authors of the *Catechism* seem to be referring to a different kind of knowing from what we normally understand by that word. They assuredly are not relying on scientific proof, at least not as we know it. As much as "creationists" would want it to be, the question of faith in God is not a discussion for biology class. (**Creationists** claim that the universe and creatures in their current state came into existence all at once in one divine act and that this theory deserves to be presented in science textbooks as much as the theory of evolution and the big bang theory do.) People of faith are talking about a different kind of knowing—a "knowing of the heart." Religious truths cannot be found under a microscope or through probing the skies at night with powerful telescopes. Nonetheless, to dismiss heart knowledge is to overlook an essential dimension of being human.

To call this type of knowledge "knowing of the heart" is not to reduce it merely to a feeling; it is not anti-intellectual. Rather, it is more like what psychologist and philosopher William James called *noetic*, related to the Greek word *gnosis* and the English word "know." (See his *Varieties of Religious Experience*, first published in 1902.) It's not the result of scientific experimentation but of spiritual experience. It involves an intense experience of illumination, of gaining insight into "knowing how things are." Perhaps we could call it an "Aha!" moment when everything suddenly fits together. Describing such knowledge in rational terms never seems to do it justice and actually diminishes it. That quality of ineffability, of not being able quite precisely to put into words, does not take away from it as a valid and essential form of knowing.

It's not as if a priest or religion teacher can hand you a book and say, "Read this and you'll know the Catholic faith." Faith is as much a matter of the heart as of the head. Saying "I believe" or "I agree" to a set of beliefs doesn't make someone Catholic. Underlying the reality of faith are experiences and commitments that cannot be reduced to words. Catholic faith doesn't mean "I know a lot about God." Catholic faith means that, through no merit of my own, I recognize that God exists and that God loves me. Catholics base that belief on Jesus, whom they know through the church and experience through their family, friends, and communities. *For Catholics, an experience of God in Jesus Christ is the basic meaning of faith.*

As a matter of the heart, faith means trusting in God; it's a relationship. Like loving, being loved, and being hopeful, faith is a gift. Think about what it means to say that faith is a gift. It can't be forced. You can't *make* someone believe. And yet the *Catechism* points out that faith in God is a very human, natural experience, as natural as breathing or holding a child's hand when crossing a street. "Trusting in God and cleaving to the truths he has revealed are contrary neither to human freedom nor to human reason" (#154). The *Catechism* says that we find this kind of trust manifest in human relations just as it exists in a relationship with God, such as "when a man and a woman marry" (#154). Although faith is a grace—that is, a gift bestowed on people—nonetheless, human beings actively receive and cooperate with that gift (just as married couples do). "In faith, the human intellect and will cooperate with divine grace" (#155).

The heart of Catholic faith, then, is trusting in God through Jesus. It is closely aligned with hope, that is, openness to the not-yet and to that which is not immediately evident. It doesn't mean not having doubts or questions. It certainly doesn't mean always living up to the ideals Catholics set for themselves. (Ask any married couple how well they succeed in living up to ideals in their relationship.) It does mean that, when times are rough, people of faith know in their hearts that they have a special companion who shares their lives. Faith means responding with profound gratitude to the great mystery of life we find ourselves in—a deep feeling of trust that God cares and is infinitely more passionate about us than we humans could ever be. "I believe; help my unbelief!"

> Listen! I am standing at the door, knocking; if you hear my voice and open the door, I will come in to you and eat with you, and you with me.
>
> Revelation 3:20

Think about and discuss the following question: Are human beings religious by their very nature?

Muslims say that nonhuman creatures, such as trees and horses, are "religious" by their very nature because they instinctively surrender to God's will, while human beings must choose whether to follow God's will. What understanding of religion is being expressed in this belief?

Head: Basic Catholic Beliefs

While Catholicism recognizes faith as (a) a personal relationship with Jesus and (b) heartfelt trust in a loving God, it is fair to say that many non-Catholic Christians place greater emphasis on this understanding of faith than Catholics do. Catholics tend to feel uncomfortable when an evangelical Christian asks them, "Do you accept Jesus as your personal Lord and Savior?" Some Christians can name the date and time of day when they "accepted Jesus into their heart." Not so for Catholics. If anything, Catholics are more likely to state what they believe, as if "faith" meant a list of such beliefs. Two historical events led to Catholicism emphasizing a "head" understanding of faith, that is, "the Catholic faith" as a set of beliefs.

In the year 325 CE, **Constantine**, the Roman emperor at the time, was upset over the bickering he saw among the Christians who inhabited the empire. He was not Christian himself, but a growing number of his subjects were, and arguments were clearly getting out of hand. There are unbelievable, but true, accounts from the time of Christian-versus-Christian intrigue and fighting over what is the right way to speak about Jesus, his relationship with God, and other fundamental teachings. Constantine gathered together church leaders at his summer palace in Nicaea, a town north of his capital city, Constantinople. Even though he was not a baptized Christian, he opened the meeting and told them to come to an agreement on a set of teachings that all Christians needed to accept. Anyone who would not comply would be banished from the empire. The church leaders—many of the world's bishops but not the pope, who lived in faraway Rome—hammered out a concise statement of core Christian beliefs. They were not trying to invent new teachings but to identify commonly accepted teachings they saw as originating with the apostles themselves and enunciated in the gospels and the other writings of the Christian scriptures. The statement of beliefs they arrived at is called the *Nicene Creed*, or "the Creed of the Council of Nicaea." More precisely, it is the Nicene-Constantinopolitan Creed, since a later council held in Constantinople made slight additions to it. It is still recited at Catholic Masses and accepted by most Protestant communities. It serves as the basis for questions asked of candidates for baptism or initiation into the church. It was designed to be a teaching tool. ("You say you believe in God and Jesus Christ? This statement summarizes for you what that means.")

Later in Christian history, when a divide occurred in Western Europe between what are known today as Protestants and Catholics, the Catholic Church again saw a need to clarify exactly what was a proper understanding of Christian beliefs and practices. Some Protestants rejected key beliefs, such as how to understand the presence of Christ in the Eucharist. There was a presumption among Catholics that faith in God and a relationship with Jesus were essential. However, the church of the time saw a need to spell out precisely what Catholics believed about many matters to distinguish Catholic beliefs from what "those Protestants" were proposing. Thus, the term "the Catholic faith" referred to a set of beliefs. To be Catholic meant to accept those beliefs.

The Nicene Creed

I believe in one God,
the Father almighty,
maker of heaven and earth,
of all things visible and invisible.

I believe in one Lord Jesus Christ,
the Only Begotten Son of God,
born of the Father before all ages.
God from God, Light from Light,
true God from true God,
begotten, not made, consubstantial with the Father;
through him all things were made.
For us men and for our salvation
he came down from heaven,
and by the Holy Spirit was incarnate of the Virgin Mary,
and became man.

For our sake he was crucified under Pontius Pilate,

he suffered death and was buried,
and rose again on the third day
in accordance with the Scriptures.
He ascended into heaven
and is seated at the right hand of the Father.
He will come again in glory
to judge the living and the dead
and his kingdom will have no end.

I believe in the Holy Spirit, the Lord, the giver of life,
who proceeds from the Father and the Son,
who with the Father and the Son is adored and glorified,
who has spoken through the prophets.

I believe in one, holy, catholic and apostolic Church.
I confess one Baptism for the forgiveness of sins
and I look forward to the resurrection of the dead
and the life of the world to come. Amen.

If you are familiar with the creed, try to read it with fresh eyes.
Which statements in the Nicene Creed are most appealing to you?
What in the creed has made it so sustaining and life-affirming for Christians today and down through the ages?
Which statements do you find most baffling?
What is your overall reaction to the creed?

Hands: Faith That Is Lived

Our moral life has its source in faith in God who reveals his love to us.

Catechism, #2087

Catholic faith is "hands-on" faith. St. Paul tells us that "if I have prophetic powers, and understand all mysteries and all knowledge, and if I have all faith, so as to remove mountains, but do not have love, I am nothing" (1 Corinthians 13:2). Faith is a response, entering into life with care and compassion. It's like saying, "Do you want love? Go out and be loving." Catholic faith is faith-in-action. A fundamental Catholic belief is that Jesus is both divine and human. Therefore, Catholics don't just look up to see God; they also look around. For Catholics, Christ is God spending time with us in multiple ways. St. Mother Teresa of Calcutta modeled this Catholic understanding of faith in action. She gathered together a group of women who spent time in the presence of Christ in the Eucharist each morning and then spent the rest of the day in the presence of Christ "in the poorest of the poor." She talked about kneeling down before Christ during Mass and then kneeling down to help people who were literally dying on the streets. She saw Christ in both disguises. Mother Teresa reminded Catholics that being a person of faith means spending time on the work that Jesus spent time on. For her work with those who are poor and downtrodden throughout the world, Mother Teresa was awarded the Nobel Peace Prize in 1979. Faith can never be separated from action, just as pronouncements of love ring hollow if never shown in deeds.

If we read the gospels, we get a sense of Jesus's message about faith as lived out in service to others. He healed, body and soul. He offered forgiveness. He was hospitable to all kinds of people, especially toward people often disdained by others. He shared meals with people whom polite society said he shouldn't eat with. Above all, he told people that God loves them and that they in turn should love one another. Jesus never separated faith from action. In fact, he even told people that if on their way to pray in the synagogue they realized that there was someone whom they had not forgiven, then they should first go seek that person's forgiveness. Good deeds take priority as expressions of faith. Pause for a moment and think about loving service as an act of faith. Why should anybody help anyone else? It can only mean that they perceive a reality greater than the obvious. We appear to be separate individuals. It takes faith to

St. Mother Teresa, founder of Missionaries of Charity

recognize a deeper truth, that we are in fact interconnected, all part of one body. Faith takes us to that deeper truth, and doing good for others is the embodiment of that truth. John Dunne gave expression to this Christian vision of faith four hundred years ago in his famous poem: "No man is an island entire of itself, every man / Is a piece of the continent, a part of the main ... any man's death diminishes me, / Because I am involved in mankind." For Catholics, every act of kindness is an act of faith.

In God's eyes our words have only the value of our actions.

St. Ignatius Loyola

Why does Catholicism assert that an act of kindness is an act of faith? Explain and illustrate what it means.
Who models faith-in-action for you? Tell their story.

Soul: Faith That Animates Us

In Sacred Scripture the term "soul" often refers to human life or the entire human person. But "soul" also refers to the innermost aspect of man, that which is of greatest value to him.

Catechism, #363

Catholicism proclaims that there is a "more than," or "greater than," dimension to the human condition. In Hebrew, the word for "soul" or "spirit" is the same word used for "breath" or "wind" (*ruah*). Catholics believe that the breath of life breathed into each of us by God doesn't end when our bodily organs cease to function. Our life is greater than our physical existence. We could dissect our entire body and account for all the memories stored in our mind and still not capture all that we are. We need more than biology class or psychology class or even philosophy class to learn about the totality of human existence. Imagine what human life would be without the soul. Images from science fiction movies come to mind in which human bodies are transformed into soulless creatures. Perhaps our worst dreams *are* true: we are surrounded by soulless "pod people"! Without souls, true human life would not exist, and faith would be impossible. Through the grace of God, we actually share in divine life. We exist in communion with God.

Catholic faith affirms this soulful "the whole is greater than the sum of its parts" dimension to human existence. Behind our thoughts and deeds, our feelings and relationships, is the soul that animates all that we are. It energizes us and makes living in response to faith possible. To speak of the soul is to humbly accept the awesome mystery that there is more to us than we imagine. Catholic faith is faith in God and in God's presence in the depth of our being.

> There are more things in heaven and earth, Horatio,
> Than are dreamt of in your philosophy.
>
> William Shakespeare, *Hamlet*, Act I, Scene 5

> Imagine that you went to college to study "the humanities," that is, a course of study about what it means to be human. What courses would you include in such a program? Anatomy and physiology? Sociology? Psychology? Anthropology? Philosophy? Make a case that a "religion" course should or should not be included.
>
> Imagine writing an autobiographical book titled *The Story of My Soul*. What might you say in it?

Faith: A Personal Quest

> A cursory glance at ancient history shows clearly how in different parts of the world, with their different cultures, there arise at the same time the fundamental questions which pervade human life. … We find [them] in the writings of Israel, as also in the Veda and the Avesta; we find them in the writings of Confucius and Lao-Tze, and in the preaching of Tirthankara and Buddha; they appear in the poetry of Homer and in the tragedies of Euripides and Sophocles, as they do in the philosophical writings of Plato and Aristotle. They are questions which have their common source in the quest for meaning which has always compelled the human heart.
>
> Pope St. John Paul II, *Fides et Ratio*, "On the Relationship between Faith and Reason," #1

Faith is a delicate matter. The death of a loved one can bolster faith or send it crashing down. A late-night intimate exchange among friends can be a "peak experience" when some sense of the meaning of life comes upon us, if only for a moment. To be human is to be a seeker. The quest can be so frustrating that we might push it aside and settle for going about our business: "I'll worry about those nagging questions about what it all means sometime in the future. Right now, I have to get to work!" For Catholics, their faith provides an anchor holding them steady so that they can go about their business in freedom and reassurance. They may sway in one direction or another as the wind blows, but their faith keeps them connected to the person, Jesus, who reveals the true nature of human life, its meaning and destiny.

Catholicism has many aspects worthy of study and analysis and even deserving of criticism. Some of what we learn from history or hear about in news reports related to Catholicism today is actually "Catholic bashing"—undeserved criticism. However, some things we find out leave us shaking our heads in disbelief. Behind it all is good news, which is where this chapter began. To lose sight of that is to miss the fundamental message of Catholic faith. It is understandable if the light of faith dims at times; that's part of the quest as well. St. Paul always seems to anticipate our concerns in his letters:

> When I was a child, I spoke like a child; when I became an adult, I put an end to childish ways. For now we see in a mirror, dimly, but then we will see face to face. Now I know only in part; then I will know fully, even as I have been fully known.
>
> 1 Corinthians 13:11–12

The last line is reassuring for Catholics. Catholic faith doesn't require "knowing God." Catholic faith is simply accepting that God knows us. As Catholics might say when faced with the great questions of life, "Leave it in God's hands."

Having read the chapter, describe your response to the following terms: religion, faith, Catholic faith.

Chapter Review

1. What does the word *gospel* mean? Why do Christians apply it to Jesus?
2. What is the origin and root meaning of the word *catholic*?
3. Why did *Catholic* come to mean "not Protestant" and "not Orthodox Christian"?
4. What did Pope Francis say to non-Catholics, including atheists, in 2017?
5. Explain the relationship between wonder and religion.
6. What does *ineffable* mean, and why is it used to explain mystery and the holy?
7. Who are the *nones* in surveys of Americans' religious affiliation? What have recent surveys said about their numbers?
8. What are characteristics of the "heart" dimension of Catholic faith?
9. Explain the "head" dimension as it applies to "the Catholic faith."
10. What is the Nicene Creed?
11. What is the relationship between faith and action in Catholicism?
12. What does the soul dimension of faith say about being human?
13. In what sense does faith serve as an anchor in the lives of Catholics?

For Further Study

Robert Barron. *Catholicism: A Journey to the Heart of the Faith*. Image Books, 2011. Captures the excitement of the Incarnational/sacramental perspective experienced in the Catholic community from its inception.

Dorothy Day. *Loaves and Fishes*. Harper & Row Publishers, 1963. Recounts how her re-encounter with Catholic faith led her to a communal life of service to those in need.

Timothy Egan. *A Pilgrimage to Eternity: From Canterbury to Rome in Search of a Faith.* Penguin Books, 2020. An honest telling of his personal story seeking grounds for faith in a secular age despite Catholicism's failings as he follows an ancient pilgrimage road.

Arthur Green. *Radical Judaism: Rethinking God and Tradition.* Yale University Press, 2010. Applies Heschel's views on religion and wonder to his Jewish faith and Judaism itself.

Abraham J. Heschel. *Between God and Man: An Interpretation of Judaism.* The Free Press, 1959. Explains why wonder is the foundation for religion.

Luke Timothy Johnson. *The Creed: What Christians Believe and Why It Matters.* An Image Book, 2005. Provides an explanation and positive assessment of the Christian creed, centering on the tenets of the Nicene Creed. It also addresses controversies and questions in readable, balanced language.

Hans Küng. *Reforming the Church Today.* Crossroad Publishing, 1990. Lays out questions that Catholicism has to address post–Vatican Council II. Much of it was written in the heady days following the Council.

Donald Nicholl. *Holiness.* Pauline Books and Media, 2005. Provides what Ronald Rohlheiser calls "a language of the soul." Explores holiness with references to multiple religious traditions.

Gaudium et Spes, ("Pastoral Constitution on the Church in the Modern World"). Documents of Vatican Council II. www.vatican.va. Discusses the role Catholicism plays in the world today. The document is attentive to developments happening in the world during the mid-1960s. Shapes the discussion of many issues facing the church since the time of the Council.

Charles Taylor. *A Secular Age.* The Belknap Press of Harvard University Press, 2007. A lengthy book that examines characteristics of a secular age and its impact on religion.

Mother Teresa of Calcutta. *A Gift for God: Prayers and Meditations.* Harper & Row, Publishers, 1975. Reflections on how Catholic faith leads to action: "Our work ... has to be built on faith—faith in Christ, who has said, 'I was hungry, I was naked, I was sick, and I was homeless, and you ministered to me.' On these words of his all our work is based."

Howard Thurman. *The Mood of Christmas and Other Celebrations*. Friends United Press, 1985. Proposes that a certain "mood" accompanies Christmas and other elements of Christianity without which humanity would be diminished.

Chapter 2
The Existence of God

We tend to think of three choices when it comes to belief in the existence of God: "I believe God exists" (theism), "I believe God does not exist" (atheism), or "I don't know if God exists" (agnosticism). The third choice, agnosticism, is usually accompanied by "and I don't care whether or not God exists; it doesn't matter to me." Catholicism is a resounding "Yes" to the existence of God. It also makes claims about the nature of God, such as that God is personal and compassionate. It professes that belief in God makes all the difference when it comes to understanding where we came from, where we are going, what we should be doing, and the meaning of life itself. In this chapter we look at Catholic teaching about the existence of God and about how we image God.

I. Origins of Belief in God

> Question the beauty of the earth, question the beauty of the sea, question the beauty of the air, amply spread around everywhere. Who made these beautiful changeable things, if not one who is beautiful and unchangeable?
>
> St. Augustine, Easter Sermon, c. 411 CE

How do you identify yourself: theist, atheist, or agnostic? Explain your position on the existence of God.
Are there other positions a person might have about the existence of God? If so, what are they?
Has your view on the existence of God changed over time? If so, how and why?
Does believing in the existence of God matter? If so, how?

"God" Seeps into Human Consciousness

> Thus, in different ways, man can come to know that there exists a reality which is the first cause and final end of all things, a reality "that everyone calls God."
>
> *Catechism*, #34

At some point, human beings or their predecessors did invent the wheel. They also invented tools and befriended dogs to be their helpmates. Some human beings discovered, no doubt through trial and error, which mushrooms one can eat and which ones to avoid. How and when did human beings realize that there is God? As discussed in the last chapter, that realization certainly began with wonder. They looked around them and came to a noetic realization that behind the changeable is that which is unchangeable. They looked into the eyes of a loved one who had just died and saw spirit residing there, more than the flesh and blood body lying lifeless before them. The sun, moon, and stars; the animals they hunted; and the fruits and berries they ate also had a spiritual quality to them, a mysterious dimension that defied simple explanation. From there it perhaps was not a great leap to arrive at the realization, stated in the *Catechism*, that there is a first cause and a final end to all that is, what we might refer to as "God." The Catholic understanding of this dynamic is that it is the work of God seeping into human consciousness. One story of revelation from God is found in the sacred writings known as the Bible, which we will look at in the next chapter.

The Axial Period

The German psychiatrist and philosopher Karl Jaspers was struck by what he saw as a transformation that took place in history from around 800–200 BCE. He saw a shift that happened throughout the world at the time. People generally were believing less in tribal gods and in spirits that found a home in the natural world (an immanent view of a god or gods) and more in one entity that exists beyond the world (a transcendent view of divinity). Accompanying this emphasis on a universal, transcendent God was also a change in emphasis about what a response to that God should be. God was less interested in proper performance of religious rituals and more concerned about moral behavior—how people treat other people. Jaspers believed so strongly that such a transformation was universal and verifiable that in 1949 he described this time period as the ***axial period***. Such a sweeping characterization of the origins of belief in one God has its defenders. In 2007 British author Karen Armstrong wrote *The Great Transformation: The Beginnings of Our Religious Traditions* largely based on the concept. Critics of Jaspers find that his thesis is overly generalized and overlooks essential differences between Hindu sages and the Buddha in India, Confucius and the founders of Taoism in China, Socrates and Homer in Greece, Zoroaster in Persia, the compilers of the Hebrew scriptures, and even the cultures of the Americas. They agree that multiple significant developments happened within a few hundred years of one another. Yes, major changes took place; but that doesn't mean that there was a wave of new insight into the human condition washing across the planet universally similar enough to warrant being labeled a discrete period. They caution that reality seldom fits so neatly into simple explanations.

The Universality of Belief

Nonetheless, it's fair to say that the majority of human beings came to a belief in one God. Even some cultures previously viewed as not believing in one God actually have a monotheistic mindset when examined more closely. This is true, for instance, of recent studies into African traditional religions. John Mbiti suggests that rather than calling African religions "polytheism" or "nature worship," it is more accurate to call them ***diffused monotheism***—one God exists who is manifest in and through people and elements of nature. The Yoruba, for instance, have a concept of one God who is the creator of all things. In his 1988 text *African Religions and Philosophy*, Mbiti gives as an example of monotheism the following traditional Pygmy hymn:

> In the beginning was God,
> Today is God
> Tomorrow will be God.
> Who can make an image of God?
> He has no body.
> He is as a word
> Which comes out of your mouth.
> That word! It is no more,

> It is past, and still it lives!
> So is God. (pp. 34–35)

Even those people who early on came to a belief in a universal, transcendent God did so cautiously, tentatively, and with trepidation. You are probably familiar with the story in the biblical book of Exodus about Moses, the greatest of all Jewish prophets, and the burning bush. A voice from the bush is asking Moses to undertake a dangerous task, so Moses asks the voice, "Who are you?" The voice replies, "YHWH." Those four Hebrew letters mean something like "I am who I am." In one sense the response says very little; in another sense it speaks volumes. God is saying, "I am"; but beyond that "I am" is mystery: "Come to some understanding of me through what I do and have done; look for me within you and around you." Jews do not say that holy name, so we are not even sure how it is pronounced, and they would never picture God.

A similar affirmation of a sacred One shrouded in mystery is found in many cultures. People of the Middle East, especially Muslims, use the Arabic word Allah for God. It means simply, "the God"; and Muslims, like Jews, do not image God. Muslim tradition lists ninety-nine names of God. "Why not round it out to an even one hundred?" you might ask, but that is precisely the point. There can be no end to the qualities residing in God. Hinduism has the concept of Brahman for ultimate reality. You will not find images or temples dedicated to Brahman. The concept is expressed more in a sound used in meditation and chanting: "*Om*," or "*Aum*." That's the sound of wind and fire, of breathing in and out. The Buddha was so hesitant to say anything about God that he is often called an atheist or at least an agnostic. No doubt he would smile at any attempt to label him. He knew how easy it is to misunderstand and misrepresent the concept of "God." Christianity refers to God as a Holy Trinity. That doctrine is not meant to limit God but to expand how we understand the One God. God is transcendent (Father); God is also immanent (Holy Spirit). For Christians, Jesus as the perfect "image" of God deserves special attention, which we will address in a future chapter and throughout the book. Nonetheless, any talk of God remains limited and must be recognized as such. The *Catechism* reminds us, "Even when he reveals himself, God remains a mystery beyond words: 'If you understood him, it would not be God'" (#230). For this reason, when

Catholics pray "Our Father" at Mass, they precede the prayer with the words: "We dare to say." At the same time, the question of the existence of God is too consequential to be dismissed.

How universal has belief in God been throughout the world and throughout human existence? We are likely living in the least "religious" era of human history, and still, at least in surveys from the mid-twenty-teens, the vast majority of people believe in some notion of God—84 percent to be exact. Of the remaining 16 percent, many of those people believe in some concept that might be interpreted as "God." It's true that religion is on the decline in the United States and Western Europe, but the opposite is true for the rest of the world. A large part of that discrepancy, of course, is the difference in the birth rates between Western societies and elsewhere; but nonetheless, belief in God is not going away, as some social scientists have been predicting would happen for over one hundred and fifty years now.

> Each of the great religious traditions affirms that as well as the social and natural world of our ordinary human experience there is a limitless world and higher Reality beyond or within us, in relation to which or to whom is our highest good.
>
> John Hick, *The World's Religious Traditions*

Poet T. S. Eliot said the following about the mystery of God: "About some things we can say nothing but before which we dare not keep silent." What does he mean? Do you agree with his seemingly contradictory statement? Explain.

Look up the ninety-nine names of God in Islam. Whether or not you believe in God, which of the names come closest to the view of God that you have? How do you define or describe God?

Find out more about the Karl Jaspers' axial period. Describe the transformations that it refers to regarding the human understanding of God.

Recently some scholars of religion suggest that we are now at the beginning of a "second axial period" when it comes to our understanding of God. How do you think people are thinking about God differently today than in the recent past?

II. Can We "Know" God Exists?

> Created in God's image and called to know and love him, the person who seeks God discovers certain ways of coming to know him. These are also called proofs for the existence of God, not in the sense of proofs in the natural sciences, but rather in the sense of "converging and convincing arguments," which allow us to attain certainty about the truth.
>
> *Catechism*, #31

During the height of the Middle Ages an Italian Dominican friar named Thomas Aquinas discovered that the ancient pre-Christian Greek philosopher Aristotle offered convincing logical arguments about why it is reasonable to posit the existence of God. Western Europe had largely been in the dark about the writings of the ancient Greeks after the fall of the Roman Empire in the West, but Muslim and Jewish scholars in Muslim-controlled Spain kept them alive and reintroduced them to the West. Along with his Muslim (in particular, Averroes) and Jewish (in particular, Maimonides) counterparts, Aquinas realized that we don't need to set aside reason when making a case for God's existence. He came up with what he called five "proofs" for the existence of God. He didn't mean that term in the modern scientific sense. He meant that belief in God is more reasonable, more logical, than the opposite position. We would need a philosophy course to understand the reasoning underlying Aquinas's way of addressing the question of God, but here's a generalized description of the type of thinking Aristotelian philosophers applied to it.

Argument from motion. Everything in the universe is moved by something or someone else. However, there exists an "unmoved mover" behind all the movement and change happening in the universe. That "unmoved mover" is what we mean by God.

Argument from causation. We are here because of our parents. Our table and chairs, the very house we live in, exist because they were created by someone. We are left with two choices: either the chain of causation has gone on forever or there was a beginning to it all. The more logical position is that there is a first cause or an "uncaused cause"—God.

Argument from necessity. Beings exist but can dissolve into nonexistence. Doesn't it follow, however, that ultimately there is "being itself" rather than nothingness? Pure being, without limitation and not dependent on anything else, is God.

St. Thomas Aquinas blended theology and philosophy.

Argument from perfection. While there are degrees to the things around us—bigger or smaller, better or worse—it follows that in the end there is perfection, the ideal—God.

Argument from design. The intricacy we see around us and in the universe might be the result of pure chance. But its infinitely sophisticated design does suggest intelligence behind it all. That supreme intelligence is God.

Using logic and reason to help understand God has its place in theology. However, the great mystics, Christian and otherwise, caution that there is too much of God for human minds to grasp. They would say that we can only say, humbly, "Ah!" to the great mystery of God. Aquinas himself was aware of the shortcomings of philosophy when approaching God. Near the completion of his monumental work on theology, he told his secretary after Mass on December 6, 1273, "All that I have written appears to be as so much straw after the things that have been revealed to me." In Catholic circles, that statement has not been viewed as a rejection on his part of his extensive philosophical work. However, Aquinas apparently had a moment of intense clarity, a noetic experience, that outstripped the vast accumulation of logical investigations he had spent his life on. He "knew" God at that moment in a way that he did not through his intellectual endeavors. It would be as if a great scholar of religion spent her entire life studying the concept of "God" but never actually experienced anything resembling an intimate encounter with God, while the uneducated man cleaning her office sang God's praises as if he and God were close friends. Aquinas knew the difference that day in 1273. Nonetheless, ever since his time Catholicism has held onto his theological and philosophical work, especially his *Summa Theologiae*, as the epitome of a thoroughly reasoned presentation of the Catholic faith.

Do you find any of Aquinas's "proofs" convincing arguments for the existence of God? Explain.

Do you ever hear references to any of the proofs in conversations or public discourse? Which arguments seem to be the most popular?

One problem with Aquinas's logical arguments is that they make a case for the existence of God, a Creator or Supreme Being, but indicate nothing about what that Supreme Being is like. Christians worship a personal God who has unconditional love for creatures, not an "unmoved mover." Do the proofs lead to a Christian understanding of God or take away from a Christian understanding?

III. Atheism: The Denial of God

To one who has faith, no explanation is necessary. To one without faith, no explanation is possible.

St. Thomas Aquinas

Early atheists

Beginning about two hundred years ago a number of European thinkers began proposing what had previously been unimaginable for most people—God does not exist. Some leading thinkers presumed that other people would eventually come to see the error of their ways and reject all religions, just as people earlier had largely rejected belief in superstition and magic. Alas, they vastly miscalculated. Today the vast majority of people worldwide believe in God in some form. What arguments against the existence of God did early atheists put forth?

"God" is a projection. Sigmund Freud (1856–1939) argued that *at bottom God is nothing more than an exalted father.* Recognized as the father of modern psychology, Freud proposed that God is merely a projection human beings make, a form of neurosis or wish fulfillment. The thought of being alone in the universe with no one to look after us is so frightening that we project that there is a "father figure" who looks after us, just as children need parents to look after them. His message? Grow up! You have created God; God didn't create you. Psychological maturity requires throwing off such childish notions as God.

Belief in God keeps us from being free. The German philosopher Friedrich Nietzsche (1844–1900) argued that the concepts "beyond" and "real world" were invented in order to depreciate the only world that exists, so that no goal, no aim or task, might be left for our earthly reality. Nietzsche claimed that we human beings will never be free until we realize that we are on our own, responsible for our own existence. Like Freud, he saw belief in God as childish. We are not adults until we venture out on our own without using God as a crutch or security blanket. He found that intellectual currents since the time of the Enlightenment in Europe led to only one conclusion: God is dead. The new reality we find ourselves in is both exhilarating and frightening. We are now free to determine our own existence.

Religion is a drug deadening our experiences of suffering and injustice. Karl Marx (1818–1883) criticized the Christianity of his day, arguing that *religion is the opium of the masses.* As industrialization was sweeping across Western Europe, he wondered why factory workers put up with the horrible conditions they experienced in mines and factories. He saw the few men who owned factories, the capitalists, as reaping all the benefits while the people actually doing all the work barely made enough to survive. Owners determined conditions in mines and factories, and more often than not those conditions were dehumanizing. Why did workers, who far outnumbered owners, put up with such an unfair situation?

Marx concluded that part of the problem was the message perpetrated by the religions of his day, especially Christianity. Religion was like opium, deadening the pain. It promised a heavenly paradise after death. Christianity preached, "Endure the trials and tribulations of this life; they are transitory and actually help us appreciate all the more where true happiness resides." Marx's message to workers: "Workers of the world, unite! Throw off your chains!" God and religion were chains holding people back from creating a "workers' paradise" on earth in which all people would be owners who shared equally in the benefits of their hard work. At the time, owners determined how long people had to work. In the new world order, workers themselves would make those decisions. At the time, owners got to go on long vacations and enjoy cultural events. In the new world order, everyone would get a vacation and go to concerts and art galleries.

How can a loving God allow suffering? The French-Algerian writer Albert Camus (1913–1960) believed that *life is absurd.* It is not quite accurate to label Camus an atheist, but he is most closely associated with what is called the "philosophy of the absurd." Camus knew suffering up close and saw its meaninglessness. For one thing, Algeria during his lifetime was a colony of France, and the native people of the country suffered greatly. The death of innocent children can certainly leave one feeling that life is absurd. "Why does God allow good people to suffer?" is perhaps the most common question that leads people to reject belief in God. You may know someone who has raised this same question: "My grandpa was such a good person all of his life. Why did he suffer so at the end of his life?" Camus's response to suffering was more subtle than blaming God. On the one hand, he insisted that we not dismiss the reality of suffering and death. On the other hand, he recommended entering into life with enthusiasm and gusto. Experience joy despite suffering.

Imagine having a conversation with the famous thinkers listed above. What would you say to each one? Are any of their arguments convincing?

Do you agree with Marx that belief in God is a disincentive for working to make this world better for people who are hurting, such as poorly paid workers? Explain your answer.

One Catholic's Response to Suffering

Catholicism does not sugarcoat pain and suffering. If anything, Catholicism emphasizes that life is a valley of tears. More often than not Catholic saints have been known for their suffering rather than their enjoyment of life. A Catholic who witnessed suffering firsthand was Dr. Takashi Nagai, a doctor in Nagasaki, Japan, who survived the 1945 atomic bomb attack on his city. He died from leukemia in 1951 at the age of forty-three. After the bombing, he spent the remainder of his life contemplating this event and placing it in the context of his Catholic faith. He was struck by the confluence of coincidences that resulted in the destruction of Nagasaki. His city was not initially the intended target. The bombers were to target a nearby Mitsubishi munitions plant, but the only thing jutting out from the clouds that day was the spire of the Catholic cathedral in the city. The bomb crew used the church spire for their target. At the time Nagasaki was the center of Japanese Catholicism. Catholics in Japan were already familiar with suffering. For hundreds of years, they had experienced persecution at the hands of other Japanese who viewed Catholicism as "foreign" and an affront to the homeland. When the bomb exploded, students at a Catholic girls' school next to the cathedral were praying their daily psalms. When Dr. Nagai made it home, he discovered his wife's body reduced to ashes. Next to her body he found her rosary beads. In all, eight thousand Catholics died instantly that day. Others, like Dr. Nagai, found themselves sickened from radiation and died early deaths.

Dr. Nagai wrote a memoir of the bombing that became a bestseller in Japan. He spent the remainder of his days in a hut he called his hermitage. He named it Nyoko-do, which translates to "Love your neighbor as yourself." In his writings and speeches, Dr. Nagai created controversy by suggesting that it was appropriate that a heavily Catholic city should be the one that was destroyed. He saw the cross as central to Catholicism. Jesus admonishes his followers to take up their cross, as he himself did. We can't expect our experience to be different from that of Jesus; only through suffering do we come to new life. Dr. Nagai's insights don't explain suffering; Catholicism doesn't provide answers to it. However, Catholic faith does suggest a response to suffering. For one thing, Catholics place their hope and trust in Jesus, who underwent suffering and death himself on the way to his triumph over them. Secondly, realizing the suffering we can inflict on others, a

Catholic response is to do all that we can to avoid causing pain and to help others in their suffering. A message Dr. Nagai took away from the Nagasaki catastrophe: Love your neighbor as yourself.

> To you do we cry, poor banished children of Eve! To you do we send up our sighs, mourning and weeping in this vale of tears!
> From the traditional Catholic prayer, "Hail, Holy Queen"

Catholicism is known for its use of crucifixes, with the body of Jesus on it, not just a bodiless cross. When a crucifix is carried in processions, it is to be clear that Jesus is hanging on the cross and not displayed as the resurrected Christ. Some cultures portray Jesus on the cross in very graphic terms, with blood and wounds prominently displayed. Make a case that the suffering and death of Jesus should or should not be such a central focus for Christianity.

Atheism Today

A group of prominent thinkers in the English-speaking world have recently called themselves the ***New Atheists***. They don't just reject that God exists; they also make the case that belief in God and religion in general are harmful. One incentive behind their militant antireligion stand was the September 11, 2001, attack that resulted in the destruction of the World Trade Center in New York City and four planes full of passengers annihilated—carried out by men who claimed to be religiously motivated. One notable atheist was Christopher Hitchens, author of the book *God Is Not Great* (2007). He called himself not simply an atheist but an ***anti-theist***. That is, he looked upon belief in God and religions as having been the cause of much that is wrong in the world. He suggested that nonbelievers have been at least as committed to doing good as believers, and often more so. Meanwhile, much that is destructive in the world today is the result of religiously motivated people. He discounted Aquinas's proofs and said that we no longer need God to make sense of the universe. We are much better off when we rely on science and rational thought in the pursuit of truth and right action. Those sentiments are echoed by two other vocal New Atheists: Richard Dawkins (*The God Delusion*, 2006) and

Sam Harris (*The End of Faith*, 2004). In the midst of publications, speaking tours, and social media messages advocating atheism, Dawkins observed that atheists were winning intellectual arguments but not changing many minds. At one public debate, after Dawkins had spoken, another scientist followed him and in so many words said, "Your arguments are very well presented, but I still believe in God."

Is Belief in God Irrational?

The argument that "religion is bad" while "science is good" is easily challenged by modern history. The Nazis' "final solution" to "the Jewish problem," doing away with all Jews, was partially legitimized by the science of eugenics. Jewish prisoners were subjected to horrific experiments in the name of science. Modern warfare is much more destructive than in the past thanks in part to scientific advancements. Advocates of religion propose that the values and worldview found in most religions can be a necessary corrective to modern science with all of its potential for good.

Catholicism affirms that the existence of God cannot be reduced to science or logical arguments, one way or the other. Some distinctions are necessary. Belief in God may be *nonrational*—that is, not capable of being proven by the scientific method or any other reasoning process. The term *irrational* is another matter. It implies that faith and reason are contradictory. They are in fact two different ways of seeking truth, two different ways of interpreting our experience. They can be different without being contradictory. From the time of the early church the dominant strain of Catholic thought proposes that *faith and reason need each other*; the one keeps the other in balance. Reason makes us skeptical when someone tries to sell on eBay a piece of toast that "miraculously" has the outline of Christ's face burnt into it. Faith reminds us that we should nonetheless be open to signals of divine presence around us. In our education for life, we need both science class and religion class. Without *faith* we could miss the ultimate mystery that surrounds us. We need to use our *reasoning* to try to make sense of it. The eleventh-century theologian St. Anselm called this process of seeking ways to speak rationally about matters of faith: "Faith seeking understanding."

Why do you think the vast majority of people throughout the world continue to affirm the existence of God?

Have you had an opportunity to hear atheists explain their rejection of God? What arguments did they give? Were they convincing?

Christian scholars who hear atheists describe the God they reject observe that more often than not they don't believe in the God atheists describe either. What perspectives on "God" should Christians reject? Are there perspectives on the concept of "God" that open-minded atheists might accept?

How do you make sense of Dawkins's observation that atheists were winning intellectual arguments but not changing people's minds about belief in God?

Find statistics about the following question and discuss your findings: Are scientists less likely to believe in God than nonscientists?

IV. Imaging God

We really can name God, starting from the manifold perfections of his creatures, which are likenesses of the infinitely perfect God, even if our limited language cannot exhaust the mystery.

Catechism, #48

Is God "Mother" and "Father"?

Proclaiming that God exists does not answer the question of how we should speak about God. The *Catechism* makes clear: Our limited language cannot exhaust the mystery. The Ten Commandments listed in the Bible caution against false representations of God. Those can be material idols or abstract "false gods" such as money or power. Actually, any way of imaging God becomes an idol when that image is taken as the *only* way to image God. The *Catechism* says that there are finite "likenesses" that tell us something about God. However, all likenesses are finite and limited, whereas God is infinite, inexhaustible mystery. In other words, all descriptions of God are metaphor: God is like a mother giving birth, a potter who creates, a watchful shepherd, a mother hen. According to the Bible, aside from Jesus the clearest image we have of God is found in the very first chapter of the first book: "God created humankind in his image, in the image of God he created them: male and female he created them" (Genesis 1:27).

That passage from Genesis raises a question: If both men and women are images (the Greek word is *ikon*) of God, then shouldn't we speak of God in both male and female terms? If we limit to only one gender the way we talk about God, image God, or pray to God, aren't we narrowing the mystery that cannot be exhausted? These questions raise many issues that have been at the forefront of Catholic theological discussion for a number of decades now. God is neither male nor female; that is not a matter of controversy. However, our English pronouns are limited to *he*, *she*, and *it*. To refer to God in an impersonal way as "it" goes against the understanding of a personal God found in all three Abrahamic faiths—Judaism, Christianity, and Islam. That leaves "he" or "she" or "he and she." Until the mid-1900s, "he" in English could refer to both sexes or to males only. For instance, the 1950s book *The Religions of Man* referred to the religions of all people, men and women, and English-speaking people generally knew that was the case. Therefore, to refer to God as "he" didn't necessarily mean that God is male. However, Christian visual images of God up until then portrayed God as a man, typically as an old man. (Remember: neither Jews nor Muslims allowed pictorial images of God at all.) The message was that when God is referred to as "he," it means male. That message was reinforced by all the references in the Bible and Christian tradition to God using male imagery.

Is it a problem to image God exclusively or predominantly as a man? Feminist theologians believe that it is a problem. For one, it is idolatrous because it limits our perception of God, who is beyond our comprehension. They propose that our understanding of God is enriched when multiple images are used. Who wouldn't be consoled by praying before an image of God who promises, "As a mother comforts her child, so I will comfort you" (Isaiah 66:13)? Feminist theologians also make the case that male-only images of God support the oppression of women. To understand that argument it is necessary to define some key terms. A *feminist* believes that (a) men and women are inherently equal, but (b) multiple factors in society work against women having equality with men, and therefore (c) people should work to bring about equality and overcome the oppression of women. A feminist is someone dedicated to uncovering ways that women are oppressed and committed to creating a more just and equal society. **Oppression** means that certain groups of people, such as women, suffer and lack power, privileges, and opportunities due to systemic factors. Feminists point to **patriarchy** (literally, "father rule") as the system that has positioned certain men as having the dominant power in a society. The God question for feminist theologians, then, is, does imaging God only as male support patriarchy and oppression of women? They point out, "When God is male, then males are gods," and women suffer for it.

In 1983 feminist theologian Rosemary Radford Reuther wrote, "Few topics are as likely to rouse such passionate feelings in contemporary Christianity as the question of the exclusively male image of God" (*Sexism and God-Talk*). Do you believe this remains true today? Explain.

Look up an article about feminine images of God in the Bible. What does it say about such images?

Do you agree with feminist theologians who say that imaging God exclusively in male language is idolatrous and oppressive? Explain.

Would you be comfortable if someone leading prayer began with the words: "Let us pray to God, who cares for us like a mother"? Why or why not?

In addition to God, Catholics have a strong devotion to Mary, the Blessed Mother. Does devotion to Mary offset the criticism of feminist theologians about male-only images of God?

What Color is God's Skin?

In the early 1970s, the singing group "Up With People" asked, "What color is God's skin?" The reply was, "It's black brown it's yellow / It is red / It is white." More recently, writer James McBride wrote a memoir titled *The Color of Water*. When he was a child, he asked his white Polish mother, who was married to a black man, what color God's skin is. His mother replied, "the color of water." (When he asked his mother if she was white, she said that she was "light-skinned," avoiding labeling herself "white" because she knew it to be a social construct in America filled with meaning beyond simply a color designation.) The same issues surrounding whether to image God as male and/or female surface in the question of how to image God in skin color, age, and ethnicity. The gospels refer to God as "Father," so it makes sense for Christians to portray God as older than Jesus. In the late fourteenth century, a French painter first portrayed God as an older, bearded white man—looking like the French model who posed for him, no doubt. The most popular image of God in Western culture is probably Michelangelo's portrayal of God the creator as an old white man, which he painted on the ceiling of the Sistine Chapel in Rome.

Is it problematic to portray God as an old white man? A few years ago, a group of scholars from Stanford University, led by Steven O. Roberts, studied the question and concluded, "Basically, if you believe that a white man rules the heavens, you are more likely to believe that white men should rule on earth." (You can read about their study in a *Stanford News* article from January 31, 2020: "Who People Believe Rules in Heaven Influences Their Beliefs About Who Rules on Earth, Stanford Scholars Find." You can also read about the study in the July 28, 2020, *Scientific American* article "Picturing God as a White Man Is Linked to Racial Stereotypes about Leadership.") Interestingly, perhaps the most popular religiously themed book of recent times portrays God as a black woman: *The Shack*, by William P. Young (2007). It spent over seventy weeks on the *New York Times* bestseller list. For many Christians, the book's stereotype-shattering portrayal was appealing and refreshing. However, despite the popularity of *The Shack*, the critique of feminist theologians still applies: the ways we image God can be idolatrous and oppressive.

Do you find evidence of what the Stanford scholars found about portraying God as an old white man? If so, give examples.

If you were commissioned with the task of decorating churches with portrayals of God, what types of images would you use?

American painter Henry Ossawa Tanner used a shaft of light to depict the power of God coming upon Mary when she became pregnant with Jesus ("The Annunciation"). Suggest ways that nonpersonal images might elicit a sense of God without diminishing the personal dimension of God.

The Holy Trinity

> God is love: Father, Son, and Holy Spirit. ... Each divine person performs the common work according to his unique personal property.
>
> *Catechism*, #257, 258

If you have spent much time with Catholics, you might have noticed that they bless themselves and begin prayer making the sign of the cross and saying, "In the name of the Father, and of the Son, and of the Holy Spirit." To become Catholic people are baptized with water accompanied by the same words. The Holy Trinity forms the framework of the Nicene Creed recited at Mass. Some Catholics even bless themselves with the three-step sign of the cross when they pass a car accident on a highway, hear a passing ambulance siren, or even when they are about to come up to bat in a baseball game. Clearly God as a Holy Trinity of Father, Son, and Holy Spirit is central to Catholic faith. Jews and Muslims are baffled by this notion of "three persons in one God." Muslims have a high regard for Jesus—according to their scripture he is the Messiah of the Jews born of the Virgin Mary. However, to equate anything or anyone with the transcendent God is the worst of offenses. In their view, the notion of a triune God runs counter to their central teaching of *Tawhid*, or the oneness of God. The heart of Jewish daily prayer, the *Shema*, also cautions against what could be perceived as watering down the oneness of God: "Hear, O Israel, the Lord is our God, the Lord is one." Even many Christians are hard-pressed to explain the Trinity: Is it monotheism or tritheism?

Christianity is unequivocally monotheistic—belief in one God. However, Christians bear witness to the dynamism of God at work and recognize "three persons" in one God. Some early Christian scholars connected the Trinity to what they called the *divine economy*. The Greek root of that word is "house," so economy means "taking care of the household." The divine economy is the means by which God works out the salvation of people. God the Father is the creator of the world, liberated the Israelites from slavery in Egypt, and sent prophets to guide people on the straight path. God the Son enters human history in the person of Jesus. God the Holy Spirit continues to be present within and among people to continue the work begun by Christ.

The word "person" or "persona" applied to the Trinity does not mean exactly what we understand by the word today. It was first used by the late second- and early third-century Latin theologian Tertullian. He was seeking to reconcile the notion of Trinity with monotheism. Each "person" is a distinct entity but always exists in relationship to the other two; together they share the same essence or substance, and each has a distinct role to play in drawing us into life with God: "The ultimate end of the whole divine economy is the entry of God's creatures into the perfect unity of the Blessed Trinity" (*Catechism*, #260). Because the word "person" has a somewhat different connotation today, and also because it describes God in the male image of "father," some people have looked for alternatives. You might hear someone begin a prayer "In the name of the Creator, the Redeemer, and the Sustainer." The problem with such language for Catholics is that it identifies the three distinct persons solely with their function. An early heresy, or teaching that was rejected by the church, was called **modalism**, which spoke of one God with three different "modes" or functions. For Catholics, the person of Jesus is more than his function; he was a distinct person who shared in the one divine essence. (We would not want to be reduced to our "function" either. We are more than a student, a teacher, a waiter, or a nurse. We are persons.)

Belief in the Trinity caused many conflicts early in Christian history that lasted hundreds of years. God as Holy Trinity has also given much comfort to Christians throughout the ages and much food for thought to those trying to make sense of the mystery of God who is beyond our comprehension. Catholics look upon the doctrine of the Trinity as a gift. Instead of the bland "unmoved mover" of Aquinas, Catholics find in scripture and early Christian writings the basis for the personal, three-persons-in-one-essence understanding of God. Although it defies simple explanation, the doctrine of the Trinity gives a richness to God and offers different avenues by which to contemplate God, like a gem shimmering in the light. One way to approach this concept of God as Holy Trinity is to ask, if you were to eliminate one or two of these persons from an understanding of God, which would it be? A loving Father, separate from but overseeing the world with compassion? The Son, Jesus, who embodied the love of God in his life, sacrifice on the cross, and hope-filled resurrection from the dead? The Holy Spirit, who continues the work of God in the community called the church and in people committed to making of their lives a home for the Spirit?

One ancient Greek word associated with the Trinity is *perichoresis*. It means "dancing around." (The English word "choreography" shares the same root meaning.) Perichoresis ascribes to God, the Holy Trinity, a dynamic of three persons in a loving relationship dancing around one another. The Trinity is God's three-person, three-dimensional work of getting people to join in the divine dance, "the entry of God's creatures into the perfect unity of the Blessed Trinity."

"Unmoved Mover" or Holy Trinity?

In his novel *Jayber Crow*, Wendell Berry has his main character musing over the notion of God. He ends up finding wisdom in the Christian understanding of God as Holy Trinity.

> From my college courses and my reading I knew the various names that came at the end of a line of questions or were placed as periods to bafflement: the First Cause, the First Mover, the Life Force, the Universal Mind, the First Principle, the Unmoved Mover, even Providence. ... I imagined that the right name might be Father, and I imagined all that that name would imply: the love, the compassion, the taking offense, the disappointment, the anger, the bearing of wounds, the weeping of tears, the forgiveness, the suffering unto death. ... Could I not see how divine omnipotence might by the force of its love be swayed down into the world? Could I not see how it might, because it could know its creatures only by compassion, put on mortal flesh, become a man, and walk among us, assume our nature and our fate, suffer our faults and our death? ... And I could imagine a Father who is yet like a mother hen spreading her wings before the storm or in the dusk before the dark night for the little ones. ... I could imagine God looking down upon it, its lives living by His spirit, breathing by His breath, knowing by His light, but each life living also (inescapably) by its own will—His own body given to be broken. (Washington, DC: Counterpoint, 2000, pp. 251–52, used with permission)

A number of Christians have used different images to try to illustrate the mystery of the Holy Trinity. You may be familiar with St. Patrick and the three-leaf clover. One early Christian writer talked about the sun and the rays of the sun. The church has also made use of a geometrical pattern to illustrate the Trinity: a triangle in a circle. Every description falls short. What would you suggest as an image that might describe the Trinity at least to some degree?

Different Catholic prayers focus more on God as Father, Son, or Holy Spirit—sometimes in the same prayer. Look up Catholic prayers and take note of references to God as Father, Son, or Holy Spirit.

Belief in God and Catholic Life

Belief in God colors a Catholic's entire life. It gives meaning to their lives and points to the source of all that they are grateful for. Belief in *one* God shapes their attitude toward other people, including people they don't know and especially people in need. If there is one God, then all people are children of God. Strangers are not the enemy but family members they haven't met yet. Catholic tradition looks to both faith and reason to probe the great mysteries of life, not dismissing one source of truth or the other. And thoughtful Catholics recognize that God is more than any image we have of God or any words we use to speak of God. Modern feminist theologians have provided new insights into how our God-talk can be idolatrous and injurious to people by overlooking the biblical insight that women and men image God. Finally, Catholic belief in God as the Holy Trinity reminds them that love is at the very heart of God's being. When they seek to be a loving presence in the world themselves, Catholics do so in the name of the Father, and of the Son, and of the Holy Spirit.

Chapter Review

1. According to Karl Jaspers, when was the axial period? Why does he call it that?
2. What does YHWH mean? What does it say about the Jewish concept of God?
3. What does the sound "*Om*" or "*Aum*" say about the Hindu understanding of *Brahman*?

4. In the mid-twenty-teens, what percentage of the world's population professed belief in God?
5. What are St. Thomas Aquinas's "five proofs" for the existence of God?
6. What experience did Aquinas have in 1773 that put his philosophical work into perspective for him?
7. Explain the critique of believing in God posited by Freud, Nietzsche, Marx, and Camus.
8. Who was Dr. Takashi Nagai, and what did he say about Catholicism and suffering?
9. Describe the attitude toward religion of the New Atheists.
10. According to the book of Genesis, who most clearly images God?
11. What two reasons do feminist theologians give for referring to God in both male and female language and images?
12. Define *feminist*.
13. What conclusion did Stanford scholars reach about depicting God as an old white man?
14. Explain the Christian doctrine of the Holy Trinity.
15. Why do Catholics look upon the doctrine of the Trinity as a gift?

For Further Study

"Aquinas & the Cosmological Arguments: Crash Course Philosophy #10." YouTube. A philosopher gives a fast-paced explanation of Thomas Aquinas's cosmological "proofs" for the existence of God and then points out their inadequacies for making the case for what people generally understand by "God."

Karen Armstrong. *The Great Transformation: The Beginning of Our Religious Tradition.* Anchor Books, 2007. Examines elements of religion as they took shape during the axial period, which she identifies as beginning around 1600 BCE and ending before 200 BCE.

Wendell Berry. *Jayber Crow.* Counterpoint, 2000.

James H. Cone. *God of the Oppressed*. HarperSanFrancisco, 1975. Cone has written a number of books exploring the connection between the black experience in America and biblical images and stories. He makes the case that Jesus's blackness is "both literal and symbolic."

Sam Harris. *The End of Faith: Religion, Terror, and the Future of Reason*. W. W. Norton, 2005. Makes the case that religions underlie much that is wrong in the world, focusing in particular on the September 11, 2001, attacks in America by men who claimed to have a religious motivation.

John Hick, "Religious Pluralism." In *The World's Religious Traditions*. Current Perspectives in Religious Studies, Frank Whaling, ed. Cambridge University Press, 1985.

Pope John Paul II. *Fides et Ratio* ("On the Relationship between Faith and Reason"). vatican.va, 1998. Affirms that "the Church is no stranger to the journey of discovery" and explores the biblical and Catholic tradition of linking theology and philosophy.

Elizabeth A. Johnson. *She Who Is: The Mystery of God in Feminist Theological Discourse*. Crossroad Publishing Company, 1992. Applies feminist critical theology that "unmask(s) the hidden dynamic of domination in the Christian tradition's language, customs, memory, historical sacred texts, ethics, symbolism, theology and ritual." Arrives at "She Who Is" as a name for God that resonates more closely than traditional terms with a biblical understanding of God for today.

Richard Rohr. *The Divine Dance: The Trinity and Your Transformation*. Whitaker House, 2016. Rohr sets out to "dust off a daring doctrine" of the Holy Trinity and move beyond the Christian teaching as something other than a math problem. ("How can there be three persons but one God?") He explores relationship as central to what the Holy Trinity means and suggests how Christians can enter into the flow of the divine dance that is the Triune God.

Rosemary Radford Reuther. *Sexism and God-Talk: Toward a Feminist Theology*. Beacon Press, 1983. A pioneering work that examines theological methodology, language and imagery about God, and implications for how we think and speak about God.

Leo Zanebettin and Patricia Mitchell. "Blessed Are Those Who Mourn: Takashi Nagai," in *A Great Cloud of Witnesses*. Word Among Us, 1998. Tells the story of Dr. Takashi Nagai, whose experience of the Nagasaki atomic bomb blast's obliteration of his family and much of the Japanese Catholic community during World War II led him to explore what Catholicism teaches about suffering.

Chapter 3
Scripture: A Gift from God in Word and Story

Catholics recognize the Bible as the inspired word of God that contains within its pages the central message of the Christian faith. That message is couched in various forms and genres of writings that were composed over a thousand years and collected in the Old and New Testaments. It includes songs, pithy sayings, stories, historical and semihistorical narratives, and a collection of laws aimed at providing guidance for a just moral order as it was understood three thousand years ago. In this chapter, we will discuss how to approach what Christians call the Old Testament and then what actually is found in it.

> And such is the force and power of the Word of God that it can serve the Church as her support and vigor and the children of the Church as strength for their faith, food for the soul, and a pure and lasting font of spiritual life.
>
> *Catechism,* #131

List five things you already know about the Bible.
List five questions that a curious person might have about the Bible.
Begin a search to find answers to these questions. Compare what you find with what others find.

I. Modern Science and the Bible

An early Catholic advocate of scientific investigation into scripture, the life of Jesus, and the cultures of biblical times was the French Dominican priest Father Marie-Joseph Lagrange who founded the *Ecole Biblique,* dedicated to a "faithful yet scientific" study of the

Bible, in Jerusalem in 1890. Founding an institute for scientific research into the Bible would seem to be an unremarkable event. Doesn't it make sense to apply knowledge from science to everything, including something as precious as the Bible is to so many people? In fact, at the time, Father Lagrange and his research school were suspect in the eyes of many Catholic leaders. Eighteen years after its founding Father Lagrange was ordered to return to France, and the school was briefly closed. What made his work and that of other scholars studying scripture so suspect?

One answer to that question lies in what was called at the time *modernism*. Beginning around the middle of the nineteenth century, many church leaders talked about modernism as a great threat to the faith. The term came to be applied to just about anything that appeared to be antithetical to the Catholic Church and faith. One element of what was labeled modernism was *the belief that science held a privileged position in the pursuit of truth over all other sources of truth,* such as "divine revelation"—the Bible. As a result, "science" and "the Bible" were pitted against each other. Holding the Bible up to scientific scrutiny meant questioning the foundational document of Catholicism and Christianity itself. That concern remains with Christians today. When they find out more about what went into the writing of the Bible, does it lead to disillusionment and lack of faith, the way discovering that Santa Claus doesn't exist deflates a Christian child's wonder and delight in Christmas gifts?

One issue that people in the Western world have grappled with since the mid-nineteenth century is the origin of the human species. In his 1859 book *On the Origin of Species*, the English naturalist Charles Darwin put forth some science-based arguments that living species evolved from one form to another. That's not how the Bible describes their origins. At the very beginning of Genesis, the first book of the Bible, the story is told about all creation taking place over six days, one species after another, not an evolution of one to another over millions of years. Can science and the Bible be reconciled? Catholics like Father Lagrange put forth the proposition that they could. For them, our understanding of the Bible is enhanced by scientific investigation into it.

In time, Catholic leaders encouraged scientific study of scripture. Pope Leo XIII did so, at least cautiously, in an 1893 encyclical. Pope Pius XII did so more forcefully fifty years later in his 1943 encyclical

Divino Afflante Spiritu. The English title of that encyclical is "The Most Opportune Way to Promote Biblical Studies." He advocated the use of modern scientific methods as being valuable in understanding the Bible. For over seventy years now, while affirming that God is behind all creation, Catholic popes have stated that evolution is the most plausible explanation for how human beings came into existence. Pope St. John Paul II addressed the question in 1996 in an address to the Pontifical Academy of Science in Rome. He pointed out that in 1950 his predecessor Pope Pius XII said that "there is no conflict between evolution and the doctrine of the faith." Pope John Paul then added that further scientific findings "lead toward the recognition of evolution as more than an hypothesis." In 2014, Pope Francis reiterated that science and faith are not at odds. Nonetheless, a 2019 Gallup poll found that 34 percent of American Catholics believe that human beings were created in their current form without evolving from other species. Fifty-six percent of Protestant Christians deny evolution.

What are the latest statistics about the number of Americans who deny evolution?

In your own schooling, what were you taught about evolution and the origins of the universe and of human beings?

Christians who believe in the Bible and also in evolution claim that the biblical stories of creation are "true" but not historically factual. What do they mean? Specifically, how do Catholic biblical scholars reconcile evolution with the Bible?

Historical-Critical Methods Applied to the Bible

The interpreter must, as it were, go back wholly in spirit to those remote centuries of the East and with the aid of history, archaeology, ethnology, and other sciences, accurately determine what modes of writing, so to speak, the authors of that ancient period would be likely to use, and in fact did use.

Divino Afflante Spiritu, #35

In the nineteenth century, the scientific study of scripture was referred to as the ***historical-critical method***. "Historical method" here means that learning about the people, places, and cultures of the biblical era can help us understand the meaning of Bible passages better. We cannot fully understand a biblical *text* unless we know something about the *context* in which it was written. In the past two hundred years, thanks to scientific explorations, more information has surfaced about ancient cultures than was known for the past two thousand years. For example, scholars have discovered that several societies in the Middle East had stories of devastating floods. (There were Babylonian and Sumerian flood stories.) It is likely that the familiar flood story in the Bible was part of ancient Middle Eastern lore, adapted to communicate a message in line with an understanding of God and humanity held by the people who shaped the biblical narrative. Similarly, the Bible describes Joshua, successor to Moses, leading the Israelite slaves in the conquest of what they perceived to be their ancestral homeland. A crucial event in that story was that the mighty walls of the city of Jericho, the oldest known city on earth, came tumbling down through the intervention of God so that the Israelites could conquer it. Archaeologists discovered that Jericho was indeed a walled city at one time but that the walls were destroyed centuries before the Israelites arrived there. It makes sense from their point of view that God destroyed the wall to signal God's approval of their asserting dominion over the land, even if it didn't happen in as dramatic a fashion as described in the biblical narrative.

The book of Exodus has Moses going up onto a mountain where he encounters God and receives ten commandments that the people were to follow as they fashioned themselves into a nation with their own law code. In 1901, archaeologists discovered a **stele** (stone column) with writing that contained a law code given, according to the account on the stele itself, to Babylonian King Hammurabi by their god of justice in order to "protect the weak from the strong." The stele dates from about five hundred years before Moses and the Israelites received their law code from their God, YHWH. Apparently, for centuries sages spread the Code of Hammurabi around the many Middle Eastern civilizations so that it likely would have been known by the Israelites as they fashioned their own laws found in the first five books of the Bible.

Do historical studies suggest that the Bible was influenced by nonbiblical sources, even sources from other cultures besides that of "God's chosen people"? Catholicism admits that in the Bible "God speaks through men in human fashion" (Vatican Council II, *Dei Verbum*, #12). The *Catechism* says, "In order to discover *the sacred authors' intention*, the reader must take into account the conditions of their time and culture, the literary genres in use at the time, and the modes of feeling, speaking, and narrating then current" (#110). The authors of the Bible were people of their time and culture; they made use of the knowledge available to them. At the same time, they had a unique experience and understanding of God that Jews, Christians, and Muslims believe came from God, either directly or indirectly. All three religions view the Hebrew Bible as ultimately of divine origin. The ancient compilers of the Bible were moved by God to transform what was available to them and communicate a divinely inspired message that became the Bible. In his letter to the Ephesians, St. Paul was talking about God speaking in Christ, but his message can apply as well to the words of the entire Bible that Christians consider the inspired word of God: "With all wisdom and insight he [God] has made known to us the mystery of his will, according to his good pleasure" (Eph 1:8–9).

Read the story of Noah and the flood in Genesis, chapters 6–8. What message does the story contain? How is God portrayed in the story?

The 2014 film "Noah" suggests that humanity's mistreatment of the earth led to the flood that destroyed it. Is this environmental take a valid application of the biblical epic? If you are not familiar with the movie, read Matt Zoller Seitz's review of it at RogerEbert.com.

Look up "archaeology and the Bible." What are some archaeological find-ings in the past two hundred years that have shed light on the Bible?

Biblical Literary Criticism

In the present day indeed this art, which is called textual criticism and which is used with great and praiseworthy results in the editions of profane writings, is also quite rightly employed in the case of the Sacred Books.

Divino Afflante Spiritu, #17

The "critical" part of the historical-critical approach to understanding scripture refers to literary criticism. The Bible is written in many different "forms of literary expression" (*Catechism*, #110). Some of the forms of expression are easy to identify. For instance, the psalms are clearly songs, and the book of Proverbs is filled with short sayings known as proverbs. The book of Job appears to be a short story, as does the book of Jonah. However, at times history blends in with more fanciful types of writing. For instance, there is evidence from nonbiblical sources that members of nomadic tribes known as *'apiru*, or **Hebrews**, were slaves in Egypt about thirty-five hundred years ago. Some of them managed to escape slavery and make their way to the fertile land of Canaan, modern-day Israel and Palestine. The second book of the Bible, Exodus, tells of their transformation from slaves to an independent nation that actually wielded power for a brief period three thousand years ago. Many descriptions of the circumstances surrounding their release from captivity don't hold up to historical scrutiny, despite making for a great Hollywood spectacle. We do have Egyptian chronicles from the time, but no mention is made in them of the firstborn sons of all Egyptians dying suddenly or of the pharaoh and all of his army being destroyed when the waters of the Red Sea came crashing down upon them. The biblical account mentions ten plagues. Some of them may refer to actual natural phenomena. In the story, they are acts of God.

Scholars engaged in biblical literary criticism painstakingly examine portions of the Bible, even individual words, in their original languages, and try to determine what they meant in their historical context and what the intended meaning of the authors was. To complicate matters, Hebrew, like Arabic, includes only consonants in written texts, not vowels. A line of Hebrew can read like abbreviations found on vanity car license plates. Also, we have no original, first draft of books of the Bible. The oldest portions were likely told orally for centuries before they were written down. Scholars who study oral cultures point out that storytellers often add their own embellishments to stories they have heard from others and over time a standard version emerges. The scribes who collected these stories did not separate the ancient stories from their own editorializing. Scholars are generally in agreement that the first five books of the Hebrew Bible underwent four major "editions" before the written text as we know it today was put into final form.

The written Hebrew Bible was compiled over the course of more than five hundred years and included portions that were even older. Do you struggle to make sense of Shakespeare's English at times? He wrote a mere five hundred years ago. Jane Austen wrote just two hundred years ago, and some of her words have evolved in meaning. For instance, she writes that someone looked upon another character with "condescension." She meant the word in a positive sense—a kind and caring feeling for the other. Nowadays, if someone is "condescending" it has a negative connotation; it means to pity someone, to look down upon another. Mark Twain's *Huckleberry Finn*, written less than one hundred and fifty years ago, is banned from some school libraries because of language deemed unacceptable today. When it comes to the Bible, we can say that the words in our favorite English translation meant the same centuries ago and in a very different culture as they mean to us today. Or, we can enlist the help of scholars using historical-critical methods to come up with a better understanding of what the written texts meant during the course of their compilation. Catholicism affirms that the effort is worth it since the Bible conveys the message of salvation, and new insights into it can help us understand that message even more clearly.

What is the Rosetta Stone? When was it deciphered? How did it open doors to a better understanding of the Bible?

What is cuneiform? When did modern scholars begin to understand it?

The Bible uses different literary forms. Describe a recent event in purely factual language, then write about it with added editorial commentary or in a work of fiction, a poem, or a song.

Biblical Fundamentalism

It's fair to say that Protestantism has been more visibly Bible centered than Catholicism. In a sense, Protestantism began as a "back to the Bible" movement. Martin Luther and other reformers of the early sixteenth century who broke with the Catholic Church looked to the Bible for justification for their positions. They encouraged people to read the Bible on their own, something that would not have been possible seventy years prior to that. The invention of the printing press made it possible for people to read scripture themselves instead of hearing what the Bible said from the few monks and clerics who could read and had access to handwritten texts. When Luther was condemned by church leaders, he spent his time hidden away in a castle, translating the Bible into a highly readable, understandable German. One of the reasons there are so many Protestant sects is that various reformers differed over their interpretation of the Bible's message. Today there are Christians who are absolute pacifists, refusing to participate in any war, as that is what they understand the Bible teaches. Some Christians, albeit a very small number, handle poisonous snakes during their Sunday services, as the Bible says believers do in Mark 16:18. When it comes to reading scripture, along with the text itself, there is always the interpretation of the text.

When the scientific study of scripture became popular in the nineteenth century, Protestants were torn about how to view it. Many welcomed historical-critical approaches and the insights they provided. Others reacted with trepidation. They felt that science was undermining the Bible, which they saw as the foundation of their faith. While Catholic leaders were cautiously welcoming scientific inquiry, some Protestants—mainly in America—felt that the "fundamentals" of the faith were in jeopardy. ***Biblical fundamentalists*** declared their belief in the ***inerrancy*** of the Bible. That is, the Bible in its entirety is without error; to admit that even one statement is false or factually inaccurate would undermine its entire validity. They held that the Bible was not to be subject to interpretation. The literal meaning, what is written, is the factual meaning. For instance, to disavow that the world was created over six days would lead to denying that Christ rose from the dead, resulting in the total collapse of Christian faith.

The disagreement between "mainline Protestants," open to historical-critical interpretations of scripture, and fundamentalist Christians continues to this day. Catholicism also believes in biblical inerrancy, but it has a different understanding of what that means. Catholic leaders have a long tradition of seeing no conflict between reason and faith, the Bible and science, so at least at the institutional level the Catholic Church does not advocate biblical fundamentalism the way Protestant fundamentalists do.

> A biblical fundamentalist reading of scripture considers the words of the Bible to mean what those words mean today. For instance, if the Bible says that someone had a child at age 187 and lived a total of 969 years (Methuselah), then that is what actually happened. Since all creatures came into being at the same time, then humans and dinosaurs roamed the earth together. Is there a danger to a strictly fundamentalist interpretation of scripture? For example, does it create unnecessary tension with modern science?

The two main approaches to scripture can be summarized as follows:

The historical-critical approach

- applies insight from historical and linguistic studies to gain a better understanding of the Bible,
- examines texts in light of the context in which they were spoken and written,
- searches for the most accurate rendering of biblical passages,
- identifies the various genres in biblical writings and treats them differently, and
- assumes that interpretation of what a text means is unavoidable and uses historical-critical tools to arrive at the most reasonable interpretation.

The fundamentalist approach to scripture assumes that

- the Bible is the unadulterated and unequivocal word of God,
- human authors merely wrote down what God told them to,
- the words of the Bible mean the same today as they did when written,
- the Bible provides a factual account of early history, even if science suggests otherwise, and
- the Bible must be read without subjective interpretation, so the literal meaning must be accepted as fact.

The Four Senses of Scripture

Was there at one time a man and a woman who lived in a garden paradise where there was no suffering or death? Did it once rain so hard for forty days that the entire earth was covered with water and only one family survived, who managed to gather a male and female of every species to join them on their ark? Did a man named Jonah live inside of a fish for three days? It is too simplistic to say that Christians considered all of these stories to be factual until modern scientists started to question them two hundred years ago. Early Christian writers were more interested in what those stories *meant* than in whether or not they were factual. They recognized the ***literal sense*** of what was written. However, they saw a ***spiritual sense*** in biblical stories. For them, in the literal sense Adam is one particular man; but in a spiritual sense he represents all humanity. The flood is a metaphor for the cleansing that happens in sacramental baptism. Jonah's three days inside a fish is a precursor and metaphor for Christ's time of burial in the tomb.

For early Christians, the literal sense of scripture was seen as filled with deeper meanings that could be applied to the Christian life. On the spiritual level, biblical passages had three senses. (1) Bible stories had an ***allegorical sense***. For instance, the *Catechism* says that "the crossing of the Red Sea is a sign or type of Christ's victory and also of Christian Baptism" (#117). Noah's ark, which saved people from the death-dealing waters around it, represents the church that offers safe harbor to people today. (2) Biblical passages also have a ***moral sense***. After Cain kills his brother Abel, God confronts Cain about his fratricidal deed (Genesis 4:8–16). Cain denies knowing anything about it, saying, "Am I my brother's keeper?" That moral question is for all of us: Are we responsible for one another? The Bible's answer is a definitive yes. (3) The ***anagogical sense*** means that biblical images and stories point to eternity. For early Christian writers, Jerusalem was not only the great city of David, home to the sacred center of the universe, the temple; it was the "heavenly city," a metaphor for heaven itself. The Exodus event, the journey to the promised land, symbolizes being freed from death and entrance into the true heavenly homeland God has prepared for people.

Early Christian commentators engaged in ***exegesis***, a Greek word that means "to draw out." They drew out multiple meanings from the many Bible stories they knew, both literal meaning and spiritual meanings. Even if the Bible was not being read extensively, it provided a language for people to communicate about the Christian mysteries and about the mystery of life itself. Often biblical messages were communicated in paintings, statues, and eventually stained glass windows. Preachers told Bible stories and drew out meaning from them. (What does it mean for us to wrestle with God? What forms of slavery do we long to be freed from?) Today, modern exegetes use the historical-critical method to draw out additional meaning from the Bible, making it a living document that engages Christians in a conversation with inspired authors who saw God's active presence in their own experiences.

Exegesis is the "drawing out" of meaning from biblical passages. Modern exegesis refers to scholars who apply historical-critical methods to draw out possible meanings of a passage in its original context.

Give an example of how someone might "draw out" meaning from a story or image in the Bible.

The Bible is meant to be prayed, not just read. How might the Bible be read for the purposes of spiritual enrichment?

II. Catholicism and the Bible

Scripture and Tradition

The *Catechism* says, "In the sacred books, the Father who is in heaven comes lovingly to meet his children, and talks with them" (#104). In his 2005 encyclical "God is Love" (*Deus Caritas Est*), Pope Benedict XVI reminded Catholics that the Bible is a love story (#17). It tells the story of a love relationship between God and a group of people who began as a band of poor, landless nomads. With God's help, guidance, and steadfast love they became a people—God's people. Like all intense love relationships, the one between God and God's people was at times contentious. In fact, the name of this people, Israel, means "one who wrestles with God," based on a story about one of the earliest nomadic chiefs named Jacob, who wrestles through the night with a stranger whom he recognizes as a messenger from God (Genesis

32:28). For Christians, the love story reaches its climax, its fulfillment, in the person of Jesus and specifically in his torturous death and in the new kind of life that was his glorious resurrection. From there, the story extends beyond the people of Israel and is available to all people. Anyone can now pick up a Bible and read this love letter from God, complete with its at times baffling stories, archaic laws, and culture-specific perspectives.

For Catholics, the Bible is the inspired word of God. Biblical inspiration doesn't mean that human authors did not put their own stamp on what we find written there. Catholicism doesn't say that the Bible is the "words" of God. It refers to the Bible as "the word of God," or at Mass as "the word of the Lord." The Bible provides special communication from God and therefore is "divine revelation," as Jesus is the Word of God in a human person. The *Catechism* asserts that in Jesus the Word of God took on human flesh, with all of its weaknesses. He was a man of a particular time and a particular culture. So also, the Bible is the word of God "expressed in the words of men" who also existed at a particular time and in a particular culture (#101).

Catholicism affirms that all we need to know for our salvation can be found in the sacred writings that make up the Bible. Catholicism does caution that we not get caught up in concentrating on the weeds and miss the beauty of the entire garden. In the words of the *Catechism*, we should be especially attentive "to the content and unity of the whole Scripture" (#112), and to aid in that process, we should read the Scripture within "the living Tradition of the whole Church" (#113). We should also approach scripture with the eyes of faith, which lies not in words but within the heart. Catholicism, therefore, sees scripture as interconnected with the church and with its tradition of interpreting scripture. The Bible is the inspired word of God, but church Tradition plays a crucial role in helping people make sense of it. Along with all Christians, Catholics believe that the scriptures "are a storehouse of sublime teaching on God and of sound wisdom on human life, as well as a wonderful treasury of prayers; in them, too, the mystery of our salvation is present in a hidden way" (*Catechism*, #122).

In your schooling, you have probably had courses in science and in literature. As a literary form, much of the Bible is more like a story than a philosophical or scientific text. How would you describe the difference in how truth is conveyed in story form as opposed to in a scientific text?

Catholic versus Protestant Attitudes toward Bible Reading

There are many "Bible-carrying Christians" in America, those churchgoers who bring their Bible with them and expect Bible passages to be the central focus of the services they attend. They might even take home a recording of their pastor's sermon on the Bible passage of the day so they can listen again during the week. They can quote lines from the Bible by heart. For them, the Bible is definitely more than a decoration on a bookshelf or a place to record family births and deaths. They may have a pocket Bible or a booklet with inspiring Bible quotes with them to read as they ride the subway or take a break at work. They look to the Bible to provide guidance about all aspects of their lives. For a long while, hotels in America placed a Bible in every room, complete with questions on the inside cover. (Feeling lonely and depressed? Battling alcoholism? Read such and such a passage.) Those Bibles were supplied by an organization called the **Gideons**, a Protestant Christian group that believed that the Bible contained the answer to all of life's problems.

What about Catholics and reading the Bible? It is fair to say that Bible-carrying Catholics are seldom seen. They listen as passages from the Bible are proclaimed at their liturgies, but they don't follow along in their own Bibles. They may keep a Bible in their home, but it isn't read on any regular basis, nor do they pepper their conversation with lines from scripture. They are likely to know the major stories in the Bible since they hear about them at Mass, but don't expect them to be able to quote John 3:16 by heart. They do not supply Bibles to hotel rooms, but they might assist in placing a card in hotels with the address of local Catholic churches where people can attend Mass. For the past fifty years, many Catholic parishes have sponsored Bible-study groups, and all Catholics recognize the central role that the Bible plays in their religious faith. A major difference compared to Protestant Christians is that they connect the Bible to Catholic Tradition and the church.

Why this difference between Catholics and Protestants when it comes to Bible reading? For the first fifteen hundred years of Christian history the average person could not pick up a Bible and read it. In fact, few books existed, and very few people could read. The printing press changed all that, and Protestantism began within decades after the proliferation of printing presses throughout Western Europe. Thanks to his translation, Luther made the Bible accessible to Germans. A few English translations surfaced about that time, but it took until 1611 for the ***King James Version,*** the literary masterpiece produced by Anglican scholars, to be published. In the eyes of the Catholic Church, reading and interpreting the Bible on one's own was dangerous. After all, even the devil can quote scripture! The Council of Trent, 1545–1563, was a major step in the Catholic Church's own reformation. Concerning Bible reading, the council cautioned Catholics to read only approved translations and to read the Bible under the guidance of the church. The Catholic Church emphasized what had been standard in Western Christianity before the printing press: The Christian message was communicated more through nonverbal means than through words.

Vatican Council II, 1962–1965, initiated a number of measures to make the Bible a more prominent feature in Catholic life. However, Catholicism continues to view divine revelation (the Bible), and "how it is handed on" (Tradition), as interwoven and inseparable.

The *King James Version* was the standard English version until after World War II, when a number of new translations were written. This translation is still used almost exclusively by some fundamentalist Christians.

If you were a member of the Gideons and wanted to make available Bibles for people facing difficult challenges in life, what biblical stories or passages would you recommend they read? You might begin with Isaiah 41:10 and John 14:27. Are there stories or sayings from other sources that you would place in hotel rooms for travelers to read and find comfort from?

The Catholic Church cautions that the Bible can be used in misguided ways. Do you know of ways in which that has happened or continues to happen today? (For example, some slave owners in the Southern United States quoted the Bible to justify slavery and even saw in the Bible grounds for considering people of African descent as inferior.)

Seeing the Big Picture—The Story of Salvation

Many people have started out on the journey of reading the entire Bible cover to cover. Few people have completed that journey. Many who have persevered would describe the journey with the famous Grateful Dead lyric: "What a long, strange trip it's been." What is a romantic love poem that doesn't even mention God (Song of Solomon, or Song of Songs) doing in the midst of it? Why are there laws about the appropriate punishment when your bull gores a neighbor's slave and kills him? Does it make any sense that King Saul was commanded by God to slaughter all the inhabitants of a village he was attacking? The final book of the Christian Bible, the book of Revelation, contains a battle scene that rivals a Marvel Comics blockbuster movie. The scriptures, written and rewritten over centuries, tend to be multifaceted and influenced by crises and concerns of their times, and they use imagery and speech patterns familiar to the audiences of their times. Catholicism asserts that there is a consistent message in the Bible and that this message is grounds for hope for all humanity.

Catholicism is based upon the belief that the Bible tells the story of (1) *creation*, (2) *the fall*, and (3) *redemption*. Each of those words refers to experiences that all humanity shares in.

Creation. We exist, "fearfully and wonderfully made," "knit together in our mother's womb" (Psalm 139:13–14).

The fall. We experience separation, dissatisfaction, wants unmet, uncertainty, and longing. "As a deer longs for flowing streams, so my soul longs for you, O God. My soul thirsts for God, for the living God" (Psalm 42:1–2).

Redemption. A redeemer is one who pays the price for a slave to be set free. For Catholics, Christ is that redeemer, our longing fulfilled: "We have an advocate with the Father, Jesus Christ the righteous; and he is the atoning sacrifice for our sins, and not for ours only but also for the sins of the whole world" (1 John 2:1–2).

For Catholics, through the twists and turns of the biblical narrative, the central theme remains steady: We are here; our life is not all we would like it to be; in Christ, we live in hope of new life on earth and beyond. The Bible is certainly filled with bewildering stories and arcane laws. And yet the central message flows along its course, like a mountain stream that makes its way from its source to its endpoint. Jews find the message of God's steadfast love in the story of their people. Muslims find the biblical message reinforced and further clarified by revelations made to their prophet Muhammad. Christians find Jesus to be the culmination of the message, as stated near the end of the very last book of the Christian Bible: "I am the Alpha and the Omega, the first and the last, the beginning and the end" (Revelation 22:13).

> My child, be attentive to my words; incline your ear to my sayings. Do not let them escape from your sight; keep them within your heart. For they are life to those who find them, and healing to all their flesh.
>
> Proverbs 4:20–22

- In your own words, sum up the overall message of the Bible as you understand it.
- Elaborate on the Bible's core message of creation, fall, and redemption. Describe how it might apply to someone's personal life.

III. The Contents of the Old Testament

The Books of the Old Testament

Bible means "the books," or even more precisely, "little books." (Some writings are as brief as one page but are still called "books.") How did these books become recognized as scripture? This is the question of **canonicity**. "Canon" means rule or measure. For instance, some people got together and decided how long an inch, a foot, a yard, and a mile are. There is a standard rule for measuring distance. If someone claims to run a mile in the fastest time ever, then it is important to know exactly how far a mile is, and everyone needs to be in agreement about that. A few hundred years before the time of Jesus, Jewish scholars gathered to "set the canon" of the Bible. That is, they decided what was to be included in their sacred scripture.

Protestants and Jews today recognize thirty-nine books as making up the canon of the Hebrew Bible. Catholics include an additional seven books because about 150 years before the time of Jesus some Jewish scholars in Egypt, where Greek was the common language, translated their Bible into Greek and included in it seven more recent writings in their translation that Jews in Israel did not include. Christianity used this translation, called the *Septuagint*, as the basis for its version of the Old Testament until Luther and early Protestants concluded that only the thirty-nine books—those written almost exclusively in Hebrew—were to be recognized as scripture. Catholic Bibles include an additional seven books, adding up to forty-six books.

Jews divide the Bible into three sections: the *Torah* (the first five books), the *prophets* (the history from the conquest of Canaan to the founding of Jerusalem after the exile in Babylon), and the *writings* (the remaining historical, poetic, and wisdom literature). Catholic translations divide what Jews label the prophetic books into two separate sections, "historical books" and "the prophets," so a Catholic Bible is divided into four sections. The first five books, called the Torah (in Greek, the *Pentateuch*, meaning "five books"), end with people who had been landless, oppressed, and enslaved looking out at the promised land. The historical books move the story along, describing historical developments from the conquest of the land onward. Prophets emerge who chastise those who have gone astray and challenge people to be steadfast in their fidelity to God. The fourth section of the Old Testament is made up of songs (psalms), poems, and what is called "wisdom literature."

Catholicism divides the Old Testament into four sections:

- The Pentateuch (the Torah or "the Law")
- The Historical Books (from the conquest of Canaan to the time the canon is established)
- The Prophets (preachers warning about being faithful to the covenant)
- The Writings (psalms, poetry, and wisdom literature)

Before reading the following brief summary of the contents of the Old Testament, look at the Table of Contents of a Bible and then read through some of the text itself to get a sense of the scope of the books of the Bible.

Abraham and the Covenant

> Now the LORD said to Abram, "Go from your country and your kindred and your father's house to the land that I will show you. I will make of you a great nation, and I will bless you, and make your name great."
>
> Genesis 12:1–2

The beginning chapters of the first book, Genesis, have stories about creation, a garden paradise peopled by only one man and one woman, a serpent-tempter condemned to crawl on its belly forevermore, banishment from paradise, a brother killing a brother, a misguided attempt to build a tower up to heaven, and a great flood. These stories have a mythical quality to them. If they began with the words, "Once upon a time ... ," we would appreciate that they are not the stuff of factual history but instead are conveying an understanding of the worldview held by a particular group of people. They were stories told to contrast their understanding of God and humanity with the worldview of the cultures around them. Who were those people?

Chapter twelve of Genesis might be a more logical place to begin your Bible reading. It introduces a man who can claim to have some actual historical substance to him—Abram, whose name is changed to Abraham. The Bible says that his birthplace was "Ur of the Chaldees," a town that actually exists in modern-day Iraq with a different name. He leaves his homeland, as directed by a God quite different from the gods of his surrounding community. He sets off with his family and becomes a nomad, traveling about lands such as Egypt and Canaan that we would recognize today. We might imagine that leaving his homeland was the start of a great adventure, but he was actually taking a great risk. He was the patriarch of a family of nomadic herders, the Hebrews, a word indicating that they were migrants, aliens who couldn't stay in any one place for long, a people without a homeland. In other words, if Abraham did indeed choose to leave his homeland, he was putting himself and his family in a precarious position. Egyptians were from Egypt, Babylonians were from Babylonia, but

Hebrews were from no place in particular. They had to make their way through territories claimed by other people. It took cunning and, in the broad sense of the word, faith to survive when moving from place to place.

Abraham and his descendants did more than survive. What sustained him was his relationship with God, which the Bible refers to as a ***covenant***. A covenant is an agreement, usually between a ruler and subjects. In the Bible, it came to describe the relationship between Abraham and his descendants with their God: "You shall be my people, and I will be your God" (Ezekiel 36:28). Leaving Ur was a test of faith. Abraham is put to an even greater test when God commands him to sacrifice his only son, Isaac. Abraham trusts God, and in time God's promise to him is fulfilled. His descendants, under the leadership of Moses, gain a homeland, and they become as numerous as the "stars in the sky."

The Exodus, from Slavery to Freedom and a Homeland

> Then the Lord said, "I have observed the misery of my people who are in Egypt; I have heard their cry on account of their taskmasters. Indeed, I know their sufferings, and I have come down to deliver them from the Egyptians, and to bring them up out of that land to a good and broad land, a land flowing with milk and honey."
>
> Exodus 3:7–8

The central event in the sweeping story of God's chosen people is the ***Exodus***, told in the second book of the Bible, and the greatest figure in the story is a man named Moses. Besides being the foundation of Jewish identity, and the lens through which Christians understand Christ's death and resurrection, the Exodus is one of the great stories in human history. The basic story has historical veracity to it. There were slaves in Egypt, and many of them traced their ancestry back to Abraham. In the twelfth century BCE freed slaves and other landless Hebrews gained strength and an identity as a people powerful enough to take control of the land of Canaan. In the biblical account, this unbelievable turnaround is attributed totally to God. That theme, the lowly raised up, the homeless given a home, a group of "nobodies" becoming the chosen ones, runs throughout the entire Bible. For instance, Jesus, a landless peasant himself, comes to be recognized by his followers as the embodiment of God. Mary, Jesus's mother, declares herself to be a lowly one who has been raised up to be the mother of Christ.

The Exodus is often viewed as the story of a battle between the Egyptian gods and the God of Moses: who is more powerful? More importantly, it is about a God who has compassion on the suffering of an enslaved people. God knows suffering. God hears their cry and intervenes on their behalf. Throughout the Bible, we discover that God is always on the side of those who are hurting and most in need. Exodus is a story of liberation, trials, and finally fulfillment. According to the story, the freed slaves spent forty years in the desert before they even saw the promised land. There were times when things got so bad that they wanted to return to slavery in Egypt. They persevered. Moses encountered God, revealed in the sacred name YHWH. During that time of trials and desert wanderings, a bond was forged among the people and with their God. They became a people with their own story, a set of laws, and an identity always linked to God.

> When Africans enslaved in America heard the story of Exodus, it held special meaning for them. What are some ways that the theme of the story might be applied to other groups, perhaps even to your own life?

King David and the Golden Age of Israel

> David reigned over all Israel; and he administered justice and equity to all his people.
>
> 1 Chronicles 18:14

The lowly Hebrews, known as the Israelites or the children of Israel after Abraham's grandson Jacob/Israel, did not simply enter the promised land and immediately take it over. It took two hundred years before control of it was secure enough that they cried out to have an earthly king like other nations had. The first king, Saul, was a military general whose reign ended in his suicide after he saw his last son killed in battle. The next king, however, succeeded in bringing real glory and prestige to Israel. The story of King David mirrors the theme underlying the stories of Abraham and the Exodus. God reveals to a holy man named Samuel that the one chosen to be king was the son of a man named Jesse, who lived in the little town of Bethlehem. Samuel went to Bethlehem and met Jesse's seven sons. However, God let Samuel know that none of these men were to be anointed as the future king. Jesse told Samuel that only his youngest was not accounted for, a mere boy who was out tending the sheep. The boy David was brought before Samuel, and God let it be known that this least likely candidate was the one to be anointed as the future king.

Like other stories in the Bible, this one is also a "David and Goliath" story. The Israelites were descendants of nomads who lacked the trappings of power possessed by Egypt and Babylonia. Nonetheless, the Israelites became God's chosen people. Under David and his son Solomon, the promise God had made to Abraham seemed to have been fulfilled. However, the coalition of tribes fell apart; the nation lost power when it separated into two—Israel and Judah.

One concept that emerged after the splitting of the kingdom into two and the subsequent conquest of them by other nations is *mashiah* or *messiah*. The term means "anointed one." Rulers were anointed with oil to signify their having been chosen to take on this responsibility. For instance, David was anointed when he became king. When the king-dom fell apart after Solomon, there was a longing within the community for a new King David, a newly anointed one, who would restore peace and prosperity to the nation.

One thousand years after David, a man came to be recognized by his followers as the messiah, even though he was not what most Jews looked for in the messiah. In

Young King David is associated wit slaying the giant and writing psalms.

Greek, messiah, anointed one, is ***christ***, a word that can be either a common noun or a proper name.

Read about King David in 1 and 2 Samuel. What qualities stand out about him?

Prophets, Mouthpieces of God

And what does the Lord require of you but to do justice, and to love kindness, and to walk humbly with your God?

Micah 6:8

As the two kingdoms were falling apart, God sent prophets to warn rulers and subjects alike that the unjust practices they engaged in would lead to their destruction. The words of the prophets are collected in books of the Bible mostly named after them: Isaiah, Jeremiah, Hosea, Micah, and others. The prophets chastised Israelites who had become wealthy for not taking better care of widows, orphans, foreigners, and other people in need in the community. They were great preachers, chosen not by kings but by God. The prophets of Israel shared common characteristics. They spoke with reluctance, even offering excuses about why they were not up to the task. And yet in the books of the prophets are found some of the most memorable lines from the Bible. They were not "smooth talkers," telling kings and the people in power what they wanted to hear. They spoke a harsh message, telling people that if they did not follow the teachings from the best of their tradition, destruction would follow. In the end they offered words of hope. Even though the children of Israel did not adhere to the covenant, God always remains faithful to God's promise.

The prophet Jeremiah reprimands people who are greedy for unjust gain, engage in shameful practices, and yet refuse to admit their wrongdoing. In exasperation, he says that they have forgotten how to blush (8:12). What does this mean?

Who do you think plays the role of a prophet in society today?

This Christmas season, listen to Handel's *Messiah*. Much of the libretto is from the prophet Isaiah.

> Read through the books of the prophets. Take note of passages that have become famous, such as this: "They shall beat their swords into ploughshares, and their spears into pruning-hooks; nation shall not lift up sword against nation, neither shall they learn war any more" (Isaiah 2:4).

Psalms and Wisdom Literature

> I called on God, and the spirit of wisdom came to me. I preferred her to sceptres and thrones, and I accounted wealth as nothing in comparison with her.
>
> Wisdom of Solomon, 7:7–8

Different parts of the Bible are attributed to different authors. The first five books, which spell out "the law," are the books of Moses. The psalms, one hundred and fifty songs often used in community worship, are attributed to King David. (When he was a boy, David played a stringed musical instrument to soothe King Saul.) David's son Solomon was considered a wise ruler, so writings on wisdom are associated with him. There are six books that are categorized as "wisdom literature." More than other parts of the Bible, the writings about wisdom speak to all people. In some of these writings, wisdom is personified ("Wisdom") and always referred to as "she." It is Wisdom who establishes order in the world. People would do well to ask God for wisdom, as Solomon did, so that their lives conform to the ways of God. The wise sayings in these writings offer practical guidance for everyday living, such as "Do not wear yourself out to get rich: be wise enough to desist" (Proverbs 23:4).

> Read the book of Job. What message does it contain? Is there wisdom in this message?
>
> St. Athanasius said, "The psalms seem to me to be like a mirror, in which one can see himself and the stirrings of his own heart; he can recite them against the background of his own emotions." Read a few psalms and determine if there is some truth in what Athanasius said.

The Bible in a Catholic Worldview

Along with the rest of Christianity, Catholicism accepts the Bible as the word of God; but it sees no conflict between science and scripture in interpreting the Bible. Therefore, in a Catholic worldview the Bible is inspired by God and true, despite containing some stories that are not what we understand to be historically accurate or based on science. The Bible is filled with meaning, even though stories and passages are at times enigmatic, confusing, and not easily understandable.

A Catholic worldview looks beyond the words themselves, the literal sense, to discover spiritual meaning in the words, sayings, and stories of the Bible. Delving into the spiritual sense of scripture means that Catholics believe the Bible to be not simply about events of the distant past but actually applicable to concerns of today. The Exodus story is about people who are enslaved but with God's help are making their way to freedom. That story is relived by everyone today searching for their true home, their true selves, and true justice and peace, unshackled from burdens that hold them back. The Song of Solomon is love poetry, pure and simple. However, Catholics read into it the passionate love God has for the beloved. Catholics hope to number themselves among God's beloved. When King David goes astray but admits his guilt and seeks God's forgiveness, his story is repeated every time a Catholic attends Mass and takes to heart the words "Let us call to mind our sins," asking for God's forgiveness. In other words, in Catholicism, the Bible is the word of God that speaks from the past to give counsel, challenge, comfort, and hope to people today.

Chapter Review

1. Define the following terms: modernism, *Divino Afflante Spiritu*, the historical-critical method, biblical fundamentalism, exegesis, canonicity, and Septuagint.

2. What is the difference between a literal and a spiritual sense of scripture? Give an example of the four senses of scripture.

3. What is the Catholic understanding of biblical inspiration?

4. What is the relationship between scripture and tradition for Catholicism?

5. Describe the difference between a Protestant and a Catholic attitude toward Bible reading.
6. What is the central message of the Bible?
7. What are the four major sections of the Old Testament as Catholicism divides them?
8. Who were Abraham and the Hebrews?
9. What is the theme of the Exodus story?
10. What characteristics does King David share with other biblical figures?
11. What role did prophets play for the rulers and people of Israel?
12. Who was associated with the authorship of the Torah, the psalms, and the wisdom literature?

For Further Study

Miguel A. De La Torre. *Reading the Bible from the Margins.* Orbis Books, 2002. Many theologians apply a liberation theology perspective to their analysis of scripture, usually focusing on the Exodus and the prophets in the Old Testament and Jesus in the New. De La Torre looks at not only poverty but also other concerns such as sexism and racism from the perspective of poor, marginalized, and oppressed people and contrasts it with the perspective of traditional mainstream theology.

Dei Verbum. Dogmatic Constitution on Divine Revelation. www.vatican.va. This constitution from Vatican Council II offers a Catholic understanding of God's revelation to humanity and especially of the Bible's place in that revelation.

Abraham J. Heschel. *The Prophets: An Introduction* (Volume 1). Harper Colophon Books, 1962. Explains the role of prophets in ancient Jewish society in Heschel's powerful literary style, e.g., "The prophet is scorched by the word of God."

James L. Kugel. *How to Read the Bible: A Guide to Scripture Then and Now.* Free Press, 2007. Provides an extensive "tour" of the Hebrew Bible and examines in particular how early scholars (second century BCE and afterward) interpreted biblical stories and passages compared to how modern-day scholars interpret them. Makes the point that the Bible has always been subject to interpretation, even within the Bible itself.

Carolyn Osiek, RSCJ, editor. *Anselm Academic Study Bible: New American Bible Revised Edition*. Anselm Academic, 2012. A number of "study editions" of Bibles are available. This one contains one hundred pages of background information helpful in reading and understanding biblical writings, such as a description of the historical-critical method, geography of biblical times, and various approaches to interpreting the Bible.

David Harrington Watt. *Bible-Carrying Christians: Conservative Christians and Social Power*. Oxford University Press, 2002. An ethnographic study of three Christian churches with the author's personal observations about the centrality of the Bible in each one and the differences among them.

Chapter 4
The Gospels: The Good News of Christ

For Christians, the Gospels are the heart of the New Testament as well as of the entire Bible. Not only are these four writings the primary source of information about Jesus, but they also provide a framework through which to understand how Jesus is the Messiah of the Jews, the Son of God, and the savior of the world. In other words, they tell us about Jesus and also what Jesus means for the people of the world. They were written from forty to seventy years after the time of Jesus to gather together in narrative form the stories that people who knew him had been handing down. A reading from one of these Gospels is a central part of every Catholic Mass. They are not only read at Mass, but also proclaimed. Everyone stands when the words of these writings are read aloud during the liturgy. In this chapter, we will look at how the Gospels relate the story of Jesus, each one from a unique perspective, but all of them making the case that Jesus is what the word "gospel" means—good news.

> It is common knowledge that among all the Scriptures, even those of the New Testament, the Gospels have a special preeminence, and rightly so, for they are the principal witness for the life and teaching of the incarnate Word, our savior.
>
> <div align="right">Vatican Council II, <i>Dei Verbum</i>, "Dogmatic Constitution on Divine Revelation" (#18)</div>

Read through the four Gospels. What is the good news they proclaim?

Which Gospel resonates most strongly with your understanding of Jesus?

What is your impression of Jesus from reading through the Gospels?

Which stories and sayings do you find most baffling?

I. The Makeup of the New Testament

Three Stages Leading Up to the Gospels: Eyewitness Accounts, Oral Tradition, Written Gospels

> The Apostles, ... by their oral preaching, by example, and by observances handed on what they had received from the lips of Christ, from living with Him, and from what He did, or what they had learned through the prompting of the Holy Spirit. The commission was fulfilled, too, by those Apostles and apostolic men who under the inspiration of the same Holy Spirit committed the message of salvation in writing.
>
> *Dei Verbum* (#7)

America's involvement in the Vietnam War ended in 1973, around fifty years ago. There are some people alive today who have first-hand recollections of the war, but even for them it is a distant memory. For most Americans it happened long ago in a land far away. The young Americans who fought in the war seem frozen in time. What was it actually like for a Nebraska farm boy or a young man fresh off the streets of Chicago to carry heavy equipment through tropical jungles and enter villages filled with frightened people who couldn't be distinguished friend from foe? Some who lived through the war have told their stories, and at times their stories have become part of family lore. At fewer and fewer family gatherings are the names of the dead even mentioned anymore. Books, films, and memorials try to keep the memory alive; each one also seeks to draw meaning from what happened. For instance, the Vietnam War Memorial in Washington lists the names of all those who died, lest we forget that real people with real families and real hopes and dreams died during it.

Jesus died around 30 CE. The best scholarship indicates that the writings we call Gospels were written around 70–100 CE. That's a gap of forty to seventy years, so in some cases greater than the time distance between the Vietnam War and today. During the period from the death of Jesus and his resurrection to the first written Gospels, the number of people who put their faith in him had grown well beyond the land where events took place. Most had never been to places like Galilee and Jerusalem. Early on, they heard testimony from people who actually knew Jesus personally—*eyewitness accounts*; but more and more, people heard stories about Jesus secondhand, from people who knew the people who were there. Stories handed down are known as **oral tradition**. The written *Gospels* we can read in the Bible were composed by people who wanted to make sure the story did not get lost. They also wanted to make sure that the *meaning* of the story did not get lost or distorted. These four authors are called ***evangelists***, meaning proclaimers of good news, the way television networks might break into regular programming to announce good news, that something wonderful has happened that makes all the difference in the world. Here's how the Gospel according to Luke puts it:

> Since many have undertaken to set down an orderly account of the events that have been fulfilled among us, just as they were handed on to us by those who from the beginning were eyewitnesses and servants of the word, I too decided, after investigating everything carefully from the very first, to write an orderly account for you, most excellent Theophilus, so that you may know the truth concerning the things about which you have been instructed. (1:1–4)

The author of Luke's Gospel is not claiming to be an eyewitness but rather is someone putting together an orderly account of what had been handed down. Because of the three-stage process leading to the final writing of the Gospels and the time gap between actual events and the written texts, it is unlikely that they were written by any of the twelve apostles. (The *Catechism* describes these three stages in Gospel development in paragraph 128.) The Catholic Church sees a direct link between the written Gospels and the apostles and "apostolic men." Internal evidence suggests that one or more of the Gospels was not written by Jews but by non-Jewish, Gentile Christians. One outlier theory makes the case that, because of its emphasis on Mary and other women, the author of the Gospel according to Luke might have been a woman scribe. Two hundred years after Jesus there is a reference to the Gospel authors as Matthew, Mark, Luke, and John. Traditions built up about who these evangelists were. For instance, a New Testament letter attributed to St. Paul refers to a Luke as a "beloved physician" who was one of Paul's companions. Longstanding tradition identifies this physician as the author of Luke's Gospel and the Acts of the Apostles. The apostle John was seen as the youngest of the twelve apostles and particularly loved by Jesus. He is associated with the Gospel according to John. Since the Gospel according to Mark talks so much about St. Peter, the author perhaps was a secretary or companion of Peter. Traditionally, the Gospel writers were depicted with symbols, mentioned in the book of Revelation, that represented their unique point of view: Matthew, a winged man; Mark, a lion; Luke, an ox; and John, an eagle.

Investigations into and debates about who wrote the Gospels and when and where they were written are interesting academic exercises. However, Catholicism shares with all Christians the belief that the four Gospels provide a window into Jesus, who is indeed *the* gospel. Therefore, "The Church 'forcefully and specifically exhorts all the Christian faithful ... to learn "the surpassing knowledge of Jesus Christ," by frequent reading of the divine Scriptures. "Ignorance of the Scriptures is ignorance of Christ"'" (*Catechism*, #133).

The traditional symbols associated with the four evangelists, the gospel writers

According to Catholicism, the Gospels were (a) the work of four individuals who wrote what had been handed down to them and incorporated their own perspective on Jesus, and (b) the word of God. Are these two statements contradictory? How can they be reconciled?

Is there "oral tradition" in your family, school, or community, stories handed down from one generation to the next? Give examples. Have they become more and more formalized over time?

Were More than Four Gospels Written?

If by "gospels" you mean accounts of sayings and deeds of Jesus written during the first few centuries after him, then the answer is yes, more than the four Gospels were written. In 1992, Robert J. Miller edited a collection he called *The Complete Gospels* in which he places the four **canonical** Gospels (recognized by the church and included in the Bible) alongside other writings from the early Christian era that speak of the words and deeds of Jesus. They are mostly fragments found by archaeologists in the past eighty years or merely referenced in other writings. Often, these noncanonical "gospels" parallel what is in the canonical Gospels; but at times they include stories not found anywhere else. A writing called "The Infancy Narrative of Thomas" describes five-year-old Jesus fashioning birds out of mud on the Sabbath. When his father, Joseph, asks him about it, he breathes on them and they come alive and fly away. Most of these writings, when mentioned at all, were declared heretical by leading Christian scholars and leaders. It appears that efforts were made to destroy such writings. Some managed to survive. One notable "gospel" is the "gospel of Thomas," found in the late 1940s in a library buried in the sands of Egypt. It is available online. Miller's 1992 collection could be expanded today to include some other writings discovered since then. For instance, there is a "gospel of Judas," not translated into English until 2006, that has an interesting perspective on Judas. Portrayed in the canonical Gospels as the one who betrayed Jesus, in this "gospel" he is the only one who truly understood what Jesus needed to do (die on the cross) and thus played a necessary role in causing that to happen. Jesus thanks Judas for what he did.

The question is, should these nonbiblical writings be considered gospels? There's a story of an old-time baseball umpire calling balls and strikes. After a borderline pitch, the batter turned to the ump and asked, "Was it a ball or a strike?" The umpire said, "It ain't anything until I call it." What is in the Bible is there because of decisions by leaders in the Jewish community (for the Hebrew Bible) and the Christian community (for the New Testament). Not every ancient Jewish writing was included in the Hebrew Bible. A group of Jewish leaders made the call about what is and what is not scripture. The same is true of the New Testament. Early Christians treated certain writings as scripture. In time, church leaders declared what is to be considered the Bible. Their decisions were not arbitrary. For the most part, the writings that make up the Bible were already treasured as the word of God before community leaders canonized them as such. For instance, when St. Paul wrote his letters to various communities throughout the Roman Empire, he was not envisioning that they would one day be considered sacred scripture along with the book of Genesis and the Psalms. As his letters became more widely known, the followers of Jesus recognized them as inspired by God and deserving to be called sacred scripture. In time, they were canonized as such.

The realization that the Gospels and other New Testament writings emerged out of the Christian community dispels two commonly held myths. For one thing, people might say that at first there was the Bible; and then the church came into existence and is based on the Bible. It is more accurate to say that "the church," the community of believers, existed before there was a New Testament. The gospel writers were giving voice to what people in the community believed, especially as it was understood to be handed down from the apostles. Secondly, we might say that in the beginning of the Christian movement there was uniformity; and then there started to be disagreements and divisions. Actually, there were different ways of describing the role of Jesus, the makeup of the Bible, and other significant questions right from the beginning. Within twenty years of the time of Jesus, in his letter to the Galatians, St. Paul was warning about false prophets spreading misleading teachings. One early Christian writer, Marcion, did not want to include the Old Testament as scripture. He proposed that only the Gospel according to Luke should be considered scripture. After centuries of struggles, more and more uniformity existed in the church than existed in the first couple of centuries.

> Read about "apocryphal gospels." What are they, and why do you think they were not included in the New Testament?

The Makeup of the New Testament

The New Testament includes letters, also called epistles, many written by St. Paul or attributed to him; the Gospels, four narrative accounts of the life of Jesus; the Acts of the Apostles, an account of the earliest days in the life of the church; and Revelation, a highly symbolic account of the end times.

The New Testament, twenty-seven books in all, is written in what is called ***Koine*** (pronounced coy-nay) Greek. It is not the Greek used in the great philosophical and scholarly writings of the classical period of learning in Greece. Koine Greek was used by Alexander the Great's soldiers during his conquest of the Middle East in the third century BCE, and it became the universal language of the area for centuries afterward. People who spoke different languages could communicate in this simple form of Greek. Shopkeepers and neighbors spoke Koine Greek to communicate and transact business despite coming from different cultures with different languages. Jews who lived outside of Israel typically were more comfortable in this language than in Hebrew or Aramaic, the language Jesus spoke. The earliest writings of the New Testament, Paul's letters, were addressed to people living in major cities of the Roman Empire. It made sense for him to write his letters in this kind of Greek. To reach as broad an audience as possible, the rest of the New Testament was also composed in Greek. The authors were not interested in creating scholarly treatises to be shared only among highly educated scholars, and they were not writing solely for a Jewish audience. They used the common language because they wanted to speak to the common people.

St. Paul died in the mid-sixties in Rome. In other words, his letters were composed before the four Gospels were written and represent the oldest writings of the New Testament. The last book of the Bible, Revelation, was likely written thirty-five to forty years after Paul wrote his letters. The Gospels show evidence of being written by people from different backgrounds and at different times during the last third of the first century. Three Gospels—Matthew, Mark, and Luke—are very similar, so much so that they are called *synoptic* Gospels, meaning similar or sharing the same point of view. (They share the same "optics.") Matthew is always placed first in the Bible, not because it was the first one written but because Christians came to see the fullest presentation of the teachings of Jesus in this Gospel. (Up until the changes following Vatican Council II in the late 1960s, over 80 percent of Sunday Mass Gospel readings were from Matthew.) Scholars generally agree that Mark was probably the first Gospel written, followed ten to fifteen years later by Matthew and Luke. The authors of the Gospels according to Matthew and Luke knew Mark's Gospel and built on it. The Gospel according to John doesn't build on Mark. It refers to some of the same incidents and teachings found in the synoptics but also includes others that are not.

The central story of each of the Gospels is the arrest, trial, torture, crucifixion, and resurrection of Jesus, what are called the *passion narratives*. (The word "passion" comes from a Latin word meaning "to suffer.") The major concern was how to make sense of someone who was arrested and killed for sedition being the Messiah of the Jews and the savior of the world. The Gospels actually reimagine this reality not as a stumbling block to belief in Jesus but as the very reason to believe in him. He was love personified, and his sacrifice on the cross was the ultimate expression of that love. In a sense, everything in the Gospels before the passion narrative is a prelude to the main event. The miraculous healings in Mark's Gospel are a foretaste of the love of God manifest most powerfully in Jesus's death on the cross. In John's Gospel, Jesus talks at length about the love of God and loving one another. He models that love on the cross, and therefore his death was not a victory for the powers of darkness but a passageway to new life. In other words, behind the differences among the Gospels is the basic message that Jesus is the Messiah of the Jews and the savior of the world. Jesus is the gospel, the good news; the four Gospels tell his story. His story provides hope to Christians who face death themselves and profess love to be their primary vocation in life.

Your word is a lamp to my feet and a light to my path.

Catechism, #141

> Read three different "reflections on the COVID-19 pandemic" or descriptions of other recent events, such as the Black Lives Matter protests in 2020 or the storming of the US Capitol on January 6, 2021. Describe differences among the three points of view.
>
> What do you associate with the word "passion"? Do you see a connection between your associations and the word's root meaning, to suffer?

II. The Four Gospels

A quick read of the Gospels suggests that they are reporting a coherent story while adding details and commentary from their own perspective. That is generally true. All of them attest that Jesus taught, preached, and performed miracles for a brief period before being arrested and crucified. All of them recount that some followers experienced his presence among them even after his death and burial. However, the four Gospels have unique perspectives on Jesus and on the implications of his life and message for the people of their respective communities. Was one community primarily from a Jewish or Gentile background? Were there philosophical undercurrents in the area where a Gospel was written that found their way into the gospel account? Were there events, such as the destruction of the temple and the end of the nation of Israel, that colored what a gospel writer wrote about Jesus? Was the Christian community in a particular area living under the threat of persecution, and did that influence what stood out to an evangelist when writing about Jesus?

This next section looks at the four Gospels and identifies core themes in each one. Entire books and courses exist that examine more closely the details of each Gospel. If you want to appreciate the similarities and differences among them, give some time to reading the Gospels along with the description of key themes described here. You might also read other commentaries on each Gospel, and then check them against your own reading of the Gospel itself.

The Gospel according to Mark: The Gospel of the Suffering Messiah

In the 1997 movie *Titanic*, two men claim to love the same woman. One man dies for her; the other seeks to control her. The Gospel according to Mark, the first written and the shortest, is a narrative of a slow progression in making the case that God is selfless, unconditional love and not a possessive or oppressive tyrant. Mark starts immediately by identifying Jesus as "Christ, the Son of God" (1:1). This declaration is affirmed by God, who says, "You are my Son, the Beloved; with you I am well pleased" (1:11). People generally didn't believe this about Jesus. His townspeople knew him only as the carpenter that he had been for thirty years. They took offense when he preached to them in the local synagogue. They grumbled, "Is not this the carpenter, the son of Mary and brother of James and Joses and Judas and Simon, and are not his sisters here with us?" (6:3). Even when he performs miraculous deeds, many Pharisees and scribes, leaders in the community, are skeptical. After all, Satan can use trickery and magic to lure people to the dark side. Even his closest friends don't understand him. He tells them, "Are your hearts hardened? Do you have eyes, and fail to see? Do you have ears, and fail to hear?" 8:17–18). Chapter 8 marks a turning point in the narrative; the apostles begin to get it. The apostle Peter affirms that Jesus is the Messiah (8:29). However, Peter has an understanding of what Messiah means different from how Jesus views it. When Jesus tells Peter that it entails great suffering, Peter rebukes him. Jesus tells Peter that he doesn't really understand his mission: "You are setting your mind not on divine things but on human things" (8:33).

Peter wouldn't be alone in associating the concepts of "Messiah," and "King of the Jews," with glory and worldly power. Many people in the Jewish community of the time did. And isn't it true that today "success" continues to be measured in terms of power and possessions? Jesus knew that the love of God was not "power over"—exercising dominion and domination for one's own benefit; it was not grasping, but letting go. He came to serve, not to be served (Mark 10:45). The Greek word is **kenosis**, "emptying." That's the way true love works, through gentle persuasion rather than heavy-handed control. Throughout the Gospel, Jesus is actively engaged in demonstrating God's love through healing the sick, driving out demons, and even feeding a hungry crowd. And yet the full message, what is called the *messianic secret*, is not revealed until Jesus dies on the cross. It is at that moment when, totally emptied of his life's blood, Jesus is proclaimed by the Roman soldier standing guard: "Truly this man was God's Son!" That proclamation is a secret, a great mystery, in that it is so manifestly different from the ways of the world in its depiction of true love and power.

A model of the temple at the time of Jesus

After Christ's death and burial, Mark's Gospel reports that women who went to anoint the body found the tomb empty except for a young man who told them that Jesus was not among the dead but was to be found among the living. Jesus himself appeared to some of his disciples, and they took up the challenge of proclaiming "eternal salvation" from east to west (16:8). The horrible and humiliating experience of Jesus leading to his crucifixion, so inconceivable even to his closest friends like Peter, becomes for Mark the great revelation of what God is truly like. The passion of Christ reveals the passionate love of God for all creation. For that, Jesus is the good news. His suffering and death were not a triumph of evil over good but an ultimate expression of the goodness of God itself.

Are there still distorted notions of "love" in personal relationships between people today (for example, possessiveness versus selfless giving)? Give examples of true and false expressions of what is called love today.

Do you associate God with selfless love? What does that mean for you personally?

The torture and execution of Jesus were not "necessary," as if God took delight in causing suffering. However, given his actions and his message, Jesus was living out an understanding of God that inevitably led to his death. Even his healing of the sick, which we might see as a good thing, was viewed by some powerful people as a threat. Give examples of how the good news proclaimed in Mark's Gospel could be viewed as a threat or lead to forceful opposition in today's world.

The Gospel according to Matthew: Jesus, Teacher and Messiah

If you wanted to make the case that Jesus was the Messiah anxiously awaited by Jews of the time, how would you do that? One expression consistently found in Matthew's Gospel is "in fulfillment of the scriptures" or "in fulfillment of the prophets." Matthew lays out the story of Jesus as a clear and definitive fulfillment of what the sacred scriptures of the Jews had been leading up to all along. Matthew includes an account of the birth of Jesus, which takes place in Bethlehem, the hometown of the great King David. Matthew provides a genealogy for Jesus, tracing his ancestry back to Abraham, the father of the Jewish people. He arranges extensive teachings of Jesus into five sermons, similar to the five books of teachings in the Hebrew Bible, the Torah. In the first of those sermons, Jesus ascends a mountain, much like Moses did when he received the ten commandments from God. Jesus is the new Moses, offering a fuller understanding of "the law and the prophets." For instance, in his Sermon on the Mount (beginning with chapter 5), Jesus repeatedly says, "You have heard [in the Torah] ... but I say to you." For Matthew, when the prophets of old talked about one who is to come to set things right, a righteous one, it is obvious that Jesus fulfills all of their criteria.

Matthew has Jesus preaching on a mountain, just as Moses received the commandments on a mountain.

Matthew's Gospel was highly prized in Christian communities for its comprehensive teachings of Jesus. Two-thirds of Matthew comes from Mark's Gospel, but Jesus has much more to say in Matthew than in Mark. The eight beatitudes are listed in Matthew. (Luke has four.) Along with Luke, Matthew gives us the words of the *Lord's Prayer*, memorized and recited by Christians throughout the world. The *Catechism* says, "The Lord's Prayer 'is truly the summary of the whole gospel'" (#2761). Matthew has the famous description of how people's lives will be judged:

> I was hungry and you gave me food, I was thirsty and you gave me something to drink. I was a stranger and you welcomed me, I was naked and you gave me clothing. I was sick and you took care of me, I was in prison and you visited me. ... Truly I tell you, just as you did it to one of the least of these who are members of my family, you did it to me. (25:35–36, 40)

A title frequently used for Jesus in Matthew is "rabbi," meaning "teacher." There were prominent rabbis at the time who were educated in the scriptures and revered for their teachings and interpretations of Bible passages. Jesus was not one of them. He was a peasant laborer who became an itinerant preacher for a few years—all the more remarkable that he would gain such a following and draw the attention of those in power. Jesus never rejected "the law" but drew out implications from it, often in ways that were difficult and challenging. He didn't soften what the law said. Some of his teachings deserve to be called *hard sayings*. Loving your enemies (5:44) and turning the other cheek (5:39) when someone strikes you don't come naturally. Murder is terrible, but Jesus says we should not even insult others or say, "You fool" to them (5:22). If someone forces you to walk a mile with them, walk two miles (5:41). These are hard sayings that have perplexed Christians throughout the ages.

Matthew goes to great lengths to make the case that Jesus was the long-awaited Messiah of the Jews. The Gospel also presents Jesus as a wise teacher whose interpretation of the Jewish law could be applied to Jews and non-Jews alike. "Do to others as you would have them do to you" (7:12) and "Love ... God ... and ... your neighbor as yourself" (22:37–39) have universal appeal and remain serious challenges for everyone.

Read the beatitudes listed in Matthew, chapter 5. How would you describe the Christian life based on these sayings?
Read through the Sermon on the Mount, beginning with chapter 5. How do you interpret the meaning of these teachings?
Read the description of judgment in chapter 25. Name specific ways its message could be applied today.

The Gospel according to Luke: Jesus, Savior of the Whole World

Catholicism is known for its commitment to caring for people who are poor and suffering. Every Catholic diocese in the United States has its version of Catholic Charities dedicated to helping people in need. Although the connection is not always explicit today, Catholic schools and hospitals were founded as charitable organizations, providing education and health care to people who would not otherwise have access to them. Many Catholics dedicate their lives to helping people, and all Catholics recognize that giving to others is an important dimension of their faith. They take to heart that "faith without good works is dead" (James 2:26). The Gospel according to Luke is a good place to start in understanding why care for those who are hurting is central to the message of Jesus.

If the world is about to end any minute now, then there's no time to dedicate to reaching out to people in need. There were some people in the earliest days of Christianity who understood the words "The kingdom of God is at hand" to mean that the end of time as we know it is imminent. The author of Luke has a different vision. The story doesn't end with Jesus's resurrection. Luke writes an entirely second volume, the Acts of the Apostles, which describes the spread of the message throughout the empire. That takes time and is ongoing. Before his ascension into heaven, Jesus directs his disciples that "repentance and forgiveness of sins is to be proclaimed in his name to all nations, beginning from Jerusalem. You are witnesses" (Luke 24:47–48). In other words, the work begun by Jesus was to be carried on by them. His message was not just for Jews but for "all nations," Jews and Gentiles alike. The mission entailed working to transform the world, not just spiritually but materially. For instance, in Luke Jesus offers this practical advice about how to live out his message: "When you give a luncheon or a dinner, do not invite your friends or your brothers or your relatives or rich neighbors, in case they may invite you in return, and you would be repaid. But when you give a banquet, invite the poor, the crippled, the lame, and the blind" (Luke 14:12–13).

That concern for people who are poor or left out is typical of Luke. In this Gospel, Jesus doesn't say "blessed are the poor *in spirit*" (as in Matthew 5:3) but more starkly "blessed are the poor" and "woe to the rich." The poor are not simply loved by God; they are deeply cherished. As in Matthew's Gospel, Jesus identifies with those who are poor. To see the face of the poor is to see the face of God. As in Mark's Gospel, Jesus is misunderstood and even rejected by his townspeople and also the leaders of his fellow Jews in Jerusalem. However, Jesus's message and his mission spread beyond the Jewish people. Luke has a genealogy for Jesus, tracing his ancestry all the way back to "Adam, son of God" (3:38). Jesus is the new Adam, the new Son of God. His ancestry is all-encompassing, as is his message. In fact, the Gospel according to Luke and the Acts of the Apostles suggest that the focal point of true faith in Jesus has shifted from Jerusalem to the Gentile world. His message of salvation is for the whole world. For Luke, the mission of Jesus extends in particular to people overlooked or suffering. Those are the people invited to his banquet.

Luke's gospel contains Jesus's most famous parables, such as that of the Good Samaritan.

Luke is the source of the most popular of Jesus's parables. They demonstrate Luke's concern for outcasts, such as Samaritans, sinners who have sunk to rock bottom, and lost sheep. Read the parables of the Good Samaritan and the Prodigal Son. How would you express their message for today?

Read through the Gospel according to Luke. Identify passages that express concern for people who are poor, needy, or outcasts.

Only Matthew and Luke have accounts of the birth of Jesus. We are used to conflating the two versions as if they are one story, but there are differences. (Luke has shepherds; Matthew has magi.) Compare and contrast the stories surrounding the birth of Jesus found in the two Gospels.

The Gospel according to John: "I am the Way, the Truth, and the Life"

The Gospel according to John is very different from the other three Gospels, the synoptics. In the synoptics, Jesus's preaching centers around the kingdom of God and includes many parables. John never mentions the kingdom and makes no use of parables. In the synoptics, Jesus performs miraculous deeds, but not to draw attention to himself. In John, Jesus performs some extraordinary miracles that he puts forth as signs of his divinity. These miraculous "signs" serve as a jumping-off point for Jesus to talk about himself in symbolic terms. For example, after restoring sight to a blind man, Jesus talks at length about how he is "the light of the world." In John, Jesus says "I am" in reference to himself forty-six times. His Jewish audience would know that the holy name for God, who spoke to Moses from a burning bush, was "I am." They recognized that Jesus was clearly associating himself with God by saying "I am."

Scholars point out that the portrayal of Jesus in John's Gospel is **high Christology**, emphasizing the divinity of Christ, compared to the more human portrayal of Jesus in Mark's Gospel. For instance, John does not emphasize Jesus's suffering during his passion. In fact, when he stands before the Roman governor, it seems that Pilate is more on trial than Jesus is. Because of the high Christology in John, it is all the more striking that this Gospel alone includes the story of Jesus getting down on his knees and washing the feet of his apostles. Jesus tells his apostles that they cannot understand the nature of God unless Jesus washes their feet and they do likewise.

The Gospel according to John has a **mystical** quality to it. That is, the reality of Christ is not confined to the limits of time and space; his true identity exists in the eternal realm. The Gospel begins with a poem or hymn proclaiming that Christ, the "Word of God," has existed "from the beginning" (1:1). That obviously doesn't mean that when the universe was first taking shape, Jesus was at the same time walking the earth. Jesus says of himself, "You are from below, I am from above; you are of this world, I am not of this world" (8:23). Jesus was a flesh-and-blood human being, but in his case "the Word became flesh and lived among us" (1:14). Jesus came from God and was God. For John, and for all Christians, that message offers great comfort and reassurance: "Do not let your hearts be troubled. Believe in God, believe also in me" (14:1). It is no wonder that Evangelical Christians recite by heart John 3:16: "For God so loved the world that he gave his only Son, so that everyone who believes in him may not perish but may have eternal life."

Much of the Gospel has Jesus performing wonderful acts and then pointing out how they are "signs" of who he is: "I am" the bread of life, the light of the world, the sheepgate, the good shepherd, the resurrection and the life, the true vine, and ultimately "the way, the truth, and the life" (14:6). Jesus knows the fate that awaits him, but he leaves a "new commandment" to sustain them when he is no longer physically with them: "Love one another. Just as I have loved you, you also should love one another" (13:34). God is love; Jesus is the embodiment of love; all who believe in him are to love. Even though John's Gospel makes no mention of the kingdom of God, it is clear that implied in his high Christology is that all are one in Christ Jesus, and everyone has a part to play.

Read through the passion narratives of Mark, Matthew, and John. What differences do you find in how Jesus experiences his suffering and death?

By the time John's Gospel was written, most Christians came from a Gentile, not a Jewish background. Therefore, the Gospel at times refers to "the Jews" as if those in the Jewish community who opposed Jesus were representative of all the Jewish people, which is clearly not the case. Read articles about "the Jews in John's Gospel" or "anti-Semitism in John's Gospel." What explanations do these authors give for how "the Jews" are portrayed in the Gospel?

Read the opening hymn that begins the Gospel. What does it say about the nature of Christ?

Read one of the discourses of Jesus in which he describes himself in symbolic language. Explain its message. (For instance, after he cures a blind man Jesus contrasts light and darkness. What is the darkness he is talking about? What is the light that he embodies?)

The Four Gospels, a Summary

Mark:

- First Gospel written, around 70 CE
- Shortest Gospel
- One of three synoptic Gospels, along with Matthew and Luke
- Applied the word *gospel* ("good news") to Jesus
- Emphasizes the actions more than the words of Jesus
- Introduces the "messianic secret," that Jesus's true identity is only known in his suffering and death
- Along with the other Gospels, gives details of the last days of Christ, a passion narrative
- Has the shortest account of Jesus's post-resurrection appearances

Matthew:

- Written between 75–85 CE
- Builds on Mark's Gospel
- Makes the strongest case that Jesus is the fulfillment of the Hebrew scriptures
- Contains an infancy narrative, including the visit of magi
- Traces Jesus's ancestry, through Joseph, back to Abraham
- Divides Jesus's teachings into five sermons, similar to the five books of Moses
- Includes the Sermon on the Mount, the eight beatitudes, and many "hard sayings"
- Contains the Lord's Prayer and the basis for judgment—helping "the least" is helping Christ

Luke:

- Most likely written between 80–85 CE
- Familiar with Mark's Gospel and builds on it along with another source
- Describes more prominent roles of women than other Gospels

- Infancy narrative begins with good news proclaimed to lowly shepherds
- Traces Jesus's ancestry back to Adam and ultimately to God
- Contains the most famous parables, e.g., the Good Samaritan and the Prodigal Son
- The message of Jesus goes out from Jerusalem to the Gentile world
- Has a particular emphasis on caring for the poor and people who are overlooked

John:

- Last Gospel written, probably in the 90s CE
- Makes no use of the synoptics and contains several stories not found in them
- Begins with a hymn about the Word of God becoming human
- A "high Christology" portrait of Jesus, emphasizing his oneness with God
- Jesus uses the phrase "I am" to speak about himself
- Signs illustrate Jesus's divinity, followed by symbolic images (e.g., the bread of life)
- Jesus assures his followers: do not be afraid, and love one another
- Suffering of Jesus is downplayed during his trial and crucifixion

Four Portraits of Christ, the Good News

> Now Jesus did many other signs in the presence of his disciples, which are not written in this book. But these are written so that you may come to believe that Jesus is the Messiah, the Son of God, and that through believing you may have life in his name.
>
> John 20:30–31

The Gospels are not biographies in the modern sense of the word. The authors don't mask the joy and the peace they find in the story they tell of Jesus. They wrote to offer reassurance to believers and to explain why their faith in Jesus is well founded. No doubt they also wrote to persuade inquisitive nonbelievers that the Christ whom their Christian neighbors believed in should be accepted by them as well. Modern scholarship has shed light on the Gospels, identifying timelines, sources, and major themes. The bishops of Vatican Council II recognized that "there is a growth in the understanding of the realities and the words which have been handed down" (*Dei Verbum*, #8). Catholic parishes often run Bible study groups, and the homilies at weekly and daily Mass tend to be more Gospel-centered than they used to be. Even the hymns sung during liturgies reflect Gospel themes more now than sixty years ago. There is now no question but that the Bible is a Catholic book, and the Gospels are the centerpiece of that book.

The four Gospels are a great gift from the early church to the world. It is primarily through them that people know Jesus. Imagine no Christmas or Easter, known to us through the Gospels. People who are suffering can find solace in the Gospels. The Gospel accounts of Jesus's suffering, death, and new life bring comfort to people facing their own death. Many people are inspired to work at making the world a better place by the stirring words of Jesus found in the Gospels. The Gospels tell us about Jesus who, as one of us, enlightened us about that which is greater. St. Peter speaks for all Christians when he says to Jesus: "Lord, to whom can we go? You have the words of eternal life" (John 6:68). Catholics find in the Gospels the story of the one who bears the message of eternal life.

Chapter Review

1. What three stages led up to the Gospels found in the Bible?

2. What is the difference between the canonical and noncanonical Gospels?

3. From a Catholic perspective, which came first, the church or the Gospels? Explain.

4. What four types of writing make up the New Testament?

5. What is Koine Greek? Why was it used for New Testament texts?

6. What are the synoptic Gospels? What does the word mean?

7. What are the passion narratives?
8. How does Mark refer to Jesus at the beginning of the Gospel?
9. How do most of his fellow Jews initially look upon Jesus in Mark's Gospel?
10. How does St. Peter misinterpret what being the Messiah means?
11. What is the messianic secret in Mark's Gospel?
12. What are some ways that Matthew's Gospel makes the case that Jesus is the fulfillment of the Hebrew scriptures?
13. What are some key passages found in Matthew?
14. What are the "hard sayings" of Jesus?
15. What is a rabbi? How does Matthew portray Jesus as a rabbi?
16. Which two Gospels include an infancy narrative?
17. Which Gospel writer also wrote the Acts of the Apostles?
18. What does Luke's Gospel emphasize as the vocation of being a follower of Jesus?
19. The focal point of the Christian mission shifts location in Luke's Gospel. Where is the Gospel finding a home for Luke?
20. Give an example of Jesus's concern for people who are poor in Luke's Gospel.
21. What are some key differences between John's Gospel and the synoptics?
22. How would Jesus's audience understand his constant use of the phrase "I am"?
23. What purpose do miracles accomplish in John?
24. What are some of the symbolic images Jesus uses to explain himself in John's Gospel?
25. What does it mean to say that John's description of Jesus represents "high Christology"?
26. What does it mean to say that John's Gospel has a mystical quality?

27. What are Jesus's followers supposed to do when Jesus is no longer physically with them?

For Further Study

Raymond E. Brown. *Responses to 101 Questions on the Bible*. Paulist Press, 1990. Anticipates many questions thoughtful people have about the Bible, especially related to Gospel accounts of Jesus. Brown's brief, highly readable responses are sensitive to concerns of general readers but also represent solid scholarship on each question.

Bart D. Ehrman. *The New Testament: A Historical Introduction to the Early Christian Writings,* 7th ed. Oxford University Press, 2019. A college textbook that describes the different points of view of the four canonical Gospels and provides helpful information on the background of New Testament writings.

Pope Francis. *The Gospel of Luke: A Spiritual and Pastoral Reading*. Orbis Books, 2021. Contains brief meditations on passages from the Gospel according to Luke, from the beginning of the Gospel to the end. They read like homilies for prayerful reflection rather than explanations of the texts. There are also parallel books on the Gospels according to Mark and Matthew, also gleaned from the homilies and writings of Pope Francis.

Donald Senior et al., ed. *The Catholic Study Bible*, 3rd Edition. Oxford University Press, 2016. Begins with helpful background information from leading Catholic Bible scholars. Uses the New American Bible Revised Edition as the text interspersed with notes and inserts to aid in understanding specific books and passages.

Burton H. Throckmorton, Jr. *Gospel Parallels: A Synopsis of the First Three Gospels*. Thomas Nelson, 1967. Places passages from Mark, Matthew, and Luke beside one another. Helpful for seeing differences between the three Gospels. More for a close, scholarly study than for general readers.

Chapter 5
Jesus: Word of God Made Flesh

Christians don't have faith in Jesus because of what he said or did but because of who they understand him to be, the very embodiment of God. In Jesus, God's loving embrace of humanity is complete. Whatever Catholicism stands for must flow from the person of Jesus. A Catholic worldview must be the worldview of Jesus. Little is known of Jesus apart from the four Gospels discussed in the last chapter, which talk almost exclusively about the last three years of his life. Nonetheless, nearly a third of the people in the world today feel strongly enough about Jesus and his message that they declare themselves to be Christian. Catholics make up a large percentage of Christians, and the Catholic Church has been a leading voice proclaiming Jesus and his message. In this chapter, we will look at the life of Jesus, his teachings, the way he taught, and what came to be believed about him by his followers, including Catholics past and present.

> A God who loves humanity: we would never have had the courage to believe in him, had we not known Jesus. … What kind of God is prepared to die for people? Which one? What kind of God loves always and patiently, without demanding to be loved in return? … A God who loves humanity: we would never have had the courage to believe in him, had we not known Jesus. … It is Jesus who reveals God's heart.
>
> Pope Francis, weekly remarks, March 3, 2021

Make a list of what you already know about Jesus. (As you read through this chapter, compare your list with the information presented here.)

If you had a friend who knew little or nothing about Jesus, what would you say to that person about him?

Why do you think that Jesus is such an appealing and compelling figure for so many people?

What do you believe is the central message of Jesus?

I. The Jesus of History

The Difference Jesus Makes

Some years ago, theologian Mary Reed Newland raised this poignant question: What would have happened if Jesus had never existed? What would have been lost to the world? That is not a frivolous question. At the time, there already was someone who throughout the region was called "Son of God"—Octavian, who became Roman emperor *Caesar Augustus* and reigned for over forty years, from 27 BCE to 14 CE. He brought peace and prosperity (for the privileged few at least) to the empire through sensible administration and ending a long civil war. However, he also slaughtered his enemies, kept a majority of people enslaved, and reigned with threats of retaliation against any who opposed him. There already was a King of the Jews—King Herod, known as "the Great" partially because of his impressive engineering accomplishments. He had an aqueduct built that brought fresh water to his seaside resort from hills many miles away. In Israel today you can still see remnants of his aqueduct, with its carefully calculated slight decline to allow the water to flow from the mountainside to the shore. Herod built a port on the Mediterranean where none existed naturally so that ships could go to and from Rome. He was a major advocate of Olympic-style games and came up with the idea of having not just one winner but three—gold, silver, and bronze. Most famously, he rebuilt the temple as the center of Jewish worship. He also was known to invite "friends" to dine with him at his palace in southern Israel, lavish them with wine, and have them join him for a dip in his pool—where he would have soldiers drown them. Late in his life he even killed his wife, his firstborn son, and other family members.

These two men deserve to be called "great" because of their accomplish-ments and the power they amassed for themselves. At the time, to have included Jesus in a discussion alongside Caesar Augustus and Herod was on the face of it laughable. Jesus was a Jewish peasant, a manual laborer who grew up in a small hamlet of a few hundred people. He spent no more than three years engaged in more public life, practically all of it traveling by foot among villages by the Sea of

Galilee. Galilee was not a hotbed of Jewish wealth and culture. Galileans were simple country folk, known to have a rough edge to them. One Galilean, Jesus's friend Peter, was famously given away by his country accent when he tried to deny that he knew Jesus after Jesus's arrest in Jerusalem.

Nonetheless, Mary Reed Newland's question remains. What did Jesus add to world civilization? Both Augustus and Herod were kings. What was Jesus's vision of a kingdom? The two other men treated their enemies ruthlessly. How did Jesus look upon enemies? Augustus and Herod relied on violence, intimidation, and fear to assert their power. What was Jesus's attitude toward violence and fear? Roman society under Augustus was built on inequality. Only a few reaped the benefits of Rome's wealth. Many more people in Rome at the time lived in slavery than as free persons. Disdain for the lowly marked the use of power by Augustus and Herod. Jesus had a very different view of the lowly members of society. He even called the meek and humble "blessed" and warned, "Woe to you who are rich!" (Luke 6:24) Instead of fear and intimidation, Jesus proclaimed the power of love.

God's Kingdom as Kinship

Jesus spoke of a kingdom. Surely, he had in mind the kingdom of Rome when he put forth his own contrasting vision of what God's kingdom is like. He told his followers that his kingdom was not of this world (John 18:36). He also made it clear that God's kingdom is not *like* the kingdoms of this world as they existed at the time. There is a way God intended the world to be, and the values and social arrangements under Augustus and Herod were not those God wanted for humankind. For Jesus, God's kingdom is a "kindom," a family of interrelated and interdependent members. All people are kin to one another in God's kingdom. That vision was appealing especially to people who felt themselves to be powerless, always teetering on the brink of not making ends meet, and hopeful for a better life. Christians still pray that God's kingdom will come on earth the way it is in heaven.

One event that starkly contrasts the difference between Jesus and the power and grandeur of Rome took place the week before Jesus's death. He entered Jerusalem from one end of the city riding a donkey he had borrowed, wearing simple peasants' robes, unarmed and unaccompanied by soldiers. Around the same time through another entrance the Roman governor, Pontius Pilate, no doubt was also coming to Jerusalem to oversee the Passover festivities. (He spent most of his time in one of his palatial palaces away from the boisterous, dirty city. He came back to Jerusalem when he needed to oversee festive occasions that could get out of hand, such as Passover.) Pilate was probably riding in a chariot or stately carriage surrounded by armed soldiers on horseback, dressed in a manner befitting a representative of the mighty Roman Empire. A few days later, Pilate would stand in judgment over Jesus, one kingdom against another, and condemn him to the execution reserved for the most disruptive insurrectionists and troublemakers who would dare question the existing power arrangement—and Jesus did indeed challenge it. His vision was drastically different, and enough people were moved by it that Jesus was seen as a threat both to Jewish leaders and Roman authorities. For doing so, Jesus died a criminal's death.

St. John the Baptist inspired many of the poorest among his fellow Jews with his baptizing and preaching: "Whoever has food must share with those who have none."

He had to know the fate that awaited him. After all, **John the Baptist**, who had preceded Jesus in criticizing the status quo, proposed a message similar to that of Jesus: "Whoever has two coats must share with anyone who has none; and whoever has food must do likewise" (Luke 3:11). When some Roman soldiers asked John what they should do, he told them, "Do not extort money from anyone by threats and false accusation" (Luke 3:14), a clear rejection of the type of force

Roman leaders were known for. As Jesus well knew, John ended up being beheaded for preaching messages such as these that Jesus continued in his own preaching.

A Tale of Two Kingdoms

The Roman kingdom was based on heavy taxation of poor people, extensive slavery, extreme inequality, patriarchy (power in the hands of a strong man), fear, threats and intimidation, peace through military might and military victories, the wealth and resources of the entire empire for the benefit of a few, and prosperity for a few requiring the exploitation of many.

God's kingdom as Jesus envisioned it is based on love as the guiding principle: service and care for one another; equality of all people; inclusion in the community of all groups, especially those who are poor; power *with* others, not *over* them; distribution according to people's needs; women as well as men serving as disciples; and rejection of violence and intimidation.

What do you think Christians today are envisioning when they pray "Your kingdom come on earth as it is in heaven"?

An ancient icon (image) found in Eastern churches is that of Christ as **Pantocrator**. He is depicted as a ruler—in fact, the ruler of all that is. He wears no crown and holds no sword or scepter. Instead, he holds the book of the gospels in one hand and his other hand is raised in blessing. How would you depict Christ the King or the kingdom of God as Jesus spoke of it?

Discuss the following statement: "Jesus's understanding of God's kingdom was unrealistic and unachievable two thousand years ago, and it continues to be unrealistic today as well."

The God of Jesus versus the Gods of Rome

Rome had a pantheon of gods. Myths even circulated that both Julius Caesar and Caesar Augustus were sons of gods. The Roman gods were capricious. You never knew where you stood with them. Human beings were playthings of the gods as the gods fought with one another for earthly and heavenly power. They were often pictured reclining around a table eating while debating and discussing human affairs. If bad things happened to people, it was because one god or goddess had gained the upper hand over another and the loser was taking out his frustration on unsuspecting human victims. All in all, the gods were like puppeteers controlling people's fate. You didn't want to incur a god's disfavor.

Jesus came out of a Jewish tradition that had a very different understanding of divine power. The God of the Jews is not many but one, "merciful and gracious, slow to anger and abounding in steadfast love," in the words of a psalm that Jesus would have been familiar with (Psalm 103:8). This God is not capricious but steadfast. God is not a ruler but *the* ruler, a "servant ruler" whose power lies not in taking but in giving without conditions: "He will not always accuse, nor will he keep his anger forever. He does not deal with us according to our sins, nor repay us according to our iniquities" (Psalm 103:9–10). "Iniquities" here refers to all the wickedness people do that leads to injustice and harm to others. Jesus spent the last years of his life preaching about this God who is love, and he told people that the vision of God's kingdom as kinship flows from this understanding of the one, true God. Accepting God's forgiveness means a commitment to cease one's iniquities and to make love and justice the guiding principles of a new way of life, the kingdom of God.

Read Psalm 103, "Thanksgiving for God's Goodness." Then write a song or poem in praise of mercy and compassion.

The Quest for the Historical Jesus

It is hard to separate the "historical Jesus" (facts about his life) from what Christians believe about him. Before beginning to read this section, list facts about Jesus that a nonbelieving historian would consider plausible based on the historical record available.

Today if we were to compile a biography of Jesus, we would want to include certain basic information about him. When was he born and when did he die? What did he look like? What did his hometown look like, and where else might he have lived? What kind of house did he live in? Did he have siblings, a wife, a family of his own? What people and events helped to shape who he was as he was growing up? What was his means of livelihood? What were his favorite pastimes? Did he laugh a lot and have a sense of humor? Unfortunately, no such biography of Jesus exists. We have little information about him apart from the four Gospels that are the centerpiece of the Christian New Testament. Those writings wanted to proclaim the good news who was Jesus himself; they didn't bother to tell us how tall he was or the color of his hair. We can glean from those sources some biographical information about Jesus, but much of what we would say about him, such as the year of his birth, whether or not he had brothers and sisters, and the extent of his travels, must be accompanied by the caveat "to the best of our knowledge."

For at least the last two hundred years scripture scholars and historians have tried to determine what can be known about Jesus with some degree of certainty. The "quest for the historical Jesus" can be broken down roughly into three phases. At first, some scholars tried to compile a life of Jesus that was compatible with all four gospels and with what was known about when and where Jesus lived. Then, about one hundred years ago, other leading scholars began to question whether we could know anything for certain about Jesus. Stories about Jesus in the Gospels were just that—stories. Trying to determine which were factual and which were "metaphorical" was next to impossible. Then, about fifty years ago several scripture scholars identified certain criteria to guide them in making reasonable assumptions about which passages of the gospels were "authentic Jesus material" and which were likely added by the authors of the gospels. As a result, historians are generally in agreement about certain facts regarding the life of Jesus.

What Do We Know about Jesus?

He was probably born by 4 BCE. (Remember: Don't be thrown off by that year being BC—"Before Christ." When the current calendar was being formulated, the exact year of Jesus's birth was unknown.) He died around the year 30 CE, when he was in his early thirties. He grew up in Nazareth, a small town in Galilee, and perhaps for some time as an adult lived in a somewhat larger town nearby, Capernaum, which was at the time a center for the olive oil business. It wasn't until he was in his late twenties or so that he took on a public role that coincided with his being baptized by a man calling for radical conversion of how people were living at the time, John the Baptist. Jesus gathered his own followers, especially twelve men named in the Gospels and known as the *twelve apostles*. Thereafter, he spent his time going from village to village in Galilee, preaching. He also gained a reputation for being a wonder-worker, especially for being a miraculous healer. In those three years of active preaching, he didn't travel far beyond the area where he grew up. He might have made the journey south to Jerusalem more than once, but he certainly went there at least once, the week before his death. He caused enough of a stir that he caught the attention of Jewish leaders who reported him to the Roman authorities. The Roman governor in Jerusalem called for him to be crucified, along with two other men that day, according to the accounts in the Gospels. After his death and burial, some of his followers, perhaps as many as six hundred people if they're all added up, claimed to have experienced his bodily presence among them in a few fleeting encounters.

It's amazing how a life that was so brief and narrow in geographical scope had such long-lasting and far-reaching impact. His story certainly confirms the saying, "God works in mysterious ways." In particular, the image of Jesus, the God-man, dying on the cross, emptying himself to make known the extent of God's love for all, has given multitudes of people hope and abiding peace. It didn't eradicate their suffering, but it did provide a window through which to see beyond the struggles and suffering that all people endure. What did his early followers and Christians since then come to believe about Jesus?

Beginning in 1995 a group of scripture scholars met regularly to try to determine what in the gospels Jesus actually said and what was added later by the gospel writers themselves. Read about this group, known as the *Jesus Seminar*. Describe the four categories they use to suggest what they see as authentic Jesus material and what are likely to be later additions.

Chapter 5 - Jesus: Word of God Made Flesh

Jesus spent most of his life in small villages near the Sea of Galilee.

II. Key Christian Beliefs about Jesus

Incarnation: God with Us

> Look, the virgin shall conceive and bear a son, and they shall name him Emmanuel, which means "God is with us."
>
> Matthew 1:2–3

At Christmastime, preachers often tell the story of a man who refuses to join his family for midnight Mass. He rejects the very idea upon which Christianity is based, that God would be present in a helpless child. He stays home, gazing out his picture window into the cold night. He notices some birds nestling by the window, shivering. Some birds even fly into the glass, seeking the light and warmth inside. Several times he goes outside to try to direct them to where they would be safe and warm. Each time his presence frightens them, and they fly off into the darkness. "Is there nothing I can do to reassure the birds that I am a friend and not a foe?" He wonders, "Is there no way to convince them that I care for them?" He then thinks, "If only I could become like them ... " With that, the man falls to his knees. He finally understands the awesome mystery of Christmas. Jesus is Emmanuel, God-with-us. Jesus is God become human for us. (See Matthew 1:23.)

Christians may scoff at the man's narrow-mindedness before his Christmas Eve revelation, but in fact, isn't his initial position the more reasonable one? We are used to seeing images of the newborn Christ child resting comfortably in a bed of straw, his mother dressed in blue kneeling watchfully by his side, and her husband Joseph standing beside her, staff in hand, the family's protector. Meanwhile, a bright star illumines the night, an aura of light emanates from the child himself, and a heavenly chorus of angels fills the sky with song. This scene appears to be more like the stuff of myth and not reality, too good to be true. Anyone, like the man in the story, who looks around at the messiness of the actual human condition couldn't possibly expect the Perfect One to enter into it. In the case of Jesus, the notion becomes even more absurd. He wasn't a king born in a palace; he was born poor and powerless, of peasant stock. He grew up in out-of-the-way Nazareth, a tiny village in the Galilean hill country, where providing even enough to feed one's family was a constant struggle. No one would go there on purpose, and no one would expect to come across a boy in a Nazareth carpenter shop who was the savior of the world!

Christians believe that Jesus is both divine and human. This "both-and" identity of Jesus is what Christians call the mystery of the *Incarnation*—God is "incarnated," enfleshed, in and through Jesus. The Incarnation is a *mystery* in the sense that it is a belief that evades complete understanding since no explanation can exhaust its meaning. It's easy to slip into looking at Jesus as only human or only divine. For hundreds of years, battles were fought among Christians about just this question: Is Jesus divine but only appears to be human? Is Jesus human, perhaps even a "super human," but not divine? Is Jesus both divine and human? Christianity settled on the third understanding, fully human *and* fully divine, as the accurate way to describe the nature of Jesus, even though that understanding is couched in profound mystery. For instance, we might imagine that, if Jesus is divine, then even as a child he knew full well all that was to happen to him, as if he had no choice in the matter. He simply went through the motions of living a human life. However, St. Paul tells us that Jesus "emptied himself of his divinity" by becoming one of us, fully and completely human (Philippians 2:7). Strike him and he feels pain. When he hears of the death of a friend, he weeps. The agony he experiences leading up to his death was not play-acting. He doesn't want to drink from the cup of suffering any more than the rest of us would. The description of Jesus's agony in the garden says that he "sweated blood" and was filled with anxiety—a very human response to what he knew awaited him. Christ's divinity is found in and through his humanity, not in spite of it.

Breaking Down Barriers

> In reality it is only in the mystery of the Word made flesh that the mystery of man truly becomes clear.
>
> *Catechism,* #359

As Catholicism understands it, in Christ Jesus, God is embracing humanity in a most profound and total way. The separation between human beings and God is overcome through the Word made flesh. Catholic teaching points out that if Jesus is not fully divine and fully human, then the restoration of humanity to participation in life with God is not complete. Jesus is the shining light of divinity that shares in our humanity, and he sheds light on what it means to be authentically human. No wonder Catholics celebrate Christmas with such joy and mark the season with gift-giving despite the crass materialism now often associated with it. The birth of Christ is God's great gift. The *Catechism* quotes an early Church Father, St. Athanasius, to extoll the glory of the Incarnation: "The Word became flesh to make us '*partakers of the divine nature*': ... 'For the Son of God became man so that we might become God'" (#460).

Incarnational language and the imagery that accompanies it seem so foreign to our modern understanding of reality. There is definitely a clash between a traditional Catholic worldview and a modern one on this matter. However, perhaps the meaning of the Incarnation can inspire modern people to have a greater appreciation for being human than they typically have. Christ emptied himself for all. When people give themselves in love to others, they are participating in God-like behavior. Mothers and fathers, sisters and brothers may not realize it, but in a Catholic worldview they are embodying God in their care for one another. Christ participates in creation; the world and all that is in it have divine origins. When human beings work at making the world a better place, they are participating in God's work of creation since God is the source of all creativity. Even little acts of kindness and greeting one another with a smile and a hello are participating in the divine activity modeled by Jesus. In other words, the mystery of the Incarnation makes a powerful statement about the mystery of being human. In his commentary on the Incarnation, St. Irenaeus said that the glory of God is present when human beings are fully alive (in Latin, *vivens homo*). A command implied in the Incarnation for Christians is this: *Get out and live as Christ lived!* St. Francis de Sales offers a thought-provoking clarification of that command: *"Be who you are, and be that perfectly well."*

The Paschal Mystery, the other great Christian belief about Jesus, reveals that entering into life fully can bring suffering and pain, but it also leads to abiding joy and is cause for hope.

> As you, Father, are in me and I am in you, may they also be in us. ... The glory that you have given me I have given them, so that they may be one, as we are one, I in them and you in me, that they may become completely one.
>
> John 17:21, 22–23

Based on the above description of the meaning of the Incarnation, what possible implications might it have for a Christian understanding of what it means to be human and of the types of activities human beings should be engaged in?

What are ways Christians could celebrate Christmas that would bring out its true meaning?

Look up the word "divinization" (in Greek, *theosis*). Explain what the Greek Fathers of the Church meant by this term.

The Paschal Mystery, Part 1: Suffering and Death

> Thus, it is written, that the Messiah is to suffer and to rise from the dead on the third day, and that repentance and forgiveness of sins is to be proclaimed in his name to all nations, beginning from Jerusalem.
>
> Luke 24:46–47

In the late 1800s, the Vatican put Franciscan priests, brothers, and sisters in charge of the sacred sites of the Holy Land. Franciscans maintain churches where Jesus reportedly performed important miracles, preached his Sermon on the Mount, and was crucified and entombed, and other holy sites. One venue for veneration by pilgrims is what is called the ***Via Dolorosa***, or the way of suffering. It winds through narrow streets in the old section of Jerusalem, much of it barely changed since the time of Jesus. Shops line the streets on both sides. Today vendors sell mostly souvenirs, while young boys selling postcards approach pilgrims: "Ten for a dollar." If you want to walk the Via Dolorosa for quiet contem-plation of the great suffering and humiliation Jesus experienced along the way, it's almost impossible to do given the hustle and bustle taking place there. How-ever, that atmosphere in itself is telling. When Jesus carried his cross, or at least the cross beam of his cross, he passed vendors selling bolts of cloth, drinks, and fruits, just like today. It was a spectacle for sellers and buyers to take advantage of. The Via Dolorosa reveals something about the Catholic understanding of the juxtaposition of the ordinary and the extraordinary. Christ, savior of the world, already near death, bowed by the weight of the cross, whipped by soldiers to move him along, made his way to his ultimate sacrifice that transformed the world. Meanwhile, shopkeepers went about their ordinary business of haggling over the price of wine. For Christians, the extraordinary event of salvation happened in the real world, not in a mythic, otherworldly realm.

Jesus went through Jerusalem streets on his way to crucifixion.

As deserving of celebration as Christmas is, it is not the most important feast of the Christian calendar. That honor goes to what Catholicism refers to as the ***Easter Triduum***, the three days from Holy Thursday evening to Easter Sunday. We might extend this special time back to the Sunday before the Triduum, Passion Sunday, or what is popularly known as Palm Sunday, the beginning of Holy Week. If the Jesus story were a fairy tale, Palm Sunday would have been a good place to end it. He enters the great city of Jerusalem with crowds of people throwing their cloaks on the ground in front of him, waving palms and chanting, "Hosannah to the Son of David" (Matthew 21:9). Having won the approval of the people, Jesus should have been welcomed by the Roman governor, given the keys to the city, and crowned the rightful king of the Jews. That didn't happen. The Hosannahs didn't last long. In fact, the accounts indicate that within days the crowd that had cheered him was calling for his crucifixion.

"God so loved the world ... "

Jesus's crucifixion, the event that his followers found most troubling, became the centerpiece of their belief in him. At first, they were disillusioned: he had promised that God's reign was about to happen, and instead, his promises died with him on the cross. At that moment, Jesus's humanity was most painfully evident; life seeped out of him as it would any mere mortal. However, his sacrifice on the cross was also a powerful indication of his divinity. Ironically, the Gospel of Mark places that proclamation on the lips of a

Roman soldier. For three hours darkness covered the land. Then, Jesus gave a loud cry and breathed his last. What did it all mean? The Roman soldier guarding him proclaimed, "Truly this man was God's son" (Mark 15:39). Through the emptying of Jesus's lifeblood, the soldier recognized Jesus as human. Dying as he did for the salvation of the world, he was recognized by the soldier as the Son of God. Not the emperor, stuffed beyond measure from the sweat and toil of others. No, this man, Jesus, who didn't take from others but gave his all for them.

The *Easter Triduum* consists of the following days:

> *Holy Thursday.* The Last Supper, agony in the garden, Jesus's arrest and imprisonment
>
> *Good Friday.* Torture, carrying of the cross, crucifixion and death of Jesus
>
> *Holy Saturday.* Jesus in the tomb; a time of resignation and questioning, waiting and hope
>
> *Easter Sunday.* Jesus raised from the dead (celebration begins with the Easter Vigil on Saturday night)

The Paschal Mystery, Part 2: Raised from the Dead

> If there is no resurrection of the dead, then Christ has not been raised; and if Christ has not been raised, then our proclamation has been in vain and your faith has been in vain.
>
> 1 Corinthians 15:13–14

In most languages the feast of the resurrection is called by some variant of the Greek *Pascha* (pronounced *pas-ka*), referring to the Jewish Passover. ("Easter" refers to a pre-Christian goddess associated with springtime and was applied by English speakers to the feast of the resurrection.) Passover/Pascha celebrates the story of the journey of the Israelites from slavery in Egypt to freedom in the Promised Land. For Christians, the Paschal Mystery tells the story of Jesus's journey from suffering and death to new life. Catholics incorporate a series of rituals over the three-day triduum to remember and celebrate that journey, culminating in the richly symbolic Easter Vigil liturgy. To label Easter as "the Paschal Mystery, part 2" is not to separate it from the days before it. At his Last Supper shared with his friends, Jesus promised that the sacrifice of his body broken and blood poured out on Good Friday would bring salvation. Through his resurrection, the new life he spoke about actually came into being.

How does Catholicism understand what the resurrection means? The main belief that Catholicism finds in Christ's resurrection is that death is not the end of his story. Just as God led the Israelites from slavery, through suffering and hardships, to the Promised Land, so Jesus conquers death itself and is raised to new life. The Catholic funeral rite says, "For your faithful, Lord, life is changed not ended." It goes on to say that the fabric knitted together during our lifetime does not become unraveled at death. Christ's resurrection is a statement about all people, not just himself. Scripture scholar John Dominic Crossan makes this point in his book *Resurrecting Easter*, written with his wife Sarah Sexton Crossan (2018). Crossan observes that none of the Gospels gives a firsthand account of Christ's resurrection itself. Each Gospel describes encounters some of his friends and followers had with Jesus after he has been raised from the dead, but not of the event itself. Mark's gospel simply says that when three women go to his tomb to anoint Jesus's body, they find not the body but a young man dressed in white who tells them, "Do not be alarmed; you are looking for Jesus of Nazareth, who was crucified. He has been raised; he is not here" (16:6).

Crossan and his wife, a photographer, decided to investigate how the resurrection was depicted in the earliest paintings and icons in existence. They discovered an interesting consistent pattern. In Western Christianity, paintings portrayed Jesus exiting the tomb by himself. In Eastern churches, as Jesus rises from the tomb, he is typically shown holding the hand of a man on one side and a woman on the other. They represent Adam and Eve, and thus all humanity. Resurrection is not just new life for Jesus, but through him for all of us. That coincides with what was one wording for proclaiming "the mystery of faith" in Catholic liturgies after Vatican Council II: "Dying you destroyed our death; rising you restored our life. Lord Jesus, come in glory." Catholic funeral liturgies include praying that the deceased "share in the joy" of Christ's resurrection. Jesus died and was raised from the dead, not for his own glory, but to make available salvation for all. If you hear the Nicene Creed recited, listen for the words "for us and our salvation." That is the purpose of Christ's Incarnation and Paschal Mystery.

> Christ has been raised from the dead, the first fruits of those who have died. ... For as all die in Adam, so all will be made alive in Christ.
>
> 1 Corinthians 15:20, 22

The Resurrection of the Body

There are understandable misinterpretations of what resurrection means. On the one hand, there can be an overly ***physicalized*** understanding of resurrection, imagining that Jesus got up Easter morning as if he had been in a long slumber and commenced to live his life very much the way he had been doing before he died. Catholic teaching is very clear that Christ's body is not the anatomical body he had before death. It's not like he woke up and felt hungry after his long ordeal or went in search of a change of clothes. The *Catechism* talks about Christ having a "glorified body," which awaits all of us as well (#997, 999). On the other hand, there can be an overly ***spiritualized*** interpretation. For instance, we might say that the spirit of Martin Luther King Jr. lives on in the civil rights movement. Catholicism views resurrection as different from that. Also, Catholicism rejects that Christ's soul or spirit emerged from the tomb, leaving his physical body behind. Jesus was not a ghost. The problem with portraying Christ as a disembodied spirit is that it falls into the dualism mentioned earlier. Incarnation means that Christ is a unity of body and soul. Describing resurrection in an overly spiritualized way divides the two in a way that can downplay Christ's humanity. The Nicene Creed professes belief in the resurrection of the body. At the time the creed was formulated, a popular philosophy was ***Manichaeism***, which proposed that the spiritual was polluted by the material and the soul was held captive by the body. If there is no resurrection of the body, it would give credence to this Manichaean worldview, which was rejected by such prominent Christian theologians as St. Augustine of Hippo, who was once Manichaean in outlook himself. The "body" that the creed affirms is not subject to physical, biological categorization or decay but is a glorified, spiritual body. The *Catechism* says that Jesus "did not return to an earthly life.

So, in him, 'all of them will rise again with their own bodies which they now bear,' but Christ 'will change our lowly body to be like his glorious body,' into a 'spiritual body'" (#999).

In Eastern Christian icons, Jesus raises Adam and Eve, and all humanity, from death in his Resurrection.

Eternal Life: Chronos versus Kairos

Wouldn't we all like to know what lies beyond the grave? Catholicism affirms that there is life after death and that it entails being one with God in Christ Jesus. For that reason, despite doubts and misgivings they may have, Catholics live in hope based on faith in a loving God made known through the sacrifice and resurrection of Christ. These three virtues, faith, hope, and love, sustain Catholics and are a "pledge of the presence and action of the Holy Spirit in the faculties of the human being" (*Catechism*, #1813). Words from the Book of Wisdom, often used in funeral liturgies, express this sentiment well: "The souls of the righteous are in the hand of

God. ... Their departure was thought to be a disaster, and their going from us to be their destruction; but they are at peace" (3:1–3). Christian tradition offers metaphors and imagery to describe the life that is not ended at death grounded in Christ's resurrection. Entering pearly gates and enjoying a sumptuous banquet are wonderful images of what heaven is like, but neither the Bible nor anyone's personal experience tells us what life after death is like.

Classical Greek offers some clarification about what the words "eternal life" mean. Greek has two words to describe time. **Chronos** refers to time as we know it, measured out in seconds, minutes, and hours. A chronology of events describes what has happened moment by moment leading up to the present. In addition to this understanding of time, Greek also refers to **kairos**, the timelessness that lies behind *chronos*: it exists now, but it is a reality and a mystery not subject to the decay that inevitably occurs through past, present, and future. (See *Catechism*, #763.) As mystery, it is present but hidden within history, chronological time. The glory of God is manifest in the ongoing, ever-developing drama taking place in time. In Catholicism, death means entering into the "fullness of time" with Christ, raised from the dead. It does not mean a long time (*chronos*); rather, it speaks of entering into what the *Catechism* calls the fullness of time (*kairos*).

How would you explain the Paschal Mystery that Catholicism considers the heart of its message of hope?

Look up the words of the Catholic funeral liturgy. What phrases express most strongly the Christian message about death and resurrection?

Look up the Greek word *kairos*. What do you understand it to mean?

Read about "near death experiences." What are the common themes in these accounts?

III. Teachings of Jesus

More Than Words: The Message Jesus Lived

There is a popular saying attributed to St. Francis of Assisi that actually originated early in the twentieth century: "Preach the gospel always; if necessary, use words." (Francis did say something similar to this, but not in such a succinct way.) The Gospels contain many words attributed to Jesus, but in his case, actions do speak louder than words. Gospel stories about him are snippets of what he stood for and what the kingdom of God is like. Jesus did not simply tell people about God's love for those who were poor or sick or outcasts. He was one of the poor himself; and, according to Luke's Gospel, at the very beginning of his ministry he told the people of his hometown that he has been anointed "to bring good news to the poor" (4:18). In that same sermon he said that he came to proclaim "liberation to captives." The synoptic Gospels describe several times when Jesus sets free people who had been held captive by demons; and, in the process, he even tells them that their sins are forgiven. He had a reputation for spending time with "sinners and prostitutes." He was known to be a healer, and the sick flocked to him so much that he had to struggle to have any time to himself.

Jesus's final act of sacrifice was not to bring glory to himself; it was an exclamation point on his message about the love of God. Accounts indicate that he was alone and abandoned by everyone during his three hours of agony on the cross. Passersby mocked him; even the other criminals crucified with him taunted him. At best, some women were there but stayed at a distance. The sacrifice of Jesus was complete. The Greek word used was that he "emptied" himself for us. No words were needed. He spoke through his body, crowned with thorns and pierced with nails, hands and feet.

Foot Washing and Meal Sharing

On the evening he was arrested, the very night before he died, Jesus did two things that he told his followers to continue doing in his name. These two actions represented what he had modeled all during his public life: he washed their feet, and he shared a meal with them. As mentioned in the last chapter, John's Gospel tells of Jesus getting down on his knees and washing his disciples' feet. He saw this gesture as one final declaration that "he loved them to the end" (13:1). Peter for one was shocked that Jesus would stoop to doing the work even a slave wouldn't be asked to do, but Jesus insisted that they wouldn't understand the extent of God's love for them unless he performed this seemingly belittling task. He tells them, "You also ought to wash one another's feet. For I have set an example, that you also should do as I have done to you," and "If you know these things, you are blessed if you do them (13:14–15, 17). Probing the message underlying this gesture even further, John's Gospel then continues on for five chapters with Jesus talking about love as the heart of his teaching.

The other three gospels describe the Last Supper itself. Here again, Jesus tells his disciples to continue sharing meals together, which he links directly to his forthcoming sacrifice on the cross: "He took a loaf of bread, and when he had given thanks, he broke it and gave it to them, saying, 'This is my body, which is given for you. Do this in remembrance of me'" (Luke 22:19). Meal sharing and foot washing are two richly symbolic gestures with very real, concrete applications. Jesus seems to be summing up his message during these last precious moments he has together with his friends before facing the horrors he knows await him. They represent very vividly what God is like and also what the Christian life entails.

Jesus washed his apostles's feet to show them the extent of God's love for them.

If you attend a Holy Thursday liturgy at a Catholic Church, you will witness the priest-celebrant actually washing the feet of some of his parishioners. On his first Holy Thursday as pope, Pope Francis caused a stir by washing the feet of some inmates at a Rome youth prison! During his public life, Jesus was not known for fasting; he was known for sharing meals. He sat down at supper with a despised tax collector as unassumingly as he did with reputable leaders in their communities. When he extended his hands in forgiveness and healing or simply said, "Peace be with you," he was living out what washing feet and sharing bread and wine at a meal imply. Many people who encountered him were moved by the message he lived out, and Christians continue to try to live it out themselves to this day.

St. Francis of Assisi told his companions to "preach through their deeds," and Jesus certainly modeled that message. What messages do you think you communicate through your deeds?

Luke's Gospel, chapter 7, verses 36–50, tells one story of Jesus at a meal. Read the story and describe what you understand to be its message.

Some Christians actually do foot washing—think of nurses caring for frail, sickly patients in hospitals or caregivers of sick loved ones at home or parents washing their infant children. But for most Christians Jesus's command to wash feet is carried out in other ways. What are some examples of how this message could be lived out? Why would Jesus say that knowing the importance of foot washing is a "blessing"?

Jesus and Parables

He began to teach them many things in parables.

Mark 4:2

Following in his Jewish tradition, Jesus was a storyteller. We might think that he told stories to simplify his message, the way a parent or teacher might tell a small child a story. "Don't waste food" and "Share with others" come through more vividly in a story than in direct statements. However, when we look at the parables of Jesus, we discover that they don't convey simple messages at all. In fact, they are more likely to be confounding and even upsetting. They are not moral tales with simple moral messages such as those attributed to the ancient Greek Aesop. Aesop's fable of the tortoise and the hare contains a straightforward message: slow and steady wins the race. The famous tale about the ants who work all summer, storing up food for the winter while a grasshopper fiddles the summer away also conveys a simple moral message: Hard work pays off; fiddling around doesn't. The parables of Jesus don't offer what at first appears to be commonsense or conventional morality. They are more likely to jolt his listeners to points of view they weren't expecting.

The prodigal son is a parable told by Jesus.

In one of his most famous parables, Jesus tells of a man going from Jerusalem to Jericho. He relates the story in response to the question "Who is my neighbor?" Jesus is talking to a gathering of his fellow Jews. Presumably his audience is to identify themselves with the traveler. Thieves fall upon the man, rob him, and leave him beaten by the side of the road. A Jewish priest and a law teacher pass by, but neither stops to help. A Samaritan passes by, stops to help the man, and then goes way beyond common courtesy in seeing that the beaten man is cared for. We are used to putting together "good" and "Samaritan," but that is not the connection Jesus's audience would have made. In fact, such a connection would be shocking to them. For centuries the standard position among Jews was that they hated Samaritans and called them dogs. Samaritans were from a region north of Judea that had split off from Judea; they often married non-Jews and had their own religious practices that Jews saw as a desecration of their own. To Jesus's listeners, then, the story must have been very unsettling. Does Jesus mean that we are to look upon hated foreigners or members of different religions as our neighbors? Are the people we look up to as "the good" (priests and experts in the law) not so good after all? Are we to expect help from unexpected sources? Jesus's listeners must have been startled by what the story implied.

Other gospel parables seem to confirm that Jesus wants to overturn commonly held perceptions. A landowner has two sons. One takes his inheritance and spends it carelessly. The other son stays home and helps his father. If you were a parent, which son would you prefer?

Read about the prodigal son and his brother in Luke 15:11–32 to see the strange message that Jesus draws out of the story.

Another gospel lesson shares this spirit of overturning commonly held perceptions. Jesus contrasts a Pharisee, an admired member of Jewish society, with a tax collector, who belongs to a group universally hated by fellow Jews. (They collected taxes on behalf of the despised Romans ruling over them.) Surprisingly, the tax collector is the one described as the favored of God.

These examples reveal that not all stories are parables. Jesus's stories tend to be "parabolic" in their messaging. They are certainly not simple moral tales, as they have often been reduced to. A shepherd who leaves ninety-nine of his sheep to go in search of one stray may be a "good" shepherd, but not a sensible one. A steward who pays workers the same amount regardless of how long they worked would not stay in business long in today's world. Here's the leap that connects the teller of parables with the parables he told: *Jesus himself, his message and his life story, is a "parable" that overturns commonly held expectations.* He didn't represent what most Jews expected from their Messiah. Why would anyone accept that he was God's Son? As previously explained, it's not a stretch to think of Caesar Augustus as

God's son. The soldier who proclaimed that Jesus was God's Son as he hung lifeless on the cross should have known better than to make such a foolish statement. A true son of God is not supposed to end his days as Jesus did. Common sense tells us that death marks the end of life, not a doorway to eternal life. Does it make any sense to think that God actually cares about you? Such foolishness! Both in his stories and in his very life and death, Jesus overturns commonly held assumptions about wealth, power, goodness, and true happiness.

> I speak in parables, so that "looking they may not perceive, and listening they may not understand."
>
> Luke 8:10

Read the following parables from Luke's gospel: the rich fool (12:13–21), the barren fig tree (13:6–9), the mustard seed (13:18–19), the great feast (14:16–24), and the lost coin (15:8–10). What common themes run through these stories? What makes them "parabolic"?

Read some of Aesop's fables or other moral tales. What makes them moral tales and not parables?

Did you ever have an experience that turned out to be an unexpected blessing? Tell the story.

The Questions of Jesus

> "What do you want me to do for you?"
>
> (Luke 18:41)

> "Do you want to be made well?"
>
> (John 5:6)

A few years ago, John Dear wrote a book titled *The Questions of Jesus* in which he points out that Jesus is asked 183 questions in the Gospels. He directly answers only three of them. Jesus is more likely to respond to a question with another question, a story, or a baffling comment. In all, Jesus himself poses 307 questions in the four Gospels.

We tend to think of Jesus as the one with the answers. As he goes about his ministry, he is actually more often the one with the questions.

He leaves us with hard questions, not easy answers. In the foreword to the John Dear book, Father Richard Rohr suggests what Jesus is doing through his constant questioning: "Jesus's questions are to reposition you, make you own your unconscious biases, break you out of your dualistic mind, challenge your image of God or the world, or present new creative possibilities" (*The Questions of Jesus*). As Rohr explains them, the questions of Jesus often serve a similar purpose to the parables he told.

Before we can come to understand Jesus, we need to undergo what is often a difficult and painful process of letting go. We tend to have many false assumptions that need to be questioned. Jesus says that the key to happiness is giving ourselves to others when we more likely would rather receive. Jesus points us toward identifying with the overlooked members of society rather than the rich and famous. Jesus's constant questioning opens up a crack in our protective armor and allows light to shine through.

> What questions have created an opening in your consciousness, allowing new insights and new perspectives for you?
> What questions do you sense that Jesus is asking of people today?

Jesus, Human and Divine, Raised from the Dead, Herald of God's Reign

Jesus revealed what God is like and also what it means to be human. He spoke constantly about a kingdom, God's reign, which differs dramatically from the way kingdoms existed at the time. Through miraculous deeds, especially healing the sick and freeing people from demons that possessed them, he demonstrated what God wanted for people. He lived a life that broke down barriers of inequality in wealth and power, proclaiming good news to people who were poor or otherwise burdened. He conveyed his message in words and deeds, especially through his ultimate sacrifice on the cross. He told stories that at first glance are baffling and asked many questions that cause people to ponder what is and what can be. All this led up to the central message that Christians find in Jesus—the Paschal Mystery. Death could not hold him; God's love was and is stronger than death itself.

Christ, raised from the dead, is celebrated by Catholics and other Christians, giving hope for eternal life to all.

Chapter Review

1. What are some key differences between the kingdom of the Roman Empire and the kingdom of God as Jesus described it?
2. What is the difference between the dominant Roman understanding of god/gods versus the Jewish understanding of God?
3. Name five facts about the life of Jesus that most historians agree on.
4. Explain the mystery of the Incarnation.
5. Describe implications for a Catholic worldview that reflect belief in the Incarnation.
6. What is the meaning of the Greek word *Pascha*?
7. To what does the Paschal Mystery refer?
8. What is the Easter Triduum?
9. How did painters in the Eastern Christian churches portray the resurrection of Jesus compared to how Western Christian painters portrayed it?
10. What is an overly physicalized understanding of resurrection?
11. What are two ways that resurrection can be overly spiritualized?
12. What does "resurrection of the body" mean in Christian tradition?
13. What is the difference between Greek *chronos* and *kairos*?
14. What two actions of Jesus convey his message about how Christians should act toward others?
15. How are parables different from moral tales?
16. How are the questions of Jesus similar to the effect of his parables?

For Further Study

Marcus J. Borg. *Jesus: Uncovering the Life, Teachings, and Relevance of a Religious Revolutionary*. HarperSanFrancisco, 2006. Borg has written many books about Jesus, often contrasting the understanding of Jesus he had in his childhood with what he learned from his academic studies about him. Other books of his, such as *Convictions: How I Learned What Matters Most* (2016), offer perspectives worth considering in clear, precise language, such as contrasting what the gospels say about Jesus pre-Easter versus post-Easter.

John Dominic Crossan. *God and Empire: Jesus Against Rome, Then and Now*. HarperSanFrancisco, 2007. Contrasts the values and worldview of the Roman Empire's *Pax Romanum*, based on violence, with Jesus's understanding of peace that rejects violence.

John Dominic Crossan and Sarah Sexton Crossan. *Resurrecting Easter: How the West Lost and the East Kept the Original Easter Vision*. HarperOne, 2018. Members of Eastern Catholic and Eastern Orthodox churches are familiar with icons of Jesus rising from the tomb on Easter, clutching the hands of Adam and Eve. The Crossans provide photographic images of such icons and explore the implications of the contrasting depictions of Christ's resurrection East versus West.

Anselm Grun. *Images of Jesus*. Continuum 2002. Several books offer insightful reflections on themes related to Jesus and his message. The author is a German Benedictine monk who writes a few pages of insightful commentary on fifty topics related to the life and teaching of Jesus. You might also consider Joseph Stoutzenberger *You Are My Friends: Gospel Reflections for Your Spiritual Journey* (2016), which contains thirty-six brief reflections.

Philip A. Cunningham. *Maxims for Mutuality: Principles for Catholic Theology, Education, and Preaching about Jews and Judaism*. Paulist Press, 2022. Addresses misrepresentations about the crucifixion of Jesus and popular misconceptions that have been used to blame Jews for his death and has led to anti-Semitism in general. Offers Catholics guidelines for teaching and preaching about Jews, Judaism, and its relationship with Catholicism.

Amy-Jill Levine. *Short Stories by Jesus: The Enigmatic Parables of a Controversial Rabbi*. HarperOne, 2014. Several scholars have written about the uniqueness of Jesus's parables as a form of storytelling. Levine examines the parables and demonstrates that through them Jesus was asking his followers not just to listen but to think as well.

Donald Spoto. *The Hidden Jesus: A New Life*. St. Martin's Griffin, 1998. Many fine books about the life of Jesus have been written recently. Spoto has written biographies of movie stars and in this book brings his probing style to an appreciation of Jesus. Other popular books on Jesus are James Carroll's *Christ Actually: The Son of God for the Secular Age* (2014) and James Martin's *Jesus: A Pilgrimage* (2016), written in a conversational style based on his travels through the Holy Land.

Leonard Swidler. *Yeshua: Jesus the Jew a Model for Everyone*. iPub Cloud International, 2020. Explores the meaning that Yeshua, the historical Jewish Jesus, holds for issues facing the world today.

Chapter 6
The Church: Carrying on the Message of Jesus

From a Catholic perspective, Christ cannot be separated from the community of his followers known as the church. For Catholics, the church community is the primary way by which people encounter Christ; indeed, together with members of the church past and present, they are the "body of Christ." Of all Christians, Catholics in particular hold the view that an experience of the good news of Christ is filtered through the church. The church is made up of real people and has a specific structure. It has a history, not all of it spotless. From the pope on down, no Catholic would claim to be sinless. And yet the church has produced more than its share of saints and has been instrumental in keeping alive the message of Christ. This chapter will look at the Catholic understanding of church, its origins and major historical developments, as well as some particular people who have modeled what it means to be church.

> [Christ] sent His life-giving Spirit upon His disciples and through Him has established His Body which is the Church as the universal sacrament of salvation.
>
> Vatican Council II, *Lumen gentium*, #48

What associations, thoughts, and feelings come to mind when you think about the Catholic Church? Are your associations more positive or negative?

What do you think is appealing about being part of the church for Catholics?

What do you think someone receives by being Catholic?

What do you think someone is committed to doing by being Catholic?

I. The Church as the People of God

The Church as a Gathering of God's People

> Once you were not a people, but now you are God's people.
>
> 1 Peter 2:10

In the 2017 film *The Greatest Showman*, P. T. Barnum gathers together a group of people who possess physical characteristics that make them outcasts in society, among them a bearded lady, the "smallest person on earth," and the fattest man. They come in all colors, shapes, and sizes. He puts them on stage to be gawked at by people willing to pay the price of admission. Barnum convinces them to join his show by telling them that people look upon them strangely anyway, so why not make a living from the peculiarities that have brought them such derision? In time, they become a community of equals who genuinely care for one another. Clearly, Barnum's motives were not exactly altruistic. But when the theater is burned to the ground by an angry mob incensed at the very existence of this "freak show," the performers mourn the loss of their "home." Trying to convince Barnum to rebuild, they sing, "Our own mothers were ashamed of us, but you gave us a real family. We had our own home."

By no means is P. T. Barnum a Christ-figure. However, the dynamics that are depicted in the movie do parallel both the beginnings of the church and experiences of church that people continue to have today. During Christianity's first three centuries, the threat of persecution hung over the heads of members of the church. A story is told of a Christian deacon in Rome accosted by a local official who had heard rumors that the church possessed great wealth. The official wanted a part of it, or he would report church members to the authorities. The deacon, St. Lawrence, told him to return in three days, and he would bring the wealth of the church to him. The official thought, "Three days! Surely this means that the church does possess great wealth if it takes that long to gather it." Three days later, Lawrence showed up with beggars, people who were blind or lame, and other so-called undesirables from the streets. He told the official that these were the wealth of the church. Enraged, the official had Lawrence burned slowly over an open fire until death.

Whether this incident actually happened or not, it provides an accurate understanding of what the church is called to be. Jesus gathered a ragtag community around him—some rich but mostly poor, lepers and formerly demon-possessed, women and men, outsiders and a few insiders, sinners and prostitutes. The church has been a community of his friends and followers ever since. If the church lives up to its name, all of them find a home there. Father Greg Boyle, a Jesuit priest who works with street gangs in Los Angeles, tells the story of a young gang member who spent time in prison. The young man told him that over the course of his time on the street, imprisonment, and then working in the community he felt himself transformed from being "nobody" to "somebody" and then finally "everybody." That's the kind of transformation that the Catholic Church seeks to engender in its members. The word *catholic* implies universality, inclusivity, "pertaining to the whole," which means Christ. A line from the Irish writer James Joyce provides an appropriate image for the Catholic Church: "Here comes everybody." The *Catechism* mentions many images for the church. The first one listed is "the people of God." It says, "God is not the property of any one people. But he acquired a people for himself from those who previously were not a people" (#2787). A sense of belonging to one group can lead to looking down on people who are not part of one's "in group." That's why the concept of *catholicity* is so important in a Christian understanding of God's people. The name Catholic is meant to engender a sense of connectedness to all, not to one separate group but to the people of God.

> It is above all the "poor" to whom Jesus speaks in his preaching and actions. The crowds of the sick and the outcasts who follow him and seek him out find in his words and actions a revelation of the great value of their lives and of how their hope of salvation is well-founded.
>
> Pope St. John Paul II, *The Gospel of Life*, #32

Look up the word "catholic." What words are associated with it?
Tell your own story of experiencing a sense of belonging.
An experience of belonging to one group can lead to looking down on members of other groups. Tell the story of such an

experience. Is such an experience neither "catholic" nor Christian? Explain.

How Did the Church Begin?

> The Spirit dwells in the Church and in the hearts of the faithful as in a temple.
>
> Vatican Council II, *Lumen gentium*, #4

The Bible contains a book, the Acts of the Apostles, which chronicles developments in the earliest days of the church. It tells the story of one incident that is rightfully called "the birthday of the church." It takes place fifty days after the Passover when Jesus died and was raised from the dead and thus coincides with the Jewish festival of **Pentecost**, meaning "fifty days." Recall that after his resurrection, friends of Jesus had occasions when they experienced him present among them, but the book reports that ten days before Pentecost, Jesus ascended into heaven. His friends realized that with his *ascension* Jesus was no longer present among them, and they felt at a loss about what to do about that. They had placed their hope in Jesus during the exhilarating short time he spent preaching and healing. Their hopes were dashed when he was arrested and executed. Their hopes were restored through their experience of the resurrection. Now they were huddled in a room in Jerusalem, wondering what it all meant and what they were to do.

Suddenly a burst of wind swept through the room, "tongues of fire" appeared overhead, and "all of them were filled with the Holy Spirit" (Acts 2:1–4). Due to this inspiration from the Holy Spirit, they knew something was different. Peter, leader of the group, went out and gave a rousing speech to his fellow Jews who were in town for the Pentecost festival. Despite coming from many different lands, they all understood what he was saying. Many of them were "cut to the heart" by Peter's moving words, and according to the account about three thousand were baptized that very day.

Pentecost represented a startling realization for the friends and followers of Jesus. He was no longer absent, but present. His presence was within them; his work was to be carried on through them. Being "filled with the Holy Spirit" restored their hope, gave them great joy, and laid upon them an awesome responsibility. As Jesus preached the good news of salvation, they were to do the same. As Jesus healed and raised up those who were poor and left out, they were to carry on that work. As Jesus risked his life to transform the world, they were to do likewise. Christ was to be present through them. They were the church—his gathering, his circle of friends, his sacramental presence in the world. Through them, the kingdom of God that Jesus spoke about was to make its way throughout the world.

To be part of the church is to be a member of the "body of Christ." The church prides itself on being *we*, not *they* or *it*. Every spring much of a bishop's time is spent going around to parishes celebrating a ceremony for mostly young Catholics called the sacrament of **confirmation**. What's the message of the sacrament? "*You* are filled with the Holy Spirit; go out and be what you are—the church of Christ." For this reason, Catholics quietly run homeless shelters, hospitals, schools, and sports programs for kids. They try to figure out how to live their faith at home and at work, in their schools and businesses. Go to any trouble spot in the world and chances are that Catholics are already there helping people in need. Catholic children throughout the world learn prayers from their parents and teachers who want to pass on words and gestures that become part of the fabric of their lives—the Our Father, the Hail Mary, and the Sign of the Cross. A steady flow of Catholics comes to church for Mass weekly, and some daily. Catholics from every continent contribute and put their own unique stamp on the faith, but all are united under one faith in Christ, one centralized authority, and a realization of their oneness in the Spirit.

> Christ with me, Christ before me, Christ behind me, Christ within me, Christ beneath me, Christ above me.
>
> From the ancient Irish prayer "St. Patrick's Breastplate"

What kinds of activities do you associate with Catholicism?

What kinds of activities do you think Catholics should be engaged in?

Why are wind and fire appropriate images for the Holy Spirit as described in the Pentecost story?

How accurate would you say is the following quote from Father Richard Rohr? Give examples to defend or refute his statement.

> "We must be honest and admit that most of Christianity has focused very little on what Jesus himself taught and spent most of his time doing: healing people, doing acts of justice and inclusion, embodying compassionate and nonviolent ways of living."

Who Makes Up the Church?

The opening heading of Vatican Council II's document on the church is "The mystery of the Church." What is so mysterious about the church? Think back on the earlier chapters of this book. A Jewish peasant who lived a brief life two thousand years ago is the embodiment of God. That's a mystery, the Mystery of the Incarnation. His torturous death leading to new life for himself and all people is a mystery, the Paschal Mystery. That the scriptures of a tribe who began as lowly nomads are considered the word of God is a mystery. God's presence in the world through flawed flesh-and-blood people, known as the church, is a mystery as well. In every instance, the mystery is that the visible reveals the invisible, the material gives flesh to the spiritual, the human manifests the divine.

When you think about the Catholic Church, what immediately comes to mind? Quite likely you think of the pope, dressed in his white robes surrounded by the medieval splendor of the Vatican. Closer to home, you might pass a Catholic church and see people streaming in and out, especially Saturday evening and Sunday morning. Or you might have a vague understanding that there are schools, colleges, and hospitals that are affiliated with the Catholic Church in some way. Of all major religions, the Catholic Church is the most structured. If Catholics want to prove they are members of the church, there is a record of their baptism in the books of a parish office somewhere. Therefore, it is accurate to say that "the Catholic Church" comprises all baptized Catholics throughout the world—over 17 percent of the world's population at present.

Thanks to the work of theologians in the decades leading up to it, Vatican Council II explored deeply the meaning of "church." Its Dogmatic Constitution on the Church begins by stating the obvious: people baptized as Catholics are members of the church. But it also states what is equally obvious to anyone who lives in the diverse world of today: "Many elements of sanctification and of truth are found outside of its visible structure" (#8). After all, "All men are called to be part of this catholic unity of the people of God ... for all men are called by the grace of God to salvation" (#13). Notice that the word "catholic" here is spelled with a small *c*. All people—not just "Catholics" (capital *C*)—are called to be the people of God. The document goes on to list groups of people who are "linked to" the church in some way: other Christians, Jews, Muslims, members of other religions, and even those who "sincerely seek God and moved by grace strive by their deeds to do His will as it is known through the dictates of their conscience" (#16).

Theologian Karl Rahner used the term "anonymous Christians" to refer to people who engage in work that Christians are called to do without identifying themselves as Christian. He meant the term to be a positive recognition of the holiness found in people of good will who are not directly affiliated with the Catholic Church. The term has been embraced and rejected by people both within and outside of the Catholic Church. Read about the term. Explain why you believe it is or is not helpful in describing the concept of "church."

Church Leadership

The Nicene Creed lists four "marks" of the Catholic Church: one, holy, catholic, and apostolic. In all of these identifying characteristics, Catholics see a direct link from Christ, who embodied holiness, to the church. What does the Catholic Church mean by declaring itself "apostolic"? Jesus appointed St. Peter and the apostles to proclaim a unified message of his good news to all the world. Catholics don't simply say that the church was inspired by the apostles; all Christians would certainly say that. They claim that leadership of the church of Christ has been handed on from the apostles down to the present day. Go to the second largest church in Rome, St. Paul's Outside the Walls, and in it you will find a mosaic of every pope from St. Peter down to today. This mosaic is a testament to the continuity that Catholics see present in the church and why they look upon the pope with such adulation.

Church leadership is hierarchical. ***Hierarchy*** means literally "rule by the holy ones." From a Catholic perspective, that holiness emanates not necessarily from any personal characteristics of church leaders but from their direct descendancy from St. Peter and the apostles. The *Catechism* calls the pope the ***Vicar of Christ*** and the successor of St. Peter (#882). That is, for Catholics the pope is a representative today of the apostle appointed by Christ to lead the church. Another title for the pope is ***pontiff***, short for *pontifex maximus*, meaning "the greatest bridge-builder." The next few chapters will discuss the significance of concrete, visible symbols in Catholicism. The pope and bishops are symbols, "sacramental signs," of Christ's continuing presence in the world. That presence is not handed down simply in a book, the Bible, or in abstract ideals, but in actual people.

Comprehending a Catholic understanding of church calls for a real balancing act in that it is a very human community, but it is also a vehicle for the work of the Holy Spirit. Some popes, especially in the late Middle Ages, were anything but pillars of holiness. The relationship between holiness and sinfulness is difficult to comprehend, a mystery. The Japanese poet Issa captures something of the ambiguous human condition in a haiku: "Where there are humans / You will find flies / And Buddhas." We humans draw flies; we also have a spiritual quality to us. We are saints and sinners. The church has its hierarchical structure made up of flawed human beings, but that structure is meant to remind people of Christ and of the importance of everyone as part of the body of Christ. No human being is exempt from "drawing flies," but each one is holy as well. Vatican Council II's document on the church points out that especially "in the poor and afflicted [the church] sees the image of its poor and suffering Founder" (#8).

In addition to the pope, bishops, priests, and members of religious orders of priests, brothers, sisters, and nuns, Vatican Council II speaks about the priesthood of the people. It talks about the family as "the domestic church" (#11). For most people, holiness—that is to say, "making whole," connecting to God, who is love—occurs initially in the family church. In his essay "Health Is Membership," Wendell Berry describes this simple, basic human experience of sanctification:

If we were lucky enough as children to be surrounded by grown-ups who loved us, then our sense of wholeness is not just the sense of completeness in ourselves, but also is the sense of belonging to others and to our place; it is an unconscious awareness of community, of having in common.

Discuss the following statement: "The Catholic Church should do away with the role of pope and bishops." As part of your discussion, survey Catholics about whether or not they agree with the statement. Ask them why.

Who were some of the grown-ups who helped develop your sense of belonging and community?

II. The History of the Church

Jews and Gentiles in Christ

> All who believed were together and had all things in common; they would sell their possessions and goods and distribute the proceeds to all, as any had need.
>
> Acts 2:44–45

> Now the whole group of those who believed were of one heart and soul, and no one claimed private ownership of any possessions, but everything they owned was held in common.
>
> Acts 4:32

Followers of Jesus have always had to deal with the realities that existed around them. In other words, Catholicism has a history. The Acts of the Apostles suggests that the early Christians lived what we today would call a communal lifestyle. Obviously, that didn't last. The early church was also a Jewish community. If people wanted to join the commune and were not Jewish, they were to follow the rules of life practiced by Jews of the time. Is that what Jesus intended? This question came to a head about twenty years after Jesus. Two key figures in addressing this question were St. Paul and St. Peter.

St. Paul, whose Hebrew name was Saul, felt as though those Jews who continued to follow Jesus were practicing Judaism in ways that he, a member of the Pharisee party, could not condone. He received permission from the Jewish establishment to persecute followers of Jesus and wipe out this expression of Judaism that was endangering all Jews. One day, on the road to Damascus, Paul/Saul was blinded, and a voice said to him, "Saul, Saul, why are you persecuting me?" (Acts 22:7). The voice was that of Jesus himself. He directed Paul to go into Damascus and meet with a man named Ananias, who restored his sight and told him, "The God of our ancestors has chosen you to know his will, to see the Righteous One and to hear his own voice; for you will be his witness to all the world of what you have seen and heard" (Acts 22:14–15).

That incident is packed with meaning. For one thing, Jesus is identifying directly with the Christian Jews who were being persecuted. Secondly, even though Paul had never met Jesus, he is presented as someone who has been chosen to carry on the role of an apostle of Jesus. (*Apostle* means "one who is sent."). Thirdly, Ananias is relating that Paul knows God's will and is a faithful witness to Christ. Apart from the Gospels, much of the New Testament is either written by Paul (in his letters) or about him (in Acts). The incident is making clear that Paul provides an accurate understanding of the will of God manifest in the person of Jesus.

Paul went about preaching the Gospel message with even more gusto than he had dedicated to quashing it. Maps depicting the travels of Paul reveal the extent of his missionary activity throughout the eastern Roman Empire. Typically, he spoke in synagogues; there were Jewish communities in many cities. He never envisioned himself as anything but Jewish, but now he saw belief in Christ as revealing the rightful meaning of Judaism. He also came to realize that the good news of Christ's Resurrection and the coming of God's kingdom was intended for non-Jews as well as Jews. Often there were non-Jews, called "God-fearers," who were drawn to Judaism, and when they heard Paul's message, they saw the possibility of aligning with this hospitable form of Judaism. (The word "Christian" didn't exist yet.) The number of non-Jewish God-fearers wanting to join the Jewish community who believed in Christ caused a dilemma for Paul and the early follower of Jesus: Did non-Jews have to convert to Judaism to join? Paul took the question to the Christian elders in Jerusalem. They debated the question and decided that non-Jews did not have to become Jewish or follow all of the traditional Jewish regulations.

Chapter 6 - The Church: Carrying on the Message of Jesus

St. Paul preaching to non-Jews in Athens

St Peter was viewed as something of the leader of the group, and he recounted that in a dream God had shown him wild animals laid out on a sheet and said, "Take and eat." To eat the flesh of wild animals was a violation of Jewish dietary laws, so Peter interpreted the dream to mean that it was not necessary for non-Jewish believers in Christ to adhere to all Jewish rules, such as the laws of kosher, especially if such rules were not part of their upbringing. The meeting, called the ***Council of Jerusalem*** (which took place in either 49 or 50 CE) and reported on in Acts, chapter 15, may not have occurred, but it represented a turning point taking place over the course of the first century. No longer was Christianity a form of Judaism. Now it was a separate entity, a community of Jews and non-Jews. By the end of the first century, the majority of Christians came from non-Jewish backgrounds. Christianity was now on its own, a "new religion," despite its clear Jewish roots.

At the time of Jesus, Jews and non-Jews lived separate lives. For instance, they could not sit down at table for a shared meal due to kosher food restrictions; and Jews set aside Saturday, the Sabbath, as a day of rest. In a multireligious society, should religious beliefs influence laws and practices? (For instance, should the Ten Commandments be displayed in law courts, Christian prayers be recited in public schools, and certain businesses not allowed to be open on Christmas and Easter?)

Emperor Nero and Emperor Constantine

> Nero fastened the guilt and inflicted the most exquisite tortures on a class hated for their abominations, called Christians by the populace.
>
> Tacitus, Roman historian, around 115 CE

Romans respected ancient religions and generally allowed people to practice them as long as they were not seditious or disruptive. Judaism fell into that category. Thousands of Jews were crucified under Roman rule when they were rebellious, but although they were oppressed in many ways Jews had functioning synagogues throughout the empire and the great temple in Jerusalem built by Herod about a decade before the birth of Jesus. Christianity did not fit into that category. It was looked upon as what we today would call a cult. Rome at the time had more than its share of cults, sometimes called *mystery cults*. Who knew what they were doing behind closed doors? One Roman writer reported that Christians gathered in secret where they ate flesh and drank blood. Surely no one wanted Christians in their neighborhood. In Rome, most Christians lived in the run-down section of the city. A fire erupted in 64 CE that burned for a week, destroying much of the city. Some writers of the time accused Emperor Nero of starting the fire to clear land for a new palace, and afterward Nero blamed Christians for it since they were a suspect group anyway. Whether or not that is true, it did signal a period of persecution of Christians that lasted off and on for a couple of centuries.

The threat of persecution changed with Emperor Constantine in 313 CE. Constantine was a general vying with another general for control of the empire. The night before a decisive battle he dreamt of a cross accompanied by the words "In this sign you will conquer." The next morning, he ordered his soldiers to paint crosses on their shields. They did so, and the battle was won. Subsequently, in gratitude, Constantine promulgated the ***Edict of Milan*** granting freedom of religion to Christians. That pronouncement marked one of the greatest transformations in the history of Christianity. By 370, not only was Christianity accepted, but it became the official religion of the empire. Before Constantine, to be Christian meant to be an outsider. After Constantine, Christians were insiders. Before Constantine, Christians generally considered joining the army and engaging in warfare as inimical to their faith. By the end of the fourth century, soldiers were expected to be Christian. Before this time, if someone wanted to progress in social, economic, or political power, it would be best not to be associated with Christianity. After Constantine, power shifted to people who called themselves Christian. In other words, Christianity became **Christendom**. The empire became "Christian," and Christianity took on the trappings of empire.

Are the teachings of Jesus compatible with the values inherent in an empire?

Would Jesus have applauded or denounced the transformation of Christianity after Constantine?

Read about the Theban Legion. What is their story?

Research the following question: After Constantine, did the Roman Empire become more Christian, or did Christianity become more like the Roman Empire?

Should a nation consider itself "Christian"? Is the United States a "Christian nation"?

The East-West Schism

Emperor Constantine took another step that has shaped Christianity to the present day. He decided that Rome was too run down and geographically too far on the fringes of the empire to be the capital. He decided that a more suitable and centralized location was a trading center on the Bosporus Strait, where Europe and Asia were only a few miles apart, named for its legendary founder Byzas. Constantine built a city there that straddled both sides of the waterway, Europe and Asia. He called it "New Rome," but people called it Constantine's City, or *Constantinople*. This move of the capital city left old Rome to fend for itself, and the divide between the eastern half of the empire, centered in Constantinople, and the western half, centered in Rome, increasingly grew. For one thing, the pope became more and more important to the

Christians of the West. The patriarch of Constantinople viewed himself as head of the Eastern church. An incident occurred in 1054 that led to each of these church leaders excommunicating the other; no longer were they in communion. Church historians refer to the separation as the ***East-West Schism***. Eastern churches took the name "Orthodox," meaning "right teaching." A smaller number of Christians in the East remained in union with Rome and came to be known as "Eastern Catholics." You might hear of a church called "Ukrainian Orthodox" and another called "Ukrainian Catholic." Their practices and worldview are essentially the same; but one group recognizes the pope as head of the universal church while the other does not. The vast majority of Eastern Christians are Orthodox, not Catholic.

One difference between Western Christianity and the Eastern Orthodox churches after the East-West Schism was the great deal of uniformity within Western European Christianity. Before the changes of Vatican Council II, if you attended Mass in France, England, or Germany, the service would be identical, down to the language used—Latin. In the East, churches in different countries maintained a great deal of autonomy. The Russian Orthodox are distinct from the Coptic Christians of Egypt, for instance. Since Vatican Council II, every pope has set as a goal ending the separation between Catholic and Orthodox churches.

Built in the sixth century, Hagia Sophia represents the grandeur of Christendom at the time.

> Look up information about Eastern Orthodox churches in the United States. What are the major churches represented in the country?
>
> Read about the specific circumstances that led to the East-West Schism. Who were the key players?

The Protestant-Catholic Divide

> Unless I am convicted by Scripture and plain reason—I do not accept the authority of popes and councils ... I cannot and will not recant anything. ... Here I stand, I cannot do otherwise.
>
> Martin Luther (on trial for heresy)

Five hundred years after the East-West Schism in Christianity, Western Europe experienced its own divide. Popularly known as the ***Protestant Reformation***, the person who played the most significant role in it was the German monk Martin Luther. In 1517, Luther was so upset over what he saw as a misinterpretation of certain beliefs and practices of the time that he wrote his bishop a list of pronouncements that he believed represented a more accurate, biblical understanding of Christianity. He felt assured that reasonable church leaders and theologians, including the pope, would agree with him. Legend has it that he also posted these "Ninety-Five Theses" on the church door in his hometown, inviting other scholars to debate his positions.

A recent development of the time made it possible for his ideas to spread beyond his immediate locale—the printing press, invented less that seventy years before Luther. By the end of the fifteenth century every major city in Europe had a printing press. Before this time, few people could read and very few books were available to be read. If Luther had lived just fifty years before his time, his readers would have been confined to a small number of clerics and scholars. Instead, Luther caused enough of a stir that in 1521 he was prosecuted in a trial overseen by the emperor acting on behalf of the pope. Luther wanted to use the occasion to debate; the papal representatives only wanted him to submit to the authority of the pope. Luther refused and was condemned to death, but he was rescued by a sympathetic monk and some German princes. Luther spent a year in hiding, translating the

Bible into German. He wanted the Bible to be the judge of his positions, not the pope's lawyers, who refused to enter into honest debate about them. He proposed that the Bible was the final authority on truth, not the pope.

Attempts were made to reconcile those who remained loyal to the pope with the growing number of people who expanded on Luther's positions. One meeting ended in a shouting match; dissenters walked out, shouting, "We protest." They came to be known as Protestants. Luther never envisioned that his ideas would lead to separation from the one, holy, catholic, and apostolic church. Protestantism became an ever-expanding movement as one person after another proposed teachings and practices further removed from those of the official church of the time. "Catholic" came to mean "not being Protestant." A person could now be Christian without belonging to the Catholic Church or one of the Orthodox churches. However, the majority of Europeans remained Catholic, and Catholic bishops met to establish their own reforms at the ***Council of Trent***, which lasted off and on from 1545 to 1563.

The church doors where Luther reportedly posted his "Ninety-Five Theses"

List conditions that existed at the time of Luther that made the Reformation possible.

Identify the role played by three other people at the time of the Reformation.

In the 1990s, Lutheran and Catholic theologians declared that there are no substantial differences in beliefs between the two communities. They determined that differences are actually more a matter of emphasis and interpretation than substance. What are the key differences in emphasis between Lutheranism and Catholicism?

Catholicism and the Modern World

> All faithful Christians are *forbidden* to defend as the legitimate conclusions of science those opinions which are known to be contrary to the doctrine of faith, particularly if they have been condemned by the church.
>
> Vatican Council I, 1870 CE

Less than two hundred years after the Reformation, new developments began in Europe that posed another challenge to the church; the "modern era" had begun. Of the characteristics of the modern world that ran counter to a Catholic worldview, one in particular seemed to undermine the very foundation of Catholicism—the glorification of modern science. What happens when scientific findings contradict what scripture and church teachings say? One vehicle used by the church to address this question was Vatican Council I, called by Pope Pius IX in 1869. A teaching that came out of the

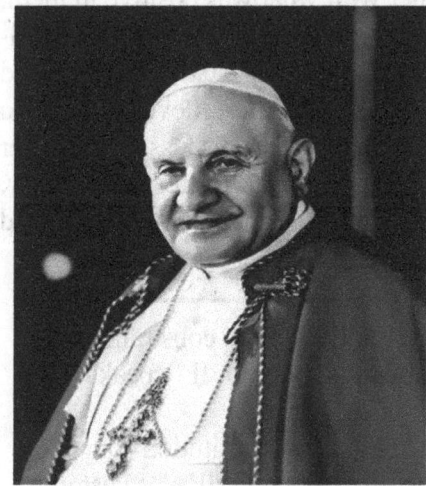

Soon after his election, Pope John XXIII called for a council to update the church.

council was the doctrine of *papal infallibility*. It states that when a pope "defines doctrine concerning faith or morals to be held by the whole church, he possesses ... that infallibility which the divine Redeemer willed his church to enjoy."

Nearly one hundred years later, the church held another council, Vatican Council II (1962–65). The council reassessed its relationship with modern developments, in particular in a document called "The Pastoral Constitution on the Church in the Modern World," which says,

> This council, first of all, wishes to assess ... those values which are most highly prized today and to relate them to their divine source. Insofar as they stem from endowments conferred by God on man, these values are exceedingly good. Yet they are often wrenched from their rightful function by the taint in man's heart, and hence stand in need of purification (#11).

Notice the difference in tone between Vatican Council I and Vatican Council II. At the time of Vatican Council I (1870), the values of the modern world appeared to be contrary to and a threat to the church. In the 1960s, the bishops at the council saw good in many modern developments and wanted to work together with what was positive in them. Advancements in the modern sciences—biology, psychology, sociology, history, and so forth—result from endowments God has conferred on people. The church wants to partner with these developments to work toward fostering the *common good*, which is discussed in chapter 13. Vatican Council I, on the other hand, had a "fortress" mentality, protecting the church from developments around it that it considered anathema.

The language of Vatican Council I is filled with constraints and condemnations, while Vatican Council II speaks of "dialogue." Explain the difference.

Read through Vatican I's "Dogmatic Constitution on the Church" and then Vatican Council II's "Pastoral Constitution on the Church in the Modern World," both available on the Vatican website. Take note of differences in tone and approach in these documents from two different time periods.

III. Mary's Role in the Church

> As mariners are guided into port by the shining of a star, so Christians are guided to heaven by Mary.
>
> St. Thomas Aquinas

Catholics hold Mary, the mother of Jesus, in such high regard that they might claim she deserves her own category, separate from the saints. Saints are not without sin; Catholic Tradition holds that Mary was sinless. In fact, it affirms that she was sinless from the very moment of her conception and has a feast day to honor her ***Immaculate Conception***, December 8. At the end of her life, she was "assumed into heaven," celebrated on the feast of the ***Assumption***, August 15. She has an entire litany of titles, from Star of the Sea to Comfort of the Afflicted and Mother of Mercy. If you see a statue of a lady in blue in a front yard, most likely the residents of that home are Catholic and are honoring Mary. Throughout the world, images of the Madonna and Child are almost as prolific as crucifixes. After the Lord's Prayer, the most popular prayer for Catholics is the Hail Mary. Catholics can use rosary beads to count off Hail Marys repeated over and over again. The Hail Mary is so synonymous with prayer itself that when a football quarterback throws up a long pass on the desperate chance that a teammate will catch it, it is called a Hail Mary pass. (Roger Staubach, quarterback of the Dallas Cowboys and a Catholic, was the first person associated with that phrase after he completed an unbelievable touchdown pass to win a game.) That sentiment of invoking Mary when everything else seems to fail is similar to praying to Mary, Untier of Knots, a title made popular by Pope Francis. Whether or not they meant it seriously, even the Beatles, in their song "Let It Be," sang of going to Mary in times of trouble. When a child falls, a mother comes running to help.

Catholics cherish the image of Mary, the Blessed Mother. She was the mother of Jesus, but in one of his last acts before death he let us know that she is mother to us all: "When Jesus saw his mother and the disciple whom he loved standing beside her, he said to his mother,

'Woman, here is your son.' Then he said to the disciple, 'Here is your mother'" (John 19:26–27). Catholics identify themselves with that beloved disciple called out to be children of Mary. If anything, Mary is even more revered in Eastern churches than by Catholics in the Latin tradition. Early in the Syriac and Greek traditions, Mary is given the title ***Theotokos***, meaning "the one who bears God," or simply "Mother of God." What about Protestants? Traditionally, Protestants downplayed the role of Mary in the story of salvation and criticized Catholics for praying to her. They did so for three reasons: (1) Little is written about Mary in the Bible. (2) It distracts from the one who is the true focus of the New Testament, Jesus. (3) It borders on idolatry in that it makes of Mary almost a goddess, like the many goddesses found in the pagan religions of the time.

The bishops of Vatican Council II debated how to describe the role of Mary in the story of salvation. They decided that she rightfully belonged in the document on the church. That decision was based on the few stories we have about Mary in the Gospels. Three times Mary is featured in the Gospels, twice in Luke and once in John. The main incident is what is known as the ***Annunciation***, celebrated at the Feast of the Incarnation, March 25. (Notice that it is nine months before the feast of Christ's birth, December 25.) Mary is betrothed to Joseph, identified as a carpenter; but they are not yet married. She is visited by a messenger from God who informs her that she has been chosen by God to conceive a child who will be "Son of the Most High" (Luke 1:32). Mary responds, "Let it be with me according to your word" (Luke 1:38). Mary's simple "Let it be" seals her position in the story of salvation. Imagine if she had said no! With that clear and forceful affirmation on her part, Mary can be called the mother of the church and the model for all Christians. She says yes to God; she is the first to witness to the Christ event. Christians seek to witness to Christ in their own lives and echo her commitment to follow God's will. She carries Christ within her and gives birth to him; Christians accept that they are to carry Christ within themselves as they interact with others and "give birth" to Christ wherever they are. Along with Mary, all Christians are to be bearers of Christ in the world. Mary's "yes" to God and to the presence of God's Son within her made her the first Christian. As mother of Christ, Mary is also mother of the church, which is the body of Christ.

Henry Ossawa Tanner portrayed Mary as a young peasant girl.

A second time Mary is featured in the Gospel of Luke follows her visit to her pregnant cousin, Elizabeth. She sings a song called the **Magnificat**, or Mary's Song of Praise. She identifies herself with "the lowly" who have been raised up and praises God for "scattering the proud" and "bringing down the powerful" (Luke 1:31–32). The tone of her song is not "Woe is me," but a recognition that if God is intervening through her, that she and her son are to be witnesses to justice. The message of her song is the same as the good news proclaimed by her son: hope for the downtrodden and justice for the oppressed, which is also the message of the church. Surely Jesus learned his love for those who are poor from this strong woman, his mother.

A third time when Mary plays a prominent role is written about in the Gospel of John. Mary attends a wedding with Jesus, who has yet to give any signs of his identity as Messiah and Son of God. The embarrassed newlyweds run out of wine at the wedding feast, and Mary turns to Jesus and says simply, "They have no wine." Jesus takes the hint. He asks the stewards to serve the water supplied for washing, which he transforms into delicious wine. Mary's gentle prodding of her son saves the day for the young couple. Catholics often pray to Mary to intercede for them rather than imploring the help of Jesus directly, giving rise to the phrase **Ad Jesum per Mariam**, "To Jesus through Mary." They appreciate the power a mother's words can have.

> Mary was made Mother of God to obtain salvation for many who, on account of their wicked lives, could not be saved according to the rigor of Divine justice, but might be saved with the help of her sweet mercy and powerful intercession.
>
> St. John Chrysostom

These are the annual Feast Days of Mary:

- December 8: Immaculate Conception. Mary is conceived pure and sinless.
- March 25: Annunciation. An angel announces to Mary that she is chosen to bear Christ, God's Son.
- May 31: Visitation. Mary visits her older cousin, Elizabeth, and sings her Magnificat.
- August 15: Assumption. Mary is brought home to heaven to be eternally with her Son.

If Mary is the model for all Christians, then stories about her are also about them. For instance, Catholic teaching holds that at the end of her life, Mary is brought to heaven. What is the implication of that story for the Christian life?

An interesting phenomenon associated with Mary is *apparitions*, appearances of Mary to various people over the last few centuries. One apparition site, Lourdes in France, has become one of the most popular pilgrimage destinations in the world. Our Lady of Guadalupe appeared to a Mexican peasant and left her image on his cloak, which now is on display in a basilica in Mexico City. Read about apparitions in various countries, such as Our Lady of La Vang in Vietnam. What are their common characteristics?

Mary has often been portrayed as a very submissive, docile person. In 1974 Pope St. Paul VI cleared up that misunderstanding by stating that Mary was neither "timidly submissive" nor "obnoxiously pious" (*Marialus Cultus*). Her words in the Magnificat are challenging, fighting words. Saying yes to the angel about accepting becoming pregnant without being married was a bold step on her part. She is listed as being among the followers of Jesus at Pentecost when the Holy Spirit descends upon them. She wasn't back in Nazareth resuming an unassuming lifestyle. Read an article about "feminist perspectives on Mary" and report on what you find.

IV. Saints in a Catholic Worldview

The Communion of Saints

> "What is the Church if not the assembly of all the saints?" The communion of saints is the Church.
>
> Catechism, #946

St. Paul referred to all followers of Christ as saints. In time, certain members of the community stood out as models of holiness and were given the title "saint." Beginning in the tenth century, people requested that the pope officially recognize certain people as saints, which led to a formal process of canonization for naming saints that includes three steps, from Venerable to Blessed to Saint. Remember the word canon, meaning rule or measure, applied to determining which books are officially recognized as scripture? A formal process to canonize saints also exists in the Catholic Church. Some saints have been canonized and therefore officially recognized as such by the church; but those standouts do not exhaust the saintliness that exists in the church and in the world. There are as many ways to demonstrate holiness as there are people. St. Francis de Sales, who wrote extensively on the devout life, said, "Be certain of this: it is an error, even heresy, to want to banish the devout life from the company of soldiers, the shops of artisans, the courts of princes and the homes of married people." Holiness can be expressed in all walks of life and through many different personality traits. De Sales reminded people, "Do not wish to be anything but what you are, and try to be that perfectly." That is the path to saintliness.

In a Catholic worldview, the church is a ***communion of saints***, past and present. People today are in communion with those who have gone before. The Protestant tradition tends to focus on Jesus exclusively. That is not the Catholic way. Devotion to saints does not detract from adoration of Christ but recognizes that Christ has been present in many ways and in many people throughout time. Catholics do not revere saints *instead of* Christ; rather, they view saints as *witnesses* of Christ and his message. The message Christ lived was one of hope and self-giving love. Saints witnessed to that message in their lives, often despite doubts and multiple personal challenges. In other words, for Catholics Christ is not just known through words in a book or in a personal, internal conversion experience. Rather, historically Christ was present in flesh and blood people and continues to be so today.

Many traditional religions, such as those of Native Americans and Africans, believe that ancestors remain present in their midst in some fashion. Can you imagine pausing and asking a beloved grandparent who has died to guide you and inspire you? Husbands and wives whose spouses have died speak at times of their loved one being present with them even after death. Saints are collective loved ones for Catholics. They pray for the intercession of saints as they go about their daily lives. Every Catholic knows that if you lose your keys, you can say a prayer to St. Anthony of Padua and he can help you find them. Pray to St. Therese, and if you do a good deed look for roses to show up in your life somehow. You might have your pet blessed on October 4, the feast of St. Francis of Assisi. Non-Catholics may look upon devotion to saints as superstition, but for Catholics, it is a recognition that Christ is present in the communion of saints, living and dead, of which we are all a part.

> Those whom we love and lose are no longer where they were before. They are now wherever we are.
>
> St. John Chrysostom

> The great and sad mistake of many people ... is to imagine that those whom death has taken, leave us. They do not leave us. They remain! Where are they? In the darkness? Oh, no! It is we who are in the darkness. We do not see them, but they see us. Their eyes, radiant with glory, are fixed upon our eyes. ... Oh infinite consolation! Though invisible to us, our dead are not absent. ... They are living near us, transformed ... into light, into power, into love.
>
> Karl Rahner, SJ, *On the Theology of Death*

Protestant churches typically are named after some biblical reference: St. Mark's Episcopal Church (Gospel writer), Ascension Lutheran Church, or simply First Baptist Church. Catholic churches are often named after a saint: St. Patrick's Cathedral, St. John Neumann Church. Since saints model holiness in particular ways, then there can be patron saints for any number of people, professions, and situations in life. A fourth-century bishop of Myra in modern-day Turkey was walking down a street one day when through an open window he heard young children crying because they had nothing to eat and their parents were without work. The bishop threw a pouch of coins through the window, much to the delight of the children. That bishop, St. Nicholas, is the patron saint of children and morphed into what Americans know as Santa Claus. The medieval St. Clare was sick and confined to her room so that she could not attend Mass that day. She saw the image of the Mass on her wall as if she were actually there. In the 1950s, the church proclaimed her the patron saint of television. In the late 1700s, a Frenchman named Benedict Joseph Labre applied to join at least four different religious orders. None of them deemed him worthy to join them. He decided to live his life traveling from place to place, begging for his food and owning only the clothes on his back. He identified himself as a "holy fool." He spent the end of his life in Rome, often visiting churches there. Many people got to know this pious beggar. One day, coming out of a church, he fell to the ground suffering some kind of medical attack. Children nearby started shouting, "The saint is dead! The saint is dead!" After his death, people actually started to speak of him as a saint, and in time he was canonized one. He is the patron saint of people who are homeless. A patron saint for students is St. Thomas Aquinas who, as a student himself, was slow to respond to questions and was called "the dumb ox" by teachers. He went on to become one of the church's greatest theologians. (You will find some of his thoughtful quotes throughout this book.)

The church continues to find models of holiness that deserve to be elevated to the status of being canonized as saints. The Vatican even solicited recommendations for who should be named the patron saint of the Internet. It decided on St. Isidore of Spain, who in the Middle Ages wrote a compendium of all knowledge that was very popular in Europe for centuries. Two twentieth-century Italians who led full, active lives were recognized for their holiness: St. Gianna Beretta

Molla, a doctor and mother who enjoyed tennis and mountain climbing, and Blessed Pier Giorgio Frassati, a young man who did everything with great gusto, including caring for sick and poor people he knew. Both were avid sports enthusiasts. During his brief life, Pier Giorgio accomplished forty-nine major mountain climbs while also caring for poor people in the evenings when he was home. Blessed Franz Jagerstatter was an Austrian farmer who lived during the Nazi era. He was married with three daughters but had led a rowdy life before marriage. (He was the first in his village to own a motorcycle and had a child with another woman before marrying his wife, Franzeska.) Nonetheless, when he was called up for military duty in the Nazi army, he refused—despite his local priest trying to convince him to serve. He saw the Nazi cause and his Catholic faith as incompatible. For this refusal, he was executed by guillotine at the age of thirty-six. He is the patron saint of conscientious objectors. In 2019 noted Hollywood director Terrence Malick made a film about Jagerstatter called *A Hidden Life*.

> Traditionally, Catholic parents choose a saint's name for their child at baptism. That saint was their patron saint. However, Catholics can look to other saints as their "patrons," based on some quality, profession, or state in life. Look up various patron saints, such as the many patron saints of mothers and grandparents, nurses and fire fighters. What led them to be that particular patron?
>
> Read more about St. Gianna Beretta Molla and Blessed Pier Giorgio Frassati. How would you describe their spirituality?
>
> If you were interested in choosing a patron saint for yourself, whom would you choose and why?

The Saints through History

> If the Church was a body composed of different members, it couldn't lack the noblest of all: it must have a Heart, and a Heart BURNING WITH LOVE.
>
> St. Therese, in *Catechism*, #826

Martyrs

Different models of holiness were prominent at different times throughout church history. For the first few centuries, due to the constant threat of persecutions, *martyrs* were the epitome of saintliness. The word means "witness." In their case, martyrs witnessed to Christ in a specific way—by dying for him, often in horrendous fashion. The sacrifices of early martyrs kept Christianity alive and actually inspired many people to join this movement filled with people willing to give their very lives for it. In fact, a second-century Christian writer professed that "the blood of the martyrs is the seed of the church." We know the

Martyr Franz Jagerstatter gave his life for refusal to serve in the Nazi army.

story of two young women martyred during this time because of a book written about them. Perpetua, a noblewoman, and her servant, Felicity, were engaged in preparation for their baptism in Carthage, Northern Africa. Becoming Christian was outlawed at the time. They were found out, arrested, and scheduled to be fed to lions as part of a spectacle the next day. Perpetua had just given birth, and Felicity was pregnant. Perpetua's father, who had wealth and some prestige, made an arrangement with the local officials: all the two had to do was renounce their faith in Christ and they could go free. Her father pleaded with Perpetua to take the offer, not just for herself but for her newborn child. Both young women refused to deny Christ. They were led to the local arena and stripped naked, and hungry lions were released from their cages. For whatever reason, the lions steered clear of the two women. As was customary in such cases, a soldier was dispatched to cut their throats and end their lives. The names of Perpetua and Felicity are invoked in one of the eucharistic prayers recited at times during Mass.

Confessors

As Christianity became more and more accepted and influential, some Christians still wanted to witness to Christ. This gave rise to what are called in the church *confessors*, people who gave their lives to Christ but were not killed for doing so. As the age of Constantine approached, a popular trend emerged. Christians who wanted to live an austere life of sacrifice gave up the comforts of family, home, and civilization to live alone in deserted places. When his parents died, St. Anthony of Egypt (251–356 CE) gave half of the inheritance to his younger sister and the rest to people who were poor. He went out into the desert and lived in an abandoned tomb for many years. People in the area recognized him as a holy man, and some wanted to join him. He established a structure for people to live alone but in a communal setting. St. Mary of Egypt (344–421 CE) also gave up a worldly life to live out the remainder of her life alone in the desert. Hermits such as these gave rise to what are known as *monks* and *nuns*. Monasteries have simple individual cells for monks and nuns to live in while joining others for communal prayer, meals, and work. They take vows of poverty, chastity, and obedience. More austere communities talk to one another only for a few hours on Sundays or when necessary, and seldom to people outside of the community. In the East, St. Macrina and her younger brother, St. Basil, are credited with beginning monastic life there. In the West, St. Benedict and his twin sister, St. Scholastica, formulated "the rule of St. Benedict" that has served as the model for most monastic communities in the Western church ever since. There are still monks and nuns living a cloistered life, separate from the outside world, dedicated to work and prayer. Women not living a monastic life who are members of religious communities engaged in service in the world are technically *sisters*, not nuns. However, the designation *nuns* has come to refer to all women who are members of a religious order.

Mendicants

At the height of the Middle Ages, two men followed a different way of living a Christian lifestyle: St. Dominic and St. Francis of Assisi. They began a different lifestyle for saintliness—*mendicant*, meaning "beggar." By the time of Francis and Dominic (early thirteenth century), living in a monastery was for many not so difficult or challenging an experience. Monasteries often owned a great deal of land surrounding the monastery, where they grew crops and tended farm animals. They developed skills in making breads, cheeses, wine, and beer. Francis of Assisi was a child of the growing middle class, son of a successful cloth merchant. In his youth he led the other young men of the town in various pranks and carousing. When his town went to war with a neighboring town, he donned armor and headed off to battle. He was quickly captured and spent time in prison until his father's money bought his freedom. Francis, however, had changed. He grew pensive and no longer joined in fun with his former friends. He left home and found refuge in a nearby rundown chapel, which he set about to rebuild. People recognized the change in Francis and thought that perhaps he would go to a monastery. Francis felt that monastic life was too secure, too comfortable, compared to how Christ had lived. He wanted to give up everything, as he felt Christ had done. He decided not to live apart from the world but to be a holy presence in it. He renounced all of his possessions and wore the humble garb of a beggar. If people gave him food, he ate; otherwise, he went without. He worked at times but never accepted pay for it. He experienced great joy in what he called service to his newfound lady, Lady Poverty. Others joined him in great numbers. Single-handedly, Francis transformed European society and showed what a lifestyle of holiness could be. Dominic did much the same in Spain, except his focus was on preaching. By singing the praises of poverty and simple living, Francis and Dominic offered an antidote to the materialism gaining ground in Europe at the time.

Modern Religious Orders

Three hundred years after the advent of the mendicant orders, new expressions of saintliness emerged. One man's story illustrates the change. St. Vincent de Paul was born a peasant in France, but some wealthy patrons recognized his intelligence and sponsored his training to become a priest. Vincent served as a priest for French nobility until one day a nobleman invited Vincent to accompany him to his summer palace. When the party arrived there, the steward of the palace told Vincent that one of the farmhands was dying and would love to have a priest hear his confession and bless him before he died. Vincent visited the man, who felt great comfort and relief from him. Vincent realized that his priesthood would be better served by helping poor people and others in need. He returned to Paris and began various programs to help prisoners and people who were homeless. A local wealthy woman, Louise de Marillac, convinced some other wealthy women to go into town and bring food to poor people. Together with Vincent, she started a community of women committed to doing this work full-time; these became known as the Daughters of Charity. These two saints began what today we call social work. Another Frenchman, St. John Baptist de la Salle, saw poor boys with nothing to do but get into trouble. At the time, education was only for families who could afford it. La Salle decided to bring together like-minded men to educate poor boys. He came up with the idea of having one teacher teaching a group of students at a time as opposed to one-on-one tutoring. He proposed having certain subjects taught at the same time every day. In other words, he invented what schools typically are today. Other men and women began communities that served people in health care, education, social work, and missionary activity in foreign countries. The Society of Jesus (Jesuits) and Ursuline sisters became synonymous with quality education. For a long time, homeless shelters and hospitals were begun and staffed by religious men and women. (Even the famous Mayo clinic owes its existence to a persistent group of nuns who were behind its founding.)

Saints Today

What models of holiness exist within Catholicism today? For one thing, the kinds of saints who were prominent in the past remain present today. Unfortunately, there are still martyrs, women and men who die putting their faith into practice. In 1980, Archbishop Oscar Romero of El Salvador was shot dead while saying Mass; a few months later four American women who worked with the poor in that country were also brutally murdered. Father Mychal Judge, chaplain of the New York Fire Department, died from fallen debris while ministering to victims of the September 11, 2001, World Trade Center attack. There are still men and women who live a monastic lifestyle. Thomas Merton, a Trappist monk who lived as a hermit at his Kentucky monastery, was one of the most influential religious

Sr. Mary Alfred Moes (d. 1899) was inspired to build the world-renowned Mayo Clinic in Rochester, MN, which at the time had only one doctor.

figures of the twentieth century. Franciscan and Dominican priests, sisters, and brothers, along with laypeople who are "third order" Franciscans, live a modern version of the charism of their founders, Francis and Dominic. Christian Brothers, the order founded by La Salle, continue to teach and administer schools. Sisters and nuns are still involved in many forms of service to their communities. So often their work goes on behind the scenes, such as caring for migrants at the southern border or teaching English as a second language to people new to America.

To learn about a more vocal group of sisters, read about the "nuns on the bus" who traveled the country seeking to influence public policy affecting people living in poverty.

However, few women in America are joining traditional religious orders, and the number of men becoming priests has diminished to such a degree that a "priest shortage" is part of discussions among church leaders. How are Catholics witnessing to their faith today? Many men and women are volunteering their time to coach children. Laypeople are keeping Catholic schools going at every level. Dedicated professionals provide healthcare. For most of them, it is not just a job but a vocation. Catholic Worker houses and other outreach programs serve the needs of homeless people. Catholics work with gang members in Los Angeles and Chicago. People support one another through AA programs. Laypeople in parishes hold weekly Bible study groups and get involved in service projects. Perhaps most importantly, parents live out their faith by showing love to their children and making their homes "domestic churches."

Who are models of saintliness today that come to mind?
What kinds of saints do we need today?

We are not on earth as museum keepers, but to cultivate a flourishing garden of life and to prepare for a glorious future.

Pope St. John XXIII

Christ and the Church

Jesus is the heart of the church, but that heart would be dormant without the church. A famous cartoon shows a man asking God, "Why don't you do something about all the problems in the world?" God responds, "I did do something. I created you." Christ is the savior of the world; but that saving action continues today in the many people of good will who carry on that work, which was the message of Pentecost. Sometimes that gathering, the church, is unrecognizable for what it is. The Holy Spirit is an artist who refuses to stay inside the lines. Jesus reminds us not to be astonished: "The wind blows where it chooses, and you hear the sound of it, but you do not know where it comes from or where it goes. So it is with everyone who is born of the Spirit" (John 3:8). Church buildings can be vivid reminders of the presence of the Spirit in brick and mortar, stained glass and steeples. The church community, with its hierarchy of pastoral ministers along with all the people of God, keeps alive the promise Jesus left his disciples and takes up the challenge of bringing the world ever closer to becoming God's kingdom.

Chapter Review

1. What did St. Lawrence put forth as the wealth of the church?
2. What does the word *catholic* mean?
3. What happened at Pentecost, and why is it called the birthday of the church?
4. What groups did Vatican Council II say were linked to the catholic church?
5. What does the word *hierarchy* mean? In the Catholic Church, what does it refer to?
6. How did St. Paul and the Council of Jerusalem transform the church?
7. What role did Emperors Nero and Constantine play in how Christians were viewed in the Roman Empire?
8. What is the East-West Schism?

9. What role did Martin Luther play in the Christianity of Western Europe?
10. What was the Council of Trent?
11. What was the difference in attitude toward the modern world between Vatican Council I and Vatican Council II?
12. How do Catholics look upon Mary, the Blessed Mother?
13. What are three annual feasts associated with Mary?
14. Why did Vatican Council II place discussion of Mary in the document on the church?
15. Who were the greatest saints of the early church?
16. What did confessors, and later monks and nuns, do to serve Christ?
17. What are mendicant orders?
18. What kinds of work did the founders of modern religious orders engage in?

For Further Study

Luigi Accatoli. *When a Pope Asks Forgiveness: The Mea Culpa's of John Paul II.* Pauline Books, 1998. In preparation for the year 2000, the pope of the time decided to issue apologies for ways that members of the church mistreated groups of people, such as heretics and apostates during the Inquisition, women, and indigenous people. The author discusses the pope's statements leading up to these admissions of guilt and his reflections on some of the darker sides of Catholic history.

Robert Ellsberg. *All Saints: Daily Reflections on Saints, Prophets, and Witnesses for Our Time.* A Crossroad Book, 1997. A short reflection for every day of the year on particular "saints," not all of them canonized or even Catholic. Ellsberg has since written a number of other books about saints, whom he describes as "people of flesh and blood, struggling to find their way."

Pope Francis. *Evangelii Gaudium* ("The Joy of the Gospel.") United States Conference of Catholic Bishops, 2013. Pope Francis exhorts all members of the church to spread the joy of the gospel and enunciates many themes that have been the hallmarks of his papacy.

Edward P. Hahnenberg. *A Concise Guide to the Documents of Vatican II*. St. Anthony Messenger Press, 2007. Offers background information on and a synopsis of the Council documents.

Lumen Gentium ("Dogmatic Constitution on the Church"). vatican.va. Lays out Vatican Council II's vision of church, which is much more inclusive and expansive than commonly held beliefs about church prior to the council.

Timothy Matovina. *Latino Catholicism: Transformation in America's Largest Church*, abridged edition. Liguori, 2013. Americans of Latin American background have been growing in numbers within the Catholic Church. The author calls for a more robust response on the part of church leadership to address the needs of this population.

Richard P. McBrien. *The Church: The Evolution of Catholicism*. HarperOne, 2008. Traces the development of the church from its beginnings to today. Focuses mainly on the institutional church and its leaders.

Jon M. Sweeney. *Strange Heaven: The Virgin Mary as Woman, Mother, Disciple, and Advocate*. Paraclete Press, 2006. Numerous books have recently been written about Mary, mother of Jesus, many of them dispelling the myth that she was meek and mild and not a strong woman. Sweeney examines many elements of the Mary myth and in the end affirms the consoling Catholic belief that, through Mary, they do not stand alone before God.

"Urban Trinity: The Story of Catholic Philadelphia." YouTube. Traces the various groups of Catholics who shaped a city from colonial times to the present.

Chapter 7
The Catholic Sacramental Worldview

The Catholic perspective on reality is sacramental. That means that God communicates through all aspects of the world around us. Matter and spirit are not as separate as they may appear. Indeed, the world is, in a sense, God's body language. In the words of the Jesuit poet Gerard Manley Hopkins, "The world is charged with the grandeur of God." Sacraments are encounters with Christ. In Catholicism, sacramentality is not confined to the seven sacraments that are central to Catholic life. Before those seven can be appreciated, it is necessary to understand the meaning of the concept of *sacrament* itself.

> Holy, holy, holy is the Lord of hosts; the whole earth is full of his glory.
>
> Isaiah 6:3

I. Seeing the World as Holy

Describe the three holiest places you know. What makes them holy for you?

What was your experience in these holy places? How did it change your life?

> In the end, the only events of my life worth telling are those when the imperishable world erupted into the transitory one.
>
> Carl Jung

Thin Places

Have you ever traveled to Ireland? If you have, you might have noticed something that most Americans aren't accustomed to. During certain times of the year, twilight can begin before 7:00 p.m. and continue past 10:00 p.m. Thus, the Irish live a sizeable portion of their lives in this in-between time of not quite light and not quite darkness. Twilight is a time of mystery, a time of crossing over between two worlds. Perhaps the prolonged twilight nurtures the Irish talent for storytelling. It also helps shape Irish spirituality.

Irish spirituality talks about **thin places**. Apparently, this notion existed in Ireland even before the Celts arrived around 500 BCE. Thin places are places where the borderline between heaven and earth, the spiritual realm and the material, is not so thick. They are times and places where the veil separating us from God is lifted ever so much. It's like a sacred twilight zone. To go to a thin place is to step onto holy ground and enter sacred time. In Irish spirituality, time spent in a thin place refreshes our spirit and renews our faith that we are indeed connected to something greater than we normally are aware of. To experience a thin place, we need to pay attention and listen, to see and hear what we might otherwise overlook. We could be in a thin place and not even notice it. Births and deaths are surely thin places—or should be recognized as such. Surely God is present whenever someone enters or leaves this life. A couple committing themselves to each other in marriage is also a thin place. Catholic spirituality proposes that something would be missing if such life-transforming events were made light of and not viewed as holy.

> Missing me one place, search another. I stop somewhere waiting for you.
>
> Walt Whitman

Sacramental Seeing

A hallmark of Catholicism is this perspective of seeing the world around us as holy. The old Baltimore Catechism, used as the primary instrument of instruction for American Catholics for a century, put it in simple question-and-answer format: "Where is God?" Answer: "God is everywhere." Thomas Merton suggested that we miss God not because there is too little of God but because there is so much. In her poem "Small Kindnesses," Danusha Lameris reminds us that even "brief moments of exchange" are sacramental, a way that the sacred enters into our everyday lives if we are paying attention:

> What if they are the true dwelling of the holy, these
> fleeting temples we make together when we say, "Here,
> have my seat," "Go ahead—you first." "I like your hat."

That vision, that everyday encounters are holy, represents the Catholic sacramental worldview. Hopkins expresses it eloquently in his poem "As Kingfishers Catch Fire":

> For Christ plays in ten thousand places,
> Lovely in limbs, and lovely in eyes not his
> To the Father through the features of men's faces.

Like Hopkins, Jesus himself found holiness in overlooked people—children, tax collectors, a Roman soldier, foreigners, prisoners, and the sick. Jesus also saw holiness hidden in the natural settings around him. Before beginning his active, public life, Jesus spent time alone in a barren place, surrounded by nature, where he could be in communion with his Father.

One way to express the Catholic sacramental worldview is to say, "Do you see the people and the world around you? Rightly understood, they can speak to you of God." In other words, God communicates *through* the stuff of the earth, not divorced from it. From a sacramental perspective, matter is not a distraction from God but a revelation of God. God reaches out to us in sensuous, material ways. Martin Luther and, after him, most Protestant leaders were scandalized at the corruption they saw in the "visible" church and in the almost superstitious way in which its ritual practices were viewed by many people. This led to a position within Protestantism that can be summarized as "See the material world around you? God is not like that." That is, the real church is a spiritual "perfect society," not represented by the men living a decadent lifestyle in the halls of the Vatican at the time. Protestants considered the thoughtless external administration of sacramental rituals as "hocus pocus"—a phrase used to mock the Latin words of consecration of the bread during Mass, *Hoc est enim corpus meum* ("This is indeed my body"). Internal conversion, not mindless mumbling of words before an altar or a statue, is holy. It takes us away from the material world, filled with its temptations and distractions.

Catholicism continued to see things differently. The Catholic view is that all reality rightly understood is sacramental. God permeates the world and our very souls. St. Thomas Aquinas expressed the Catholic view in this way: "What is there awkward about visible and bodily things ministering to spiritual health? Aren't they the instruments of God, who was made flesh for us and suffered in this world?" This sacramental perspective flows from the notion of God as the Holy Trinity. God is not distant but is close at hand. God the Father wants to communicate to us so much that he sent his Son to dwell among us as one of us. Father and Son desire so much to be with us everywhere and always that they sent the Spirit. That's why we can look around us and within us and see God there. A sacramental worldview also flows naturally from the Christian doctrine of the Incarnation. In Jesus, the visible, bodily Word of God in the flesh is holy. To see ourselves, others, and the world around us as sacramental means to see them as God sees them. The world is sacramental, filled with thin places, if we but look with the eyes of faith.

> Every spark of life is equally sacred; for in the humblest atom and the most brilliant star, in the lowest insect and the finest intelligence, there is the radiant smile and thrill of the same Absolute.
>
> Paleontologist and theologian Pierre Teilhard de Chardin, SJ

> Look up the term "thin places" as it applies to Irish spirituality. How is it described? How might it be applied to your own life?
> What are steps you could take that might further develop a sacramental view of the world and other people?

Sacramental Blindness: Dualism and Secularism

> God is the Creator of the human body as well as the soul. Neither of these is evil, nor does God hate either of them; for He hates none of the things that He has made.
>
> St. Augustine

People in certain cultures are more attuned to the holy than people tend to be in our secularized society. Native American cultures immediately come to mind. The Lakota look upon elements of nature as having "spirit"—*wakan*. The spirits of animals, trees, and even the grasses of the plains are *wakan* and are an expression of the Great Spirit, *Wakantanka*. Black Elk (1860s–1950), a holy man of the Oglala Lakota and also a convert to Catholicism, spoke about his experience of "seeing in a sacred manner the shapes of all things ... as they must live together like one being." He said that the Lakota and birds share the same religion; both build their homes in a circle, which is the way the world works. In the Japanese Shinto religion, archways, called *torii*, are found beside lakes and in front of mountains to remind people that natural settings are temples in themselves; no need to erect a separate building to be reminded of the holy. In predominantly Muslim countries, devout Muslims take a break from their activities five times a day to pray and remind themselves that "God is greater" (*Allahu Akbar*). In this way they seek never to stray too far from a sense of the holy. The ancient Hindu scripture *Bhagavad Gita* has God saying, "I permeate all the universe. ... All beings exist within me." Hindu practices are all about achieving a deepened consciousness of that reality. Sacramental awareness runs through Judeo-Christian tradition as well. The Psalms depict sun, moon, and stars, mighty waters and mountains, and all creation as the holy work of God. All creation can serve as a reminder of the sacred mystery that envelopes us. And St. Francis of Assisi stands out in Christian tradition as someone who found fellowship with other creatures in praising God.

St. Francis of Assisi modeled befriending nature and viewing all creation as

Why has the message of God's communicating in everyday, earthy ways not always been evident in Catholic teaching or practice? Two movements run counter to this message: ***dualism*** and ***secularism***.

Simply put, the worldview of dualism proposes that (1) a great divide exists between the material and spiritual realms, and (2) the material world is bad while the spiritual is good. In this worldview, sensual, bodily experiences lure people away from contemplating God. Human beings are created in God's image because of two non-sensual, spiritual qualities they possess: intellect and will. Through intellect and will, human beings can keep in check the allure of materiality, especially pleasures associated with "the world and the flesh." A dualistic worldview leads to looking upon the earthiness of ourselves and our world in a negative light. The experience of the earthy as holy gets lost.

Secularism vs. Romanticism

Secularism entered Western Europe in the mid-1600s. It too separated the material from the spiritual, but in this case it downplayed the significance of the spiritual. While Native Americans look upon other creatures as *wakan*, secularists view the natural world as made up of physical entities having no deeper, spiritual quality to them. A movement that fought back against the reductionist tendencies of secularism and its reliance on empirical science as the sole source of truth reached its peak in Europe in the early nineteenth century: *Romanticism*. You may be familiar with the Romantic poets of England: Wordsworth, Shelley, Keats, and William Blake. Wordsworth wrote about "Our cheerful faith, that all which we behold / Is full of blessings." There's a story about Blake walking with a scientist/secularist friend who says to him, "Surely when you look at the sun you see a round glowing orb in the sky." Blake replied, "When I see the sun, I see choirs of angels singing, 'Alleluia.'" Perhaps if we looked upon the sun from a sacramental perspective, as St. Francis of Assisi did, we too would join in singing, "Alleluia."

If we live in a secular culture, we likely suffer from *sacramental blindness*. We fail to see the sacred hidden within the beauty of the visible world around us. St. Paul wrote that creation should bring us to an awareness of God because, in modern terms, the earth is God's body language: "Ever since the creation of the world his eternal power and divine nature, invisible though they are, have been understood and seen through the things he has made" (Romans 1:20). Catholicism proclaims that we come from God, but we have forgotten the way back. However, like Hansel and Gretel in the dark forest, we may notice pebbles leading us to an awareness of the sacredness in our midst. The encounters we have with other people are sparks of the divine presence that we can miss unless we fine-tune our "God sense." A walk along the beach can be not only physically exhilarating but also spiritually uplifting. Church buildings are not intended to block out "the world," as if they are the sole repository of the good and the holy. From a Catholic perspective, there must be a connection between "sanctuary" and "street." Times spent in church can evoke awareness of our connection to that which is greater than we typically notice. They are meant to be sacramental, thin places where we can remember that God is with us at all times. Sacramental awareness reminds us that the ongoing, unfolding drama of time itself is holy.

> A Christian life is a sacramental life; it is not a life lived only in the mind, only in the soul; through the bodies of men and women Christ toils and endures and rejoices and loves and dies.
>
> Caryl Houselander

What difference does it make whether we have a dualist, secularist, or sacramental perspective on ourselves, other people, and the world around us? Describe each perspective. Describe each one using specific examples.

Do you have moments of sacramental blindness and also of sacramental seeing? Name some ways that someone might further develop a sacramental view of the world and other people.

The Problem of Evil and a Sacramental Worldview

The Catholic emphasis on the sacramentality of creation and the everyday as means by which God communicates serves as an antidote to the dualistic view that sees the material world as a distraction from the "truly holy," which is not of this world. However, are there people, things, and events in this world that are *not* sacramental and cannot be recognized as such? Are some things simply not a manifestation of the sacred but are instead a grave distortion of all that is holy? Christianity does have a history of glorifying suffering as a means to bringing people closer to God, but it takes a very special grace to reach that awareness. It's hard to think of children dying of starvation as African deserts expand, or who witness their friends ending up victims of neighborhood gang wars, as sacramental. It would seem to be cold-hearted to do so. Is God present in and through such catastrophes? When we can no longer make sense of something, we have reached the breaking point of sacramental spirituality. Evil and suffering cannot be dismissed for what they are—awful realities in our world. A Catholic worldview does not dismiss or overlook the cross; Jesus, holiness itself, underwent suffering and a torturous death.

Workers in a Nazi concentration camp. Is there a limit to the presence of God?

We know from the story of Jesus that "the holy" is not always pleasant or joyful. Sometimes it rips our hearts out. Traveling through Europe, one discovers many holy places —magnificent cathedrals, quaint little chapels, and monasteries. But is there any holier ground than the death camps where millions of Jews and countless others were murdered during the Holocaust? We dare to call these sites holy, even though we cannot enter them without breaking down in tears and screaming at God, "How could this have happened?" We would never joke about or make light of death camps. They are too holy. Closer to home, visit the Vietnam War memorial in Washington. The atmosphere is one of reverential silence. If a relative of yours died in that war, you might touch the name carved into the memorial and pray. The same respectful attitude surrounds the site in lower Manhattan where the World Trade Center buildings once stood. Unfortunately, mass shootings across the United States in recent years have resulted in places now viewed as shrines, where we place flowers and candles to honor the sacredness of those who have died. Only when we recognize evil and the pervasiveness of senseless human suffering do we understand why Catholic churches prominently display Christ on the crucifix. There is holiness even in the worst of human tragedies, although we wouldn't dare to make sense of them. The Catholic sacramental vision reminds us to gaze upon pain and suffering in our world with great reverence, even as we wring our hands in anger and sorrow.

Does a sacramental worldview help in, or detract from, addressing the problem of evil?

Which sparks a spirit of compassion for suffering more: dualism, secularism, or a sacramental worldview?

II. Symbol and Ritual

Symbolic Thinking and Sacramental Awareness

All nature is a vast symbolism: Every material fact has sheathed within it a spiritual truth.

Edwin Hubble, Astronomer

To understand a sacramental worldview, we need to understand symbols and rituals and the roles they play in human experience. The root meaning of the word *symbol* is "to throw together." Two entities, apparently on different plains (the material and the spiritual), are thrown together. Symbols are material objects and sensual experiences that speak to us about deeper realities. All of our bodily senses offer material for the symbolic. ("She came out of that situation smelling like a rose." "Your words are very touching.") When songwriter Paul Simon wrote, "I am a rock / I am an island," we knew immediately where the rest of the song was going: "For a rock feels no pain / And an island never cries." Is there any other way to speak about God than with symbolic language? Medieval English mystic Julian of Norwich describes God using the following symbolic imagery: "He is our clothing that lovingly wraps and folds us about; it embraces us all around as it hangs upon us with such tender love" (*Revelations of Divine Love*, chapter 5). The richest symbols are drawn from nature, not manufactured and then assigned a meaning, like a flag or a stop sign. Natural symbols have meanings inherent in the qualities that they possess. For this reason, they are universal and can speak to our very humanity. That being said, natural symbols tend to have multiple associations. Think of how precious and life-giving fire was for the Tom Hanks character in the movie "Cast Away." Fire is not so life-giving when it rages out of control in the forest fires across the American West.

Symbolic thinking is a uniquely human capacity. Psychologist Carl Jung reminded us that human beings are "symbolizing animals." He saw playing with symbols as having a conversation with one's subconscious; or, more accurately, symbols are subconscious images bubbling forth into our consciousness. For Jung, human beings share a "collective unconscious." That's why natural symbols speak across cultures. Catholic sacraments link natural symbols to the mystery of Christ's message of salvation. Being able to see spiritual associations in that which is physical is quite a gift. If our symbolic consciousness were dulled, we would be robbed of a great source of vibrancy and meaning. How sad it would be if we never looked at a tree, a cloud, or an ocean and didn't free our minds to leap to possible associations they might have on a spiritual level. Without an appreciation for the human capacity for symbolizing, all religion would be relegated to being a relic from the past, perhaps best discarded as magical thinking.

Rituals as Symbolic Actions

A handshake has a literal, practical meaning: I come with an open hand, not a closed fist; I come in peace, not to fight. However, it now symbolizes more than that. It means "Welcome," "Happy to meet you," "Good to see you." (During the years of COVID quarantining, people felt lost because of not being able to shake hands or have physical contact with others.) Similarly, a kiss means more than what the physical act entails. That's why when Judas betrays Jesus with a kiss it is particularly offensive. A kiss means love or at least care for another, a gesture of peace. Judas violates the very nature of the symbolic richness of a kiss. To say that rituals are symbolic does not mean that they have no real-life implications. A classic example from Catholicism is people wishing one another peace at Mass and then afterward cutting each other off while driving out of the church parking lot. A kiss is supposed to mean something. So is wishing someone peace.

Even though both are often actions that are frequently repeated, **rituals** are not the same as *routines*. Brushing one's teeth every day is a great routine; it lacks the symbolic power of bowing when greeting an elder or getting down on one's knees in prayer. Extended rituals can serve as a way to get us out of our everyday existence. Dance, drama, parades, and athletics are in a sense extended rituals. Of themselves they serve no practical purpose, even though scoring the winning basket in a basketball game can bring a whole community together in celebration. Dance involves bodily movement akin to a handshake and a kiss. In some cultures, it serves as the primary way to leave one's cares behind and become enraptured in an experience of God's presence. (Think of dancing all night around a drum at a Native American powwow.) Celebrations almost always include rituals. When children decorate their bikes with red, white, and blue streamers for the Fourth of July, they are participating in a celebration marking the birth of the nation. Words may accompany rituals, but it is the objects and actions that speak more forcefully. In fact, words often diminish the sensual impact of a ritual. Rituals are used to link people to their past. One of the unfortunate aspects of the COVID-19 pandemic of 2020 was that so many ritual celebrations were missed. "Virtual Thanksgiving dinner" didn't measure up to the real thing. Rituals are communal affairs. Think of the upheaval that resulted from some athletes kneeling during the playing of the national anthem at ball games. In their eyes, they were using the occasion to declare that the ritual was a sham because too many people were being victimized by representatives of the very nation they were supposed to be honoring. Those who disagreed found that the athletes' actions were an affront to the nation being honored through this sacred ritual.

When Ritual Becomes Mindless Routine

At times, ritual has had a bad reputation. Ritual meant mindless repetition, going through the motions of a ceremony without giving any thought to what they meant. Ritual can become dead ritual, doing something out of habit. If a Catholic attended Mass and went through the motions of standing, sitting, and kneeling when everyone else did but thought nothing of it, the ritual would be empty of meaning and could even be detrimental to expressing what the ritual was meant to be. However, when ritual "works," it can be very powerful. All religions have rites and ceremonies meant to help people connect with their deeper self, their community, their shared past, and that which is greater than what they are usually aware of. A ritual such as the Mass, a baptism, or a wedding is designed for people to experience the great mystery of God present in their lives through Christ. Without symbolic consciousness, sitting through those rituals can be deadly. For Catholics, the sacraments are the work of Christ through the Holy Spirit. However, it is up to the people themselves to bring the proper disposition to the rituals. In the words of the *Catechism*:

> The assembly should *prepare* itself to encounter its Lord and to become "a people well disposed." The preparation of hearts is the joint work of the Holy Spirit and the assembly, especially of the ministers. (#1098)

These are some characteristics of ritual:

- Symbolic action (not directly intended to serve a practical purpose but with real-life implications)
- Repetition (a characteristic shared with routine, which lacks the sacramental dimension)
- Communality (shared within a family or community)
- Part of celebration (birthdays, holidays, religious holy days)
- Connection of people with their past (traditions)
- Words or songs (but words are secondary to the symbolic actions)

Religious rituals, present throughout history and in all cultures, connect people to the mystery often overlooked in everyday consciousness. Catholic sacraments are rituals in which people experience God through the work of Christ in the Holy Spirit.

Symbols and Rituals as Ingredients of the Seven Sacraments

We need to bring an understanding of symbol and ritual to the experience of sacraments if we are to appreciate them. Each of the church's official sacraments involves symbols and rituals. For instance, the ritual for ordaining a priest involves a bishop "laying hands" on the candidate's head. Of itself, that gesture doesn't seem to be particularly powerful or meaningful. Why is this action different in the context of ordination? A bishop is ordained when two bishops before him place their hands on his head. Those bishops were ordained in similar fashion, in a continuous chain going back to the apostles. Jesus healed and blessed people with the laying on of hands—power going out from him to them. Even before the time of Jesus, in Jewish tradition laying on of hands marked the transfer of power and blessing from one person to another, often from father to son. Psalm 139:5 describes God laying hands on the psalmist's head. The New Testament also has many references to blessing, healing, and transferring of the Spirit through the laying on of hands.

If you have an occasion to observe one of the seven Catholic sacraments, look for symbols and rituals such as a water bath, dabs of oil on parts of the body, bread shared and eaten, or rings exchanged. The sacraments make use of objects and actions that have layers of meaning. Water, for instance, means both life and death. Imagine coming upon a pool of fresh water in the desert (life) and then being swept away by a wave in the ocean (death). The church didn't invent the symbols and rituals in its sacraments, as if they entailed a secret password or handshake that only insiders understood. Typically, the actions and objects involved in the sacraments have meaning by their very nature—natural symbols. At least on their basic level, bread and wine don't need to be explained, nor does placing a ring on a spouse's finger. The act of people gathering together for liturgy, the "public work" of the Christian community, doesn't need explaining either. Joining others in prayer and worship has meaning by its very nature. In the sacraments, natural, familiar symbols and rituals are transformed into sacred signs of God's presence through Christ.

> God chose to take created reality and raise it to the level of a sacrament so that through it the very love of God could touch us.
>
> Bishop Donald W. Wuerl, *The Catholic Way*

Mystery & Tradition

Candles, a universal symbol.

Describe three abstract concepts in purely scientific language: love, peace, family, happiness, sadness, depression, or friendship (e.g., peace means the absence of conflict). Then describe the same concepts using symbolic imagery (e.g., the prophet Isaiah says that in the "peaceable kingdom" the lion will lie down with the lamb). Discuss the difference between the two types of description. Which comes closer to communicating the depth and richness of each concept?

Describe some symbols and rituals that are meaningful for you. Explain why.

What religious symbols are most meaningful for you?

Would you characterize emojis as symbols or mere signs? Explain.

III. Jesus, the Church, and the Sacraments

Jesus, the Primary Sacrament

Catholics are used to thinking of sacraments as referring to "the seven sacraments," which we will look at in the next two chapters. They can miss the broader context in which the seven have their meaning. One reason Catholics have a history of separating the seven sacraments from the rest of their spiritual life is that many Protestants early on rejected elements of the theology behind them. A traditional Catholic definition of sacrament is that it is *an outward sign instituted by Christ to give grace*. Protestants emphasized internal personal conversion rather than external rituals, which rules out oral confession of sins to a priest and, for some, infant baptism. In the Protestant tradition, asking for God's forgiveness internally is considered a true sign of conversion to Christ instead of mouthing words to a priest in confession. Only when someone is mature enough to accept Jesus Christ (conscious, personal conversion) would baptism make sense. Thus, for many early Protestants, baptizing infants was viewed as a superstitious practice. Also, Protestants centered their beliefs solely on the Bible. They saw baptism and Eucharist directly referenced there but not the other sacraments.

If a sacrament is an outward (visible, tangible) sign of God's presence, then **the primary sacrament** is not a *what* at all but a *who*—Jesus. The *Catechism* puts it this way: "In the body of Jesus 'we see our God made visible and so are caught up in the love of God we cannot see'" (#477). God's grace finds its perfect expression in Jesus; that's the mystery of the Incarnation. In turn, Christ acts through the sacraments. The sacraments themselves are meaningless apart from Jesus. The traditional definition of a sacrament includes the phrase "instituted by Christ." Jesus was a healer, so there are sacraments of healing. Jesus transformed people into his body, the church; there are sacraments of initiation. Jesus served others; there are sacraments of vocation through which people can serve their communities.

Catholic sacramental theology addresses the question, how do we meet the living God? For Christians, the answer is, first and foremost, Jesus. Catholics don't separate Jesus from creation. The universe and all that it contains manifest the glory of God. We can't appreciate the Catholic sacramental vision unless we have a sense of reverence and awe for the goods of creation. That's why the following questions represent a false dichotomy: "Why do I have to go to church? Can't I worship God on the beach or walking in the woods?" From a sacramental perspective, of course, we can discover God all around us. If we don't find Christ in the woods or on the beach, then we have separated him from the very world he entered into to transform. The seven sacraments, however, are graced moments that flow from the mission of the church given by Christ. They link Catholics directly to his saving act of dying and rising to new life. They are for individual persons but also situate Catholics in the community of Jesus. There are many ways to encounter Christ. The church has identified seven through which God's grace will be given and be effective for salvation.

> What was visible in Christ has now passed over into the sacraments of the Church.
>
> Pope St. Leo the Great

- The text says that "going for a walk in the woods" and "going to church" should not be viewed as either/or experiences of Christ's presence. How could someone integrate activities that are strictly church related with a broader sacramental experience? (For instance, how could hearing words of forgiveness in confession help people in their dealings with others?)
- Imagine that you meet someone who questions the sacramental system of Catholicism. How would you explain their purpose and the relationship between Jesus and the seven sacraments from a Catholic perspective?

The Church as Sacrament of Christ

> The church is in Christ like a sacrament or as a sign and instrument both of a very closely knit union with God and of the unity of the whole human race.
>
> Vatican Council II, "Dogmatic Constitution on the Church," #1

Jesus is the sacrament of God; ***the church is the sacrament of Jesus***. The people who make up the church are an outward sign (visible, tangible) of Christ present to us. Getting away from the hustle and bustle of busy lives can be refreshing and rejuvenating. Hopefully, such experiences increase for Catholics their capacity to appreciate how they are Christ to one another at work, at school, in church, even in shopping malls. St. Pope John XXIII reminded Catholics that, to an unbeliever, you may be the only scripture they ever hear; you may be the only sacrament they ever encounter.

Thomas Merton, the most famous American monk, entered a Trappist monastery in the 1940s and lived there until his death in the 1960s. Trappists live a life of silence, regular prayer, and communal work apart from contact with the "outside world." Merton was also a prolific writer who captured people's imagination with his honest and vivid descriptions of his spiritual struggles and insights. He tells of an incident when he went into Louisville, Kentucky, for a doctor's appointment. Standing on a street corner, he suddenly experienced the intense feeling that he was connected to all the people who passed by; he and they made up one body. He realized that part of his motivation for entering the monastery was to get away from the world. He knew on this day that that was an impossible and, in fact, un-Christian task. We are all connected to one another. His time in the monastery actually intensified his realization of the oneness we share. From his solitary hermitage Merton kept up with events in the world and produced thoughtful and influential writings on prayer and contemplation, peace, social justice, other religions, and other pressing issues of his day.

In a sense, the sacraments are like our time in a monastery. They are not "holy times" with no connection to the rest of our lives. Sacraments remind us of the holiness of all time. If the church is a sacrament, then it follows that its members are sacramental. What an awesome responsibility people take on when they join the church! For Catholics, this means that they accept that others come to know Christ through them; they are to be channels of grace and the peace of Christ. Our neighbors may never meet the pope, a bishop, or even a priest, but they meet individual members of the church. Catholics are called upon to be a sacrament to them. Other people are also a sacrament to us, outward signs giving grace.

Charles de Foucauld: A Sacramental Presence in a Muslim World

One person who modeled this "sacramental presence" was the Frenchman Charles de Foucauld (1858–1916). Foucauld was an aristocrat and a soldier who ended up serving in North Africa. In time, he came to love the people he met there; and, even though they were Muslim, their spirit of hospitality and adoration inspired him to reconnect with his Catholicism. He became a priest and lived among the Tuareg people of

Algeria. He didn't try to convert them to Christ but rather to model a Christian life himself. He learned their language and was available for humble service to them, despite coming from French nobility. His ministry of presence was as a member of the church, a sacrament of Jesus. One symbolic image for Foucauld and the church as sacrament is "leaven." Through their commitment to Christ in baptism and confirmation and modeled in the Eucharist, Catholics are committed to being leaven in the bread of the world, causing everyone to rise.

Charles de Foucauld lived as a sacramental presence among non-Christians in early twentieth-century Algeria.

What are some ways the church and its members are sacraments?
What are some ways that you have seen people you know serve as a sacramental presence to others?
Have you ever experienced yourself as a sacramental presence?

> Only the Holy Spirit is capable of building the church with such badly hewn stones as ourselves.
>
> Carlo Carretto

Why Seven?

There are seven days of the week, seven days of creation, and seven sacraments. Catholic Tradition lists seven gifts of the Holy Spirit and seven deadly sins. Jesus told his disciples to forgive others "seventy times seven" times. The use of this number is no accident. Like other dimensions of scripture and spirituality, numbers have deeper meanings. **Seven** means fullness, completeness. It combines four (the four corners of the earth) and three (the heavens). Seven represents the fullness of heaven and earth.

According to Catholic teaching, the seven sacraments provide the fullness of grace. **Grace** refers to life with God. The sacraments are viewed as specific graced events in a Catholic's encounter with Christ. To appreciate the sacraments, it's important to understand how they fit into a person's spiritual journey. Here are four characteristics common to all of the sacraments.

For one thing, individual Catholics may not even be aware of grace at work when they participate in the sacraments. That's okay. It's God's work. People participate in that work, both the participants and others through whom God works. In the words of theologian Karl Rahner, grace "is always and everywhere at work in the world"; but each sacrament has a "special character" that sets it apart from other manifestations of grace.

Secondly, sacraments are not isolated events; they are celebrated as communal rituals. Each one is connected to the larger church community. Even that most private of sacraments, reconciliation, has a communal dimension. Through the sacrament Catholics seek to make things right with God, but they also celebrate their desire for reconciliation with the church and anyone they might have offended.

Thirdly, each sacrament is part of a larger, ongoing process of conversion. While each sacrament celebrates a particular transformation, conversion itself is a process that takes a lifetime. God is present in people's lives in different ways during different times in their lives.

Finally, each sacrament comes with responsibility. Marriage is not only for the benefit of the couple. Through their marriage, they commit to a life of service to family and community. Confirmation celebrates accepting that, with the help of the Holy Spirit, Catholic youth are ready to make the transition to adult commitment to serve others. Even in the baptism of infants, the community gathered—led by parents and godparents—promises to guide the child as he or she makes the way to adulthood.

From Greek Mysterion to Latin Sacramentum

In the sacraments, the realm of the sacred enters into the common, everyday lives of people, bringing them into an experience of the mystery of union with God in Christ. In fact, the original Greek term for sacrament is *mysterion*—related to our word "mystery." The Latin church translated that word as *sacramentum*, meaning a holy, secret mystery. (Notice the root of the word *sacram/sacer*, meaning "sacred" or "holy.") The term was used for the secret initiation into the Roman army accompanied by the oath of loyalty all members of the Roman legions took. With each sacrament, Catholics enter into incomprehensible mystery, sacred time, and sacred space. The holy, all around us but hidden, comes to light in the sacraments of the church.

> Sacraments ... are actions of the Holy Spirit at work in his Body, the Church.
>
> *Catechism*, #1116

IV. Sacramentals: The Richness of Catholic Spirituality

> There is scarcely any proper use of material things which cannot thus be directed toward the sanctification of men and the praise of God.
>
> Vatican Council II, "The Constitution on the Divine Liturgy" (#61)

Besides the official sacraments, Catholics have available to them a vast array of prayers, devotions, sacred actions and gestures, and holy objects that can serve as a source of blessing for them. Sacred objects and actions are called ***sacramentals***—a term that connects them to but also distinguishes them from the seven sacraments. Sacramentals offer opportunities for Catholics to engage in devotional practices apart from the official sacraments themselves. Sacramentals include crucifixes and medals, blessed rosary beads, candles, palms blessed on Passion (Palm) Sunday, and ashes on Ash Wednesday. In every case a sacramental is not mere ornament. Rather, it provides an opportunity to excite the mind to the contemplation of the divine.

The simple act of entering a church can involve a series of sacramentals—blessing oneself with holy water, genuflecting, lighting a candle, and saying a prayer before a statue, for instance. Medals and what are popularly known as "holy cards"—bearing an image of Jesus,

Mary, or a saint with a prayer on the back and small enough to fit into a wallet—are sacramentals. (Attend a Catholic funeral and you likely will receive one—a way to remember the deceased and to mark the person's dying as a holy event.) Different cultural groups have special prayers and devotions that may include sacramentals. If you travel to Mexico City you might notice young men on their knees making their way to the basilica that houses the image of Our Lady of Guadalupe. Or an Italian church might sponsor a procession in which a statue of the Blessed Mother is carried through the neighborhood. Some Catholic parishes hold novenas, nine days of special prayers and liturgies related to a particular saint or concern. Stations of the Cross during Lent and crowning a statue of Mary in May are regular practices in American parishes. The Catechism makes clear that sacramentals can be administered by laypeople. Think of a father or mother who blesses his or her child every night, making the sign of the cross on the child's forehead. That's a sacramental act. Picture a family pausing to say grace before a meal or all participants in a track meet among Catholic schools reciting the Hail Mary before the events begin: "Every baptized person is called to be a 'blessing', and to bless" (*Catechism*, #1669).

To the eye alive, nothing is without its wonder.

Lucien Stryk

Name and describe some sacramentals, spiritual objects and actions other than the seven sacraments, with which you are familiar.

Which sacramentals speak most powerfully to you? If none come to mind, what sacred objects or actions have you observed as being significant for other people?

Do you or would you have a holy object such as a crucifix, statue of the Blessed Mother, or rosary beads displayed in your home? Why or why not?

Sacramental Vision and Our Lives

Sacraments and sacramentals display sensitivity to our makeup as bodily creatures. We communicate more impactfully through nonverbals than through the words we say, and we respond more to nonverbal messages than spoken ones. Every study done on communication supports this assertion. Healthcare professionals know the importance of nonverbals, as do parents, teachers, and childcare workers. The Council of Trent, convened soon after the Reformation, explained the reasoning behind the Catholic use of sacraments and sacramentals, partially to counteract those Protestants who were rejecting them: "Without external helps [human beings] cannot easily be raised to the meditation of divine things" (Session XXIII, #5). Jesus is not just a spoken word; he is a material, bodily word—the Word made flesh. For Catholics, God continues to speak in material, bodily ways through sacraments, sacramentals, and the sacramental people whom we encounter every day. The universe itself is God's body language as well. Science, poetry, music, and the arts can inspire us to hear the voice of God speaking through creation. Hearing that voice requires developing sacramental sensitivity.

> Make a case that cultivating a sacramental vision is or is not necessary for experiencing the fullness of human life. What would be missing without such a vision?

> God made the world for the delight of human beings—if only we could see His goodness everywhere. His concern for us. His awareness of our needs: the phone call we've waited for, the ride we are offered, the letter in the mail, just the little things.
>
> St. Mother Teresa of Calcutta

Chapter Review

1. What are "thin places" in Irish spirituality?
2. What is the Catholic sacramental worldview?
3. What is the difference between sacramental blindness and sacramental seeing?
4. What two developments in Western culture led to sacramental blindness? Describe each development.

5. What was the Romantic movement in Western culture? How did it respond to the emphasis on the empirical sciences of the time?

6. What is the root meaning of the term *symbol*? What are natural symbols?

7. What is the meaning of the term *ritual*? How is it different from *routine*?

8. What are the characteristics of ritual?

9. What does it mean to say that Jesus is the primary sacrament?

10. How did the Baltimore Catechism define sacrament?

11. What does it mean to say that the church is a sacrament of Jesus?

12. What is the meaning of the number seven as used in scripture and Christian tradition?

13. What four characteristics describe the role of sacraments in a Catholic's life?

14. What are the Greek and Latin words for "sacrament"? What does each term say about the sacraments?

15. What are sacramentals? What is an example of a sacramental?

For Further Study

Philippe Beguerie and Claude Duchesneau. *How to Understand the Sacraments*, Crossroad, 1991. Explains the background of the Catholic concept of sacrament, such as Jesus and church as sacrament and the role symbols and rituals play in human life. The second half explores the history and theology of the seven sacraments.

Thomas Berry. *Meditations with Thomas Berry.* Selected by June Raymond, additional material by Brian Swimme. GreenSpirit Book Series, 2021. Brief reflections on the holiness of the universe and of processes at work in nature. Fr. Thomas Berry, who died in 2009, was a leading inspiration to those who saw an intimate connection between matter and spirit, physicality and divinity.

Karen E. Eifler and Thomas M. Landy, eds. *Becoming Beholders: Cultivating Sacramental Imagination and Actions in College Classrooms*. Liturgical Press, 2014. Chapter 1 itself, by Michael J. Hines, is worth reading for its explanation of how a sacramental vision is central to a Catholic worldview: "The fundamental principle of Catholic liturgy is that everything and the kitchen sink have a place within it." That which makes God's love evident for someone is sacrament.

John O'Donohue, in conversation with John Quinn. *Walking in Wonder: Eternal Wisdom for a Modern World*. Convergent Books, 2015. Filled with insights from a poet and philosopher who reflects the spiritual sensitivity of his Irish heritage, such as, "We are sent here to search for the light of Easter in our hearts, and when we find it we are meant to give it away generously."

Karl Rahner. *Meditations on the Sacraments*. Crossroad, 1977. Although labeled "meditations," these commentaries on the sacraments present Rahner's theology of sacrament, which influenced the perspective of Vatican Council II and leading Catholic theologians of the time. Written in language that is accessible to non-theologians.

Klemens Richter. *The Meaning of the Sacramental Symbols: Answers to Today's Questions*. The Liturgical Press, 1990. Provides background on both the primary and secondary symbols used in Catholic sacraments such as incense and candles. Explains the meaning of symbol as the union of "outer" and "inner" reality.

Sacrosanctum Concilium ("Constitution on Divine Liturgy"). vatican.va. This document from Vatican Council II explains the Catholic theology of sacrament, centering on the eucharistic liturgy. It called for review of all sacramental practices so that "they be given new vigor to meet the circumstances and needs of modern times," which led to major changes to the sacraments from 1966 to 1973.

Edward Schillebeeckx. *Christ the Sacrament of the Encounter with God*. Sheed & Ward, 1987. The classic presentation that situates the seven sacraments in relation to Christ as the primary sacrament.

Chapter 8
The Sacraments of Initiation

Seven sacraments make up the cornerstone of Catholic spirituality. They serve as stepping stones in the life of the members of the church, from initiation to table fellowship to service. Early in Christian history sacramental rituals came to be recognized as a means of connecting with Christ. Over time, seven such sacraments came to be seen as unique graced experiences, although their theology and format have changed somewhat from the time of their origins. An investigation into the sacraments, specifically their meaning and implementation, followed Vatican Council II, resulting in major changes taking place from the late 1960s to the early 1970s. Despite the changes, Catholicism continues to be identified with certain sacramental practices: baptism (especially of infants), the *Eucharist* (popularly known as the Mass), the sacrament of reconciliation (commonly called "confession"), and a priesthood made up exclusively of men who are for the most part unmarried. (There are married Catholic priests, but they are the rare exception.) Sacraments are primary ways for Catholics to encounter Christ, just as Christians in the Evangelical tradition encounter Christ primarily in the Bible. This chapter looks at what each sacrament celebrates, how it is celebrated, and questions and controversies related to it.

The seven sacraments are divided into three categories:

- The sacraments of initiation: baptism, confirmation, and Eucharist
- The sacraments of healing: reconciliation and anointing of the sick
- The sacraments of service to the community: marriage and holy orders

> Tell the story of an experience you have had with one of the seven Catholic sacraments, either your own experience or one that you have observed. If you have never attended a sacrament, interview someone who has and tell the story of their experience.

> The sacraments are the manifestation of the Father's tenderness and love towards each of us.
>
> Pope Francis

> The sacraments of Christian initiation—Baptism, Confirmation, and the Eucharist—lay the foundation of every Christian life. ... The faithful are born anew by Baptism, strengthened by the sacrament of Confirmation, and receive in the Eucharist the food of eternal life.
>
> *Catechism*, #1212

I. Baptism: Initiation into New Life

A Radically New Worldview and Lifestyle

During his public life Jesus invited everyone he met to join him in changing the direction of their lives. For Catholics today, the sacraments continue to be Christ's invitation to refocus their lives. Here's part of a sermon given by a fourth-century archbishop of Constantinople that describes with a flourish the mystery of conversion into Christ that happens in the sacraments:

> Before yesterday you were captives, but now you are free and citizens of the Church; lately you lived in the shame of your sins, but now you live in freedom and justice. You are not only free, but also sons and daughters, not only sons and daughters, but also heirs; not only heirs but also brothers and sisters of Christ.
>
> Saint John Chrysostom, *To the Newly Baptized*

What was involved in the conversion that marked initiation into the Christian community? St. Paul gives the following account of the conversion Jesus called for:

> In Christ Jesus you are all children of God through faith. As many of you as were baptized into Christ have clothed yourselves with Christ. There is no longer Jew or Greek, there is no longer slave or free, there is no longer male and female; for all of you are one in Christ Jesus.
>
> Galatians 3:26–28

Elsewhere in his letters St. Paul references overcoming these same three divisions dominant in his culture. It's likely that the line "no longer Jew or Greek, slave or free, male and female" was actually part of the initiation rite at the time. (Stephen J. Patterson makes this case in *The Forgotten Creed: Christianity's Original Struggle against Bigotry, Slavery, and Sexism* [2018].) Here was Paul, renowned follower of Christ, within a couple of decades after Jesus, affirming that to become Christian means to address three social problems that still plague us today: racism (Jew/Greek), classism (slave/free), and sexism (male/female). This was no pie-in-the-sky "Let's all get along" message. It was a challenge laid out by Jesus and carried on by his earliest followers. To be Christian means to break down barriers and work for equality.

The Catholic Church today continues this process of initiation, beginning with baptism and culminating in full participation in the Eucharist. For adults, this movement from baptism through confirmation to Eucharist happens in one ceremony—usually at the Easter vigil. When infants are baptized, their first Communion is delayed until around the age of seven and confirmation until even later. In Eastern Catholic and Eastern Orthodox churches, infants receive baptism, confirmation, and Eucharist (in the form of consecrated wine) in one ceremony. Whether or not the three sacraments of initiation are celebrated at the same time or separately, they are organically connected. We can look at each sacrament separately as long as we realize that together they celebrate the conversion Jesus offers his friends and are part of initiation into his family, the church, in which all are one.

> What are some ways that the Catholic Church, Catholic-affiliated organizations, and individual Catholics are

working to address racism, classism, and sexism in society today?

When we let [freedom] ring from every village and every hamlet, from every state and every city, we will be able to speed up that day when all of God's children, black men and white men, Jews and Gentiles, Protestants and Catholics, will be able to join hands and sing in the words of the old Negro spiritual, "Free at last. Free at last. Thank God almighty, we are free at last."

Martin Luther, King, Jr., "I Have a Dream" speech, 1963

Initiation into New Life

When we arrive at a friend's house for dinner after a long journey, we're probably invited to wash up first to refresh and renew ourselves. Baptism represents coming home after being a stranger in a strange land, out of touch with our true identity as children of God. In the biblical account, Adam came into existence in a garden paradise. He, and by extension all humanity, went astray—estranged from God. Jesus, the "new Adam," restores humanity to its rightful home, reunited with God. The new life celebrated in baptism is the restoration of the original blessing bestowed on humanity by God. The central ritual of the sacrament of baptism is immersion in a bath of water or at least pouring water onto a person's head. Even when the person being baptized is a newborn, the water part of the sacrament is a moment in a process. Much has taken place preparing for this event, and the event itself represents a commitment on the part of the person, their family and friends, the local church community, and the universal church itself. That commitment on everyone's part doesn't end when the water dries.

At the beginning of Christian history, baptism was as simple as going down to a nearby stream and being dunked in the water while the words, "I baptize you in the name of the Father and of the Son and of the Holy Spirit" are said. These words are exactly the words Jesus told his disciples to say at the end of Matthew's Gospel. Soon baptism became more formal. Preparation for baptism was a long process, perhaps as much as a few years. During this preparation time, candidates known as **catechumens** had a sponsor who guided them in their journey through initiation. The last, intense period of preparation was the Lenten season of forty days of prayer and fasting before Easter, when baptisms typically took place. The rite of initiation, consisting of water baptism, anointing with oil, and full participation in the Eucharist for the first time, took place at the Easter vigil. If you attend the vigil services in a Catholic church on the evening before Easter Sunday, you will notice that it is filled with references to water and light, two symbols central to baptism. You will hear sung the ancient hymn called the *Exsultet*, a proclamation of the joyous wonders being celebrated. You might also witness the exciting event of new members being initiated into the church.

Baptisms in its early period also involved a physical turning from west to east. Candidates would face the west, the direction of darkness, and renounce Satan and the allure of sin. Then they would turn to the east, the direction of the rising sun, and proclaim their faith in the Son of God. Baptisms took place in a building (baptistry) separate from the church building where Eucharist was celebrated. Baptisms involved total immersion in a pool of water, three steps down and three steps up to represent the Holy Trinity. Candidates stripped naked, were doused with oil, and then clothed in a new white garment. They were now ready to participate in the breaking of the bread.

We can only imagine what it must have been like when people seeking to join the Christian community had to wait years before they could join in the eucharistic celebration and partake of Communion. (Remember that early on becoming Christian meant that you might be subject to arrest and death, even to being publicly gouged to death by lions!) The sense of entering into new life must have been intense and palpable, as well as unnerving. You were leaving the familiar behind and setting out on a journey into the unknown.

Today, the RCIA program (Rite of Christian Initiation of Adults) is used for the initiation of adults into the Catholic community. It is modeled after the process of initiation as it was practiced in the early church. In time, most adults in Christian lands were baptized, which left infants as the only ones to receive this sacrament almost exclusively. Even today, we think of baptism as a celebration for infants. In fact, until the late 1960s the baptismal rite was written as if the recipient were an adult. The words of the baptism ritual were addressed to infants *as if they were adults*. That's one reason why godparents were so important in the ritual before Vatican Council II;

they spoke for the child. After the council, the church set up commissions to examine each sacrament and revise each one as needed. As a result, two distinct ceremonies for initiation into the church were established. There is now a ritual specifically for infants and another for adults. Initiation of adults, the Rite of Christian Initiation of Adults, is really not one rite but a whole series that culminates in baptism, confirmation, and Eucharist and continues with additional assistance and instruction even after baptism. The period following the initiation rite is called *mystagogia*, a fifty-day period when the newly initiated have an opportunity to reflect on what they have experienced.

> By God's gift, through water and the Holy Spirit, we are reborn to everlasting life. In his goodness, may he continue to pour out his blessings upon these sons and daughters of his. May he make them always, wherever they may be, faithful members of his holy people.
>
> Rite of Baptism

Based on your reading of the text, how would you explain the meaning of baptism as practiced in the Catholic Church?
If you were charged with designing a program for entrance into the Catholic Church for someone your age, what would it involve?

Original Sin

We may think of sin as referring either to actions that people do or to actions they should do but don't. Catholicism talks about another kind of sinfulness. It identifies the source of that sinfulness in the biblical story of Adam and Eve, the primordial human beings. Primordial means "existing from the beginning," and therefore it is a story meant to describe the human condition itself that has existed from the beginning of human history and continues into today. Building on that story, Catholicism refers to the sinfulness of humanity's universal "fallen state" of alienation from God and longing for wholeness. (Have you ever had a feeling of "being out of touch"—even with your own true self—or drawn to what is unhealthy and even harmful? That is a reflection of Original Sin. Welcome to the human race!) Adam and Eve, representing primordial humanity in the Bible, fell from grace, or fell out of their intimate relationship with God. Human beings long for a restoration of grace or life with God. Original Sin refers to a state of being, a deprivation. In that sense it is the reverse side of the good news of Jesus. None of us is immune from this capacity to misuse our freedom. Even the great St. Paul admits, "For I do not do the good I want, but the evil I do not want is what I do. Now if I do what I do not want, it is no longer I that do it, but sin that dwells within me" (Romans 7:19–20).

Original Sin is a concept that reminds us that we are needy creatures who long for salvation, healing, wholeness. As limited creatures, we can't get there on our own. Original Sin describes a weakness in our nature, a wound that we carry within us that needs healing, a deprivation that longs to be set right, and an inclination or tendency to oppose God's will with our own misguided choices. As St. Paul himself realized, any attempt on our part to counteract this tendency comes up flimsy and inadequate. The good news is that the troubles and any misdirected inclinations that come with being human pale in comparison with the promise of Christ, who faced them head-on and conquered them. Sin, original or otherwise, is no match for Christ. The *Catechism* contrasts "the universality of sin and death with the universality of salvation in Christ" (#402). It proclaims that most essential element of Christian teachings: the selfless sacrifice Christ made "leads to acquittal and life for all men" (#402). That's the dynamic of baptism and Original Sin. Baptism celebrates the victory of Christ over the seemingly invincible tyranny of evil, and that victory is manifest whenever people show care and compassion for one another as Jesus called upon everyone to do.

Original Sin is an often misunderstood concept in Catholicism. ("Do you mean to tell me that my beautiful newborn baby is a sinner!" "Is my dear, sweet grandpa who was never baptized going to hell?") Read the section on Original Sin in the *Catechism of the Catholic Church* (#396–412). What do you think Catholic teaching about Original Sin says about the human condition and the role of Christ in it? How would you describe the human condition?

> Write an essay or short story whose theme is alienation and/or belonging.

Symbols and Rituals

Four symbols are associated with baptism: water, oil, a candle, and a white garment. However, as with all of the sacraments, the Christian community is the primary symbol. Have you ever celebrated a birthday alone? Singing "Happy Birthday" to yourself by yourself is sad rather than joyous. No cake, no matter how delicious, succeeds in making the occasion what we would want it to be. If baptism marks initiation into the body of Christ, then at least some representatives of that body are to be present. In the revised sacrament, godparents don't speak for the child or the adult candidate; rather, they represent the church community that welcomes the newcomer. Nonetheless, the four symbols and their accompanying rituals bring out the meaning of the sacrament.

Water. When spaceships travel to distant planets, what is the first thing that's looked for? Signs of water. Where there is water, there is the possibility of life. Life on earth began in the seas that cover most of our planet. Human beings begin their existence in a watery cocoon inside their mother's womb. Our bodies are over 80 percent water. Beware of dehydration; it can kill you. Christianity isn't the only religion to recognize the symbolic power of water. Muslims precede their daily prayers with a ritual cleansing. Devout Hindus bathe in the waters of the holy Ganges River to be cleansed of their sins and prepare themselves for salvation. Clearly, water is associated with life in a symbolic sense and is life-giving in a real sense. Water also can bring about death, so always swim where lifeguards are present. During water baptism in the time of the early church, being plunged into the water three times represented being plunged into the waters of death and coming out of it into new life. Water is also associated with cleansing. Soap alone isn't enough; water cleanses. The ritual proclaims that through the waters of baptism the initiate joins the Christian community that has been set free from alienation from God, just as the Israelites were led safely through the waters of the Red Sea to the Promised Land.

Oil. Used in baptism and also in confirmation and anointing of the sick, oil has three main associations. It stands for strength and protection: as Roman soldiers of old would cover themselves with oil before entering battle, so initiates are anointed with oil as a preparation for entering the water. Secondly, oil is a balm that heals people of what ails them just as baptism does. Thirdly, oil was used to mark someone as royalty. In the baptism ceremony, oil is used before the water bath for strength and protection and afterward to signify entering into the "royal priesthood" of Christ: "May this sign (of the cross with oil on head, heart, and hands) be a constant reminder to you of Christ and of his great love for you" (Rite of Baptism).

Candle. On Holy Saturday, the day before Easter, all the candles are doused and all the lights turned off in Catholic churches. Beginning the Easter vigil, priests light a fire, the Easter fire, outside of the church and light the Paschal candle that is carried in procession into the church and placed in a position of prominence in the sanctuary. During baptisms, candles are lit from the Paschal candle. The connection is obvious. Through his resurrection, Christ is the light of the world, and the newly baptized "have been enlightened by Christ." They are then commanded, "Walk always as a child of the light and keep the flame of faith alive in your hearts" (Rite of Baptism).

New Garment. On Chinese New Year, it is customary to wear new shoes. They remind the wearer of the new beginning that awaits them in the coming year. Nowadays children might dress up in their new "Easter outfits" to mark the day. In baptism, a new white garment signifies off with the old self, on with the new. The white garment also signifies a burial shroud such as the dead were covered in during biblical times. Again, the theme of dying and rising runs through all the symbols of baptism.

Tell the story of an experience you have had with one of the symbols associated with baptism (water, fire, oil, new clothes). What real or symbolic impact did the experience have on you?

We have been buried with him by baptism into death, so that, just as Christ was raised from the dead by the glory of the Father, so we too might walk in newness of life.

Romans 6:4

Questions and Controversies

Should infants be baptized? Some non-Catholic Christian groups, notably Baptists, only baptize people who are old enough to make their own decision about whether or not to accept Christ and join the church. Catholicism sees a biblical foundation for infant baptism in references to groups of people being baptized all at once, such as the story of a woman named Lydia who was baptized along with her entire household—presumably including the children (Acts 16:15). More importantly, Catholic theology recognizes that all sacraments are gifts of the Holy Spirit. Parents don't say to their children: "When you get older you can decide whether or not to go to school." Or "When you get older you can decide what language you want to speak." Parents give their children many gifts, such as education, language, and family values. Some parents even give their children the gift of learning two languages, Chinese and English or Spanish and English, for example. For Catholics, baptism is a gift of the Holy Spirit mediated through family and the community of faith. It represents God embracing the newborn baby and whispering in its ear, "You are my beloved child."

What about people who are not baptized? The Catholic Church, along with other Christian groups, have grappled with this question for centuries. One way the question was put in pre–Vatican Council II Catholicism was, what happens to unbaptized babies? That question led to some interesting practices. Grandmothers would visit their newborn grandchildren and take them into the bathroom of a hospital, pour water on them and say the words of baptism "just in case." Besides the well-intentioned but questionable theology behind such practices, it does raise the question about the necessity of baptism for salvation. The Catholic Church holds onto the teaching that baptism is necessary for salvation as it is stated in the Gospels. However, it doesn't claim to understand the will of God on such matters. Unbaptized babies should be "entrusted to the mercy of God" (*Catechism*, #1261). Since the Middle Ages the term "limbo" had been used for the state of uncertainty in which unbaptized people spent eternity. The *Catechism* does not include the term at all, and in 2007 Pope Benedict XVI dismissed the term as an "unduly restrictive view of salvation." The *Catechism* leaves the fate of those who are unbaptized in the loving embrace of Christ: "Since Christ died for all, and since all men are in fact called to one and the same destiny, which is divine, we must hold that the Holy Spirit offers to all the possibility of being made partakers, in a way known to God, of the Paschal mystery" (#1260).

> If you were Catholic with a newborn child, would you seek baptism at that time or let the child decide when he or she is older? Explain your choice.
>
> What are some family values you received as a child? Would you want to pass them on if you have children of your own?
>
> Part of baptism is receiving a name. Tell why your parents named you what they did. If necessary, ask them. If you are Catholic, do you have a patron saint who shares your name, or are you planning on being the first saint with your name?

II. Confirmation: Mission and Witness

> Confirmation is the sacrament of mission and of witness: the fulfillment of the task given to us for the Church and for the world.
>
> Karl Rahner, *Meditations on the Sacraments*

Catholics are people on a mission. The mission is to serve as instruments through which Christ acts to transform the world so that it resembles more and more the reign of God, the world as God intends it to be. Christ provides the blueprint; in the sacrament of confirmation young Catholics commit themselves to active participation in this work. The ritual references seven gifts of the Holy Spirit that they have been cultivating throughout their lives and now are celebrated as endowments radiating within them from the Holy Spirit:

> Give them the spirit of wisdom and understanding,
> The spirit of right judgment and courage,
> The spirit of knowledge and reverence.
> Fill them with the spirit of wonder and awe
> In your presence.

Isn't a person endowed with the Holy Spirit at baptism? In the Western church, as Christian communities grew beyond major cities, bishops permitted priests to represent them in celebrating baptisms. However, bishops reserved the right to "confirm" the initiation at a later date. Over time, this led to a separate sacrament focused on the reception of the Holy Spirit. Of course, in one sense baptism already confers the blessing of the Spirit. St. Paul makes this point in 1 Corinthians 12:13: "For in the one Spirit we were all baptized into one body—Jews and Greeks, slaves and free." ***Confirmation*** came to be associated with taking one's place as an adult member of the church, another step in the process of initiation. In other words, being Christian involves doing more than the minimum. Confirmation marks the time when members of the community commit themselves to contributing to the mission of building up the church and the world. The words of the ceremony speak of becoming "witnesses" and "active members of the church." The Holy Spirit is called upon to strengthen those being confirmed for this important work.

Symbols and Rituals

Confirmation incorporates two rituals used in other sacraments as well: laying on of hands and anointing with oil. The laying on of hands, a bishop placing hands on the person's head, represents calling down the Holy Spirit. Anointing with oil represents the dual significance of strengthening, such as a soldier preparing for battle, and being sealed with the gift of the Holy Spirit. Every sacrament invokes the power of the Holy Spirit, but here the Spirit is called upon to be the helper and guide of those being confirmed. As they seek to live the Christian life, they'll need all the help they can get.

Another word for gifts of the Holy Spirit is ***charism***. The *Catechism* says: "Whether extraordinary or simple and humble, charisms are graces of the Holy Spirit which directly or indirectly benefit the Church, ordered as they are to her building up, to the good of men, and to the needs of the world" (#799). In other words, there are great tasks that some young people are called to do through confirmation. More often, the task may be as "simple and humble" as dealing with challenges such as loneliness or personal depression and anxiety or channeling one's ADD or autism for the good of oneself and others. In fact, some great accomplishments have been achieved by people who struggled with personal challenges as well—think of Abraham Lincoln and St. Francis of Assisi, for instance. Both dealt with what today we would call depression; both had a charism within themselves that they tapped into for good. Joshua Wolf Shenk wrote about "Lincoln's Great Depression" in the October 2005 issue of *The Atlantic* magazine: "With Lincoln, we have a man whose depression spurred him, painfully, to examine the core of his soul, whose hard work to stay alive helped him develop crucial skills and capacities, even as his depression lingered hauntingly; and whose inimitable character took great strength from the piercing insights of depression, the creative response to it, and a spirit of humble determination forged over decades of deep suffering and earnest longing." (Look at the National Alliance for Mental Illness [NAMI] website for an enlightening list of famous people who dealt with psychological struggles and achieved greatness.)

Confirmation is a time to seek to know one's charisms and to seek ways for using them in creative and life-giving ways, whatever one's unique circumstances might be. For some people, simply staying alive is hard work, and being there for others is even harder. Another person's work might be not walking around held back by depression or, for young people, dealing with being ostracized by their former friends. Confirmation affirms that the Holy Spirit, residing in our hearts, brings "heavenly aid."

Questions and Controversies

At what age should the sacrament be administered? Before Vatican Council II, confirmation was offered in America to children between fourth and seventh grade. The commission set up to examine the sacrament after the council considered several possibilities. Perhaps it should be administered along with baptism as Eastern churches do. Perhaps it should be delayed until Catholics reach adulthood, sometime after the age of sixteen at least. The commission decided to hold onto the link that had been established between the sacrament and adult commitment to living a Christian life. Some dioceses, especially ones that have a strong Catholic school system, continue to offer the sacrament to students in the later grades, fifth to seventh. Other dioceses choose to hold off offering the sacrament until sometime between eighth grade and later in high school. In a sense, age is not the issue; preparation and motivation are. Whatever the local practice, young people seeking confirmation are to engage in some type of service program leading up to their reception of the sacrament to demonstrate their intention to contribute in positive ways to the community. Preparation also includes more intense study of the faith. Often each candidate is interviewed by a representative of the parish to hear why he or she wants to receive the sacrament. It is no longer a matter of getting confirmed just because everyone else in that grade is doing it. At whatever age, the message of the sacrament is the same: "Under the guidance of the Holy Spirit give your lives completely in the service of all, as did Christ, who came not to be served but to serve" (Rite of Confirmation).

> God our Father, complete the work you have begun and keep the gifts of your Holy Spirit active in the hearts of your people. Make them ready to live his gospel and eager to do his will.
>
> Rite of Confirmation

At what age would you recommend offering the Sacrament of Confirmation? Why?

In light of the goal of the sacrament, what would you include in a program as preparation for your reception of confirmation?

III. Eucharist: Christ's Sacrifice Made Present

> By the mystery of this water and wine may we come to share in the divinity of Christ, who humbled himself to share in our humanity.
>
> From the Preparation of the Gifts at Mass

For Catholics, the Eucharist is celebrated to mark just about any occasion—feast days, holy days, weddings, funerals, graduations, the opening of a school year. If a friend or family member dies, some fellow Catholics will likely request that the Eucharist be celebrated for the deceased. Of course, Eucharist on Sundays is special; but a sizeable number of Catholics attend Mass daily as well. For Catholics, any kind of worship service that does not include a celebration of the Eucharist seems lacking, regardless of how great the hymn singing or sermon preached. The Eucharist is the focal point of Catholic spiritual and sacramental life. Protestant churches typically hold communion services once a month, in a few rare cases once a year, and in some Christian communities not at all. Catholics treat with such reverence the consecrated eucharistic bread that portions of it are placed in a special container in church called a tabernacle ("tent") where it is kept from one liturgy to the next. A candle remains burning near the tabernacle to remind Catholics of the presence of Christ there. If a church is open, which has become infrequent these days due to the fear of theft or desecration, Catholics could stop in for a "visit before the Blessed Sacrament," respectfully genuflecting before the tabernacle and praying before going about their business. Protestant churches would not think of keeping eucharistic bread from one communion service to another, and no need to genuflect in church since Christ is not present there the way Catholics believe he is in the eucharistic bread.

To appreciate the centrality of the Eucharist, it is necessary to understand the event that started it all. The night before he died, Jesus shared a last supper with his closest friends and followers, the apostles. During the meal, Jesus broke open a loaf of bread and passed it around and then passed around a cup of wine as well. He said three things that the apostles probably didn't quite understand at the time. "This is my body, broken for you." "This is my blood, poured out for you." "Do this in memory of me." Jesus knew what awaited him—his arrest, the torture that followed, and his humiliating, excruciating crucifixion itself. In the upcoming hours, the "bread" that was going to be broken was indeed his very body. The "wine" that was poured out was indeed his very blood. He identified his ultimate sacrifice in two simple, everyday—but essential—elements: bread and wine. He wanted his apostles to remember him by gathering around a table and sharing a meal. No doubt the apostles didn't quite "get it" at the time. Only after his death and then the joyous accounts of his new life after death did they realize what a gift Jesus had left them. There are only a few post-resurrection stories about Jesus. The two stories in Luke's Gospel involve Jesus and a meal. Two disciples meet him on the road to Emmaus. They don't recognize him until they come to an inn and sit down at table for a meal. They realize who he is when he "[takes] bread, [blesses] and [breaks] it, and [gives] it to them" (Luke: 24:30). Later, he appears to some of the apostles and asks them, "Have you anything here to eat?" (Luke 24:41). In John's Gospel, Jesus appears to apostles who are out fishing. When they arrive ashore, Jesus begins cooking the fish they had caught and says, "Come and have breakfast," as he takes bread, gives it to them, and does the same with the fish (John 21:12–13).

Believing Christ's promise that he is present "whenever two or three are gathered in his name" (Matthew 18:20) requires an act of faith. Gathering for a meal in which Christ is present, especially in blessed bread and wine, is a natural extension of that promise. The belief that Christ is truly present in the bread and wine, as he said he would be, goes to the heart of the Catholic understanding of sacrament. What do Catholics understand is going on in the sacrament of the Eucharist? For one thing, they recognize that Christ is present in multiple symbolic but real ways with every eucharistic liturgy. Christ is present in the gathering of the people; after all, they're the body of Christ. Christ is present in the proclamation of the gospel; that's why people respectfully stand during the reading of the Gospel at Mass. Christ is present in the person of the presider, the priest who leads the body of Christ in worship. And Christ is present in the consecrated bread and wine.

Catholics differ from some other Christian groups in their understanding of Christ's presence in the bread and wine. The term **transubstantiation** was coined in the Middle Ages to describe the Catholic understanding of the

An artist's rendering of the Last Supper

transformation that happens to the bread and wine at Mass. Building on ancient Greek thought, medieval philosophy observed that all persons and things are made up of appearances and substance. (The color of your hair and the girth around your middle are *appearances* that can change without indicating a *substantial* change in you.) During the liturgy the substance of the bread and wine changes but the appearances remain the same. In other words, if we were to place a Communion wafer under a microscope before and after its consecration, its physical makeup would be exactly the same. However, it would be *substantially* different. According to the *Catechism*, the transformation of the bread and wine into the body and blood of Christ surpasses our understanding (#1333). Scientific analysis will not bring us to an appreciation of it.

Every celebration of the Eucharist looks back to the Last Supper. It is a remembrance for Catholics of the great gift Jesus gave them that night. The word Eucharist means thanksgiving. The Greek word for remembrance, *anamnesis*, also comes into play here. It is the opposite of the word *amnesia*, "forgetting." Christianity would fall apart if Christians suffered eucharistic amnesia, forgetting the great sacrifice of Jesus who gave his body and blood on the cross. In the Eucharist, remembering is re-membering, re-embodying. Every eucharistic celebration is rightly called "the holy sacrifice of the Mass." (The term **Mass** comes from the concluding words of the Latin Mass: *Ite, Missa est*, "Go, it has been sent," that is, the sacrifice has been completed.) Giving thanks through the breaking of the bread of Communion and drinking from the cup makes the sacrifice that Jesus made on the cross a present reality. (Drinking the wine became less frequent in the Latin church for practical reasons. In Eastern churches, a cube of bread is dipped in wine so that in Communion both bread and wine are received.) Jesus gave his life on the cross; he gives his body and blood in the bread and wine and the celebration of the Eucharist. His sacrifice was not just for his time but for all time. For Catholics, the Eucharist is the primary way that the barriers of time dissolve and Christ is present here and now. In the words of the *Catechism*, "To receive communion is to receive Christ himself who has offered himself for us" (#1382).

Participation in the Eucharist, then, is for Catholics the centerpiece of their life with Christ. It connects them to the past—Jesus and the apostles at the Last Supper and the sacrifice of his body and blood on the cross. It is a present reality, communion with Christ and the Christian community. It is also a foretaste of the future "heavenly banquet" when all will be united fully with Christ in eternity. "Thus from celebration to celebration, as they proclaim the Paschal mystery of Jesus 'until he comes,' the pilgrim People of God advances, 'following the narrow way of the cross,' toward the heavenly banquet, when all the elect will be seated at the table of the kingdom" (*Catechism*, #1344). Not to be lost in the Catholic appreciation for the Eucharist is the moment of receiving Communion. It is a time when Catholics can feel most intimately their connection to Christ, the Good Shepherd who dwells within them. They are not alone in this world so often filled with sorrows. The world is not in their hands but God's. They have a friend in Jesus who now dwells within them. Prayer feels richer with the bread, the body of Christ, once again consumed. To which Catholics say, "Amen."

Symbols and Rituals

The Congregation. In Catholicism, there's no such thing as a "private Mass." It is always a communal service. That's one reason why altar servers were assigned to Masses: so that at least one other person besides the priest would be present to represent the Christian community. The COVID crisis of 2020 called this stipulation into question: Can a congregation be present virtually rather than physically? As with all of the sacraments, the Eucharist is the work of Christ filtered through his body, the church. The Greek word *leitourgia*, which comes into English as "liturgy," means "public work." The eucharistic liturgy is the work of the community, which represents the entire people of God. It is fair to say that at every moment, Mass is being said somewhere in the world by a gathering of the faithful. Before the changes ushered in after Vatican Council II, Mass seemed to be a private affair. Everyone faced the same direction and avoided eye contact with anyone else, maintaining respectful silence whenever they were in church. Altars faced the wall. The priest recited the Mass in Latin while the congregation sat or mostly knelt silently, often with heads bowed. After Vatican Council II, even the standard design of churches changed, from pews all facing in one direction to semicircular or even circular design. The altar came out from against the wall so that the priest stood behind it and faced the congregation. People were encouraged to welcome one another. The priest-celebrant addressed the congregation directly, and they were expected to say aloud the responses and also join in with singing (although even now Catholic hymn singing seldom matches the lively, full-throated singing done in many non-Catholic Christian churches.) The changes are meant to emphasize that the people who participate in the Mass are Christ present in real ways.

The Liturgy of the Word and the Liturgy of the Eucharist. The Catholic Mass has two distinct parts to it that both reflect Jewish roots. The first half of the Mass is the Liturgy of the Word, which centers around scripture readings, especially from one of the Gospels. Early Christians incorporated the Jewish synagogue service into the liturgy, with its prayers, blessings, chanting psalms, scripture reading, and homily. The second part of the Mass is the Liturgy of the Eucharist, a sacred meal such as was common practice among Jews, especially during Passover. With each Eucharist, Catholics receive light (wisdom and guidance from scripture) and nourishment (from partaking in the sacred meal).

Bread and Wine. There's a story about God calling together representatives of all the creatures to decide whom God should send to remind people that God is with them and cares for them. Every creature said, "Send me! Send me!" The sun made its case: where would people be without the light of day and the warmth of the sun? But then clouds and rain spoke up: People need cooling off from the hot sun, and rushing waters can proclaim God's mighty power. Various animals and plants also made their case, as did the moon and the stars that light the night. God heard each offer but wanted something more intimate, more personal, more commonplace. Bread stepped forward and offered its services. People are hungry each day, and bread can be a reminder that God nourishes them. Bread is meant to be shared, bringing people together to remember that God loves them. Bread is cultivated and ground and kneaded and baked by human hands. Surely God wants to be present through the people who work together to care for one another. God decided to send bread, and each day people enjoy this simple gift, remember God, and give thanks.

Bread and wine are examples of those natural symbols that make up the sacraments. They exemplify the "spirituality of the ordinary" that runs through Catholicism. Monks in monasteries, whom we might picture as praying all day long, actually spend much of their time in simple tasks that are to be "ordinary, obscure, and laborious"—cooking, cleaning, perhaps farm work. Catholic novelist Flannery O'Connor described one of her characters in this way: "He was as ordinary as bread." When in John's gospel Jesus says, "I am the bread of life," it didn't need explaining. Bread conjures up many different associations—health and happiness, hearth and home, sharing and celebration. Bread represents all food and every meal. Lack of bread is devastating; where that condition exists, it is a human tragedy. Wine represents thirst-quenching drink but adds a festive touch to any meal. Catholic language about the bread and wine in the Eucharist speaks about them in terms of actions, not things. Eucharist involves "breaking the bread" and "sharing the cup." This language reinforces that the Eucharist represents Christ giving his body and blood in his sacrifice on the cross.

Bread and wine at Mass also represent the heavenly banquet that God has prepared for all people, when God will wipe away the tears from their eyes and remove the cloud of sorrow that hangs over them (Isaiah 25:6–8). Catholics who are gravely ill find much solace in receiving Communion, a foretaste of paradise they pray awaits them. In the words of theologian Karl Rahner, the Eucharist for Catholics "sustains them through the changeable to the enduring, what is already the sign and the promise, the sacramental presence of that toward which they are heading, the eternal salvation, infinite rest, life that no longer declines" (*Meditation on the Sacraments*).

Questions and Controversies

Mass Attendance. For decades now, regular Mass attendance has steadily declined among people who self-identify as Catholic. Polls have tried to determine why this has been happening, and church leaders have tried to come up with ways to reverse this trend. Of course, the Catholic Church is not the only church that suffers from diminished attendance. Some churches have even instituted a Back to Church Sunday each fall when there is increased focus on welcoming back former members. Various Catholic dioceses have run similar campaigns, such as Catholics Come Home, making sure that people feel welcome to reconnect with local parishes.

The Real Presence of Christ in the Eucharist. A 2021 Pew Research poll suggests that many Catholics do not accept, or at least understand, the Real Presence of Christ in the Eucharist and instead look upon the bread and wine as "merely symbols" of Christ. That poll caused quite a stir in the church because the Real Presence is a central teaching of Catholicism. The poll's findings have been called into question regarding its wording as well as its interpretation of the answers received. It is more likely that the great majority of Catholics view the Eucharist as more than what we generally understand the word "symbol" to mean. That is, rather than *merely* a symbol, more accurate language for a Catholic's experience of the Eucharist would be that it is *more than* a symbol. If a Catholic is dying and receives Communion, he or she is experiencing Communion as more than "merely a symbol." When young Catholics receive their first Holy Communion, they are generally not thinking that it is merely a symbol. The eucharistic minister holds up the host and says, "Body of Christ," to which the young person responds, "Amen." A minister would never say, "Receive a symbol of Christ."

While it defies scientific explanation, belief in the Real Presence is based on the words of Jesus himself and has been a central tenet of Catholicism for two thousand years. Jesus understood it to be a great gift that would nurture and sustain people through the travails of their own lives as he was about to sacrifice his own. Catholicism affirms that Christ's presence in the Eucharist is no mere symbol. The depth of meaning of Christ's presence in the Eucharist, like all mysteries, can never be fully understood. To appreciate it requires developing the sacramental vision that underlies a Catholic worldview. What is "real" is not confined to what can be understood scientifically or rationally. Catholicism proposes that Christ present in the Eucharist is a direct link to his sacrificial love and to his promise of sharing in the heavenly banquet. In the context of the Eucharist, the bread and wine are *really* the body and blood of Christ.

The Eucharist and Everyday Life. A major area of concern for Catholics is the connection between the Eucharist and living the Christian life. Every sacrament is meant to be lived; it's not just the physical ritual itself. Since the Eucharist provides spiritual nourishment, a natural question is, how does the sacrament inspire people to act when so many people lack even the physical nourishment they need? The Eucharist and social justice concerns go hand in hand. Inspired by the Eucharist, people who have bread look for ways to make "a place at the table" for those who lack bread. In the words of Pope Francis, "Do I, who have so often been fed by the Body of Jesus, make any effort to relieve the hunger of the poor?" Scripture scholars point out that the word used in "eat my body" has the much more graphic meaning of gnawing and chewing, like a dog who spends hours gnawing on a bone. We receive Eucharist, but we also need to work at it in our daily lives. A traditional prayer says, "Lord, give bread to those who are hungry; and hunger for thee to those who have bread." Pier Georgio Frassati, declared by the church "Blessed," a step toward sainthood, said about his experience of daily Mass: "I receive Christ every day in Eucharist, and I return the favor each evening by visiting the poor."

We must find the Lord not only in the table of the Eucharist, but in the table of the world around us. If we do not see Jesus in the table of the world, we will really not find Jesus in the table of the Eucharist; if we do indeed find Jesus in the table of the Eucharist, we should leave the Eucharistic celebration with eyes of faith that allows us to find Jesus throughout the table of the world.

Kenan B. Osborne, OFM

Even if you are familiar with Catholic services, attend a Mass and look at it with fresh eyes. Take note of what is most striking to you in the words, the gestures/rituals, the overall ambiance in the church or chapel, and the body language of members of the congregation.

Before receiving Communion, Catholics say "Oh Lord, I am not worthy." Pope Francis writes, "The Eucharist ... is not a prize for the perfect but a powerful medicine and nourishment for the weak" (*Evangelii Gaudium*, #47). Interview a few Catholics to get a sense of how Catholics look upon their reception of Communion as essential to their spiritual life.

After reading the above text about the Eucharist, and based on your own experience of it if any, what do you find most appealing about the sacrament? Seek out a few Catholics who attend Mass regularly. Ask them what they find most appealing about the Eucharist.

Sacraments of Initiation: Pathways to Grace

Initiation implies a transformation. The sacraments of initiation represent a transformation from paranoia to metanoia, from fear to trust, from alienation to communion, from self-absorption to engagement with others in transforming the world for good. Whether for an infant or an adult, baptism represents the loving embrace of Christ filtered through a welcoming community of family, friends, and the entire church community. Confirmation celebrates the giving back that comes with becoming responsible adults empowered by the Holy Spirit who acts through all the support and connections experienced in a person's life. The Eucharist offers nourishment that comes from remembering the sacrifice of Christ on the cross, partaking of the ongoing presence of Christ in the worshiping community and eucharistic bread and wine, and celebrating the promise and possibility of peace and wellbeing on earth as it is in heaven.

Chapter Review

1. What are the three sacraments of initiation?
2. What three contemporary social problems can be linked to the transformation St. Paul associates with baptism?
3. What is a catechumen? When were catechumens typically fully initiated into the church?
4. What two distinct initiation ceremonies began after Vatican Council II?
5. What does it mean to describe Adam and Eve as the "primordial" human beings?
6. What is the human condition referred to by the term Original Sin?
7. What are the four physical symbols used in baptism?
8. What reasons are given for the Catholic practice of infant baptism?
9. What is the church's underlying message regarding unbaptized persons?
10. What does the sacrament of confirmation celebrate?
11. What is a charism?
12. What two events in the life of Jesus explain the meaning of the bread and wine in the Eucharist?

13. Explain the term "transubstantiation."

14. Every Eucharist is a remembrance of the past, a present reality, and a promise for the future. Explain.

15. How did church design and celebration of the Eucharist change after Vatican Council II?

16. What connection with everyday life should be drawn from participating in the Eucharist?

For Further Study

Pope Francis. *Meeting Jesus in the Sacraments*. Our Sunday Visitor, 2015. Reflections on the sacraments in Catholic life in which he emphasizes that "they are not simply observances, they are portals through which the Lord brings us all the power and graces that flow from his death and Resurrection."

Joseph Martos. *Doors to the Sacred: A Historical Introduction to Sacraments in the Catholic Church*. Liguori Publications, 2014. A comprehensive study of historical developments of the seven sacraments.

Thomas H. Morris. *The RCIA: Transforming the Church*. Paulist Press, 1989. Before Vatican Council II there was no separate rite of initiation/baptism for adults and infants. Separating them resulted in the RCIA, the Rite of Christian Initiation of Adults, which opened up new avenues for exploring what it means to be Catholic. This book describes the steps involved in RCIA and issues that may arise in its implementation.

Stephen J. Patterson. *The Forgotten Creed: Christianity's Original Struggle against Bigotry, Slavery, and Sexism*. Oxford University Press, 2018. Makes the case that "no longer Jew or gentile, slave or free, male and female" was part of Christian initiation in the early church and that it represented Christianity's stand against discrimination and inequality.

Thomas Richstatter, OFM. *Sacraments: How Catholics Pray*. St. Anthony Messenger Press, 1995. One of a number of books that offers a brief introduction to each of the sacraments.

Chapter 9
The Sacraments of Healing and Service

According to the Gospels, Jesus gained a reputation for being a healer. However, when he did heal people, invariably he also told them: "Your sins are forgiven." In imitation of Jesus, the Church has two sacraments of healing—reconciliation, also called penance, and anointing of the sick. As the Christian community grew, many ways of serving in the community emerged. Two sacraments came to be identified as sacraments of service: the holy orders of deacon, priest, and bishop, and marriage. This chapter looks at what each of these four sacraments celebrates, how they are celebrated, and some of the questions raised about them.

I. Sacraments of Healing

Reconciliation

> Return to me with all your heart. ... Return to the Lord, your God, for he is gracious and merciful, slow to anger, and abounding in steadfast love.
>
> Joel 2:12–13

If baptism is the sacrament of welcome, then reconciliation is the sacrament of "Welcome back!" The gospel story that serves as an inspiration for this sacrament is the prodigal son parable found in Luke 15. In the story, a son leaves home and leads a prodigal (wasteful) life spending the inheritance his father had given him. When he reaches rock bottom, he decides to chance going home and asking if his father would take him in as a servant. Little did he know or expect that every day his father had been going out to a hillside hoping for his wayward son's return. Seeing his son in the distance, the father rushes out with open arms to greet him. He displays no hint of anger or "I told you so," only unconditional rejoicing that his son has returned.

The early church soon discovered that there were "backsliders" who did not live up to the ideals of the Christian life but who wanted to remain in or return to the community. Over time a formal process for reconciliation with the community became standard. It was used exclusively for the most serious of offenses, behaviors that clearly indicated that someone was outside the good graces of the community. In many ways it resembled a reinitiation. Penitents were publicly identifiable. Only a bishop could oversee the ceremony that would readmit them as members in good standing, and only after they had spent a long time demonstrating sorrow for their wrongdoing. The opportunity to rejoin the community was available only once. Of course, members of the community failed to live up to their ideals in less egregious ways as well. People sought forgiveness for those offenses from the community in various ways, such as at the beginning of the Eucharist.

Then, around the sixth century, a new practice began that shaped what came to be known as *confession*. Before they became Christian, the Irish people were great warriors—men and women alike. (Perhaps Notre Dame University's mascot the "Fighting Irish" actually has a basis in history!) When they became Christians, many of these Irish warriors gave themselves equally intensely to living their Christian faith. Many became monks or nuns and lived very austere lives, battling not each other but the powers of evil. One practice they used to help them in their spiritual discipline was to report their sins and failings to the head of the monastery, who would suggest a penance to do to make amends and overcome the problem. People outside monasteries began to want the same opportunity to confess their sins, to be directed in performing appropriate penances, and to receive assurance from a holy monk that their sins were forgiven. Irish monks introduced this practice to Western Europe, giving people a personal experience of God's forgiveness. Since priests—men—heard confessions, screens were provided for women so that neither priest confessors nor women confessing would be embarrassed or hesitant to speak of any manner of sin. This gave rise to the small "confessional box" still found in many churches. A similar practice of personal confession to monk-confessors began in the Eastern churches at about the same time.

At times this practice emphasized judgment and even condemnation more than forgiveness and welcome home. It mimicked a courtroom scene in which the priest was the judge and the person confessing was the penitent pleading guilty. (Notice that modern prisons came to be known as *penitentiaries*—places for wrongdoers to do "penance.") Changes introduced after Vatican Council II sought to balance out the experience of the sacrament. While the sacrament maintains its personal character through private confession of sins, current practice emphasizes that there is always a *communal* dimension as well. It is not meant to be "all about me." Sometimes parishes hold communal penance services accompanied by opportunities for private confession. The sacrament is also more closely linked to *scripture*, in particular to the message of forgiveness that Jesus repeats over and over again. Even the name of the sacrament underwent a change. Use of the term reconciliation emphasizes the "Welcome back!" message more than the terms confession or even penance. Each of these terms actually refers to a step in the process of accepting God's forgiveness and being restored to grace that happens over a lifetime.

Come home. God never says, "Where have you been?"

Symbols and Rituals

Blessing from a Priest. In the sacrament, confession of sins is not a counseling session or a time for spiritual direction. In this way it is like all sacraments. Some priests may be good counselors, but that's not the purpose of confession. In confession people acknowledge their wrongdoing and their desire to overcome anything that separates them from God. As a sacrament, it is an act of worship. Like every sacrament, it is Christ at work in a sensual, visible way. The priest in confession represents Christ and the church. Reconciliation is an outward sign of Christ's message: "Take heart, son, your sins are forgiven" (Matthew 9:2). The priest, representing Christ, extends his hands over the penitent to represent the loving embrace of Jesus. If confession is made in a confessional box, the priest raises his hand and makes the sign of the cross over the penitent, even though separated by a screen. The sacrament is not the work of the penitent or of the priest or of the church. It is the work of Christ filtered through them.

Questions and Controversies

"Why do I have to confess my sins to a priest?" Guilt is a debilitating burden to bear. Dwelling on all the wrongs we have done is not life-giving. If we are like most people, we can do ten kind, gracious deeds and make one misstep, and what lingers in our consciousness is that one act we feel guilty about. What does Jesus and the Bible have to say about this darkness that can envelop us? Is there any remedy that the church can offer? If we are immersed in the message of scripture, we find there Jesus's clear message that God forgives sins: "If we confess our sins, he who is faithful and just will forgive us our sins and cleanse us from all unrighteousness" (1 John 1:9). If we accept that message, it can be very freeing, a cause for celebration and also an impetus to recommit ourselves to a more unburdened, free life. However, can't people simply pause and pray to Jesus, asking that his message of forgiveness enter into their hearts? Why confess sins to a priest? The question goes right to the heart of Catholic sacramental theology and practice. Jesus gave his apostles, and by extension the successors to the apostles, the power to forgive sins (John 20:23). For centuries, that power was exercised sparingly for major offenses and informally for minor ones. At first, individual confession of sins to a priest-confessor was not viewed as the official expression of a sacrament of reconciliation. It gained traction. People appreciated doing more than turning inward to ask God's forgiveness, even for minor offenses. They wanted the external confirmation of forgiveness from the sacramental presence of a priest, who represented Christ and the church in a personal, visible way. Hearing "Your sins are forgiven" out loud from such a holy source was more reassuring than trying to convince yourself by yourself that you are right with God. Ask yourself: Is thinking to yourself, "The person I love loves me" enough? Would the experience be enhanced if once in a while that person actually said to you out loud, "I love you"? Personal confession is not meant to be an added burden but the means of relief from a burden that can prevent people from entering into a free and full life.

"What should I confess?" A priest who serves as chaplain for retired nuns at their motherhouse commented that one of his duties is to hear the confessions of the sisters. A question immediately comes to mind:

What are these sisters, in their eighties and nineties and even older, confessing? What sins are they committing? To some degree that question represents a misunderstanding of the sacrament. For centuries the emphasis was on listing specific sins that a person committed, which is still expected as part of the sacramental practice. However, that emphasis led to a legalistic view of what happens in confession. Christ, or the priest representing Christ and the church, was viewed as a judge who passed sentence on the sinner. It also fostered scrupulosity in some people who came into the confessional. Scrupulous people are overly fearful that something they thought or did, no matter how innocuous, was a sin and warranted punishment. In extreme cases it is an expression of obsessive-compulsive disorder. Hopefully the elderly sisters who sought out the chaplain for confession were not suffering from OCD, and it is also unlikely that sinful behavior was running rampant in the motherhouse. Instead, it is more likely that they have a different understanding of the sacrament. It is an opportunity to hand oneself over to God and to celebrate the gift of Christ's mercy, which even the most fervent of believers want to be reassured about over and over again. All of us fail to love others as completely as we might. After all, even popes regularly go to confession. The sacrament is meant to be used as a vehicle for ongoing conversion into becoming the person we want to be, a process that takes a lifetime. Finally, the sacrament offers "spiritual consolation" and "consists in restoring us to God's grace and joining us with him in an intimate friendship" (*Catechism*, #1468).

Interview someone who has been to confession about what the experience was like. How did they feel afterwards?

How would you explain the purpose of the sacrament of reconciliation to someone unfamiliar with it?

What might the experience of feeling forgiven by God be like? How might it affect one's life?

How would you answer those who say that "I confess my sins directly to God; I don't need to tell them to a priest"?

Anointing and Pastoral Care of the Sick

> Are any among you sick? They should call for the elders of the church and have them pray over them, anointing them with oil in the name of the Lord.
>
> James 5:14

Even a casual reading of the Gospels reveals that Jesus was a healer. Compassion for sick people was a hallmark of his character. According to the Acts of the Apostles, both St. Peter and St. Paul were also blessed with an ability to heal. The letter of James indicates that praying over the sick and anointing them with oil were practiced from the beginning of Christianity. Today the sacrament is not limited to anointing; rather, it is actually formally known as the ***rite of anointing and pastoral care of the sick***. The church has rites for combining anointing with the sacrament of reconciliation or with receiving Communion and even with confirmation. Some parishes hold communal healing services and include prayers for the sick during Sunday liturgy. In other words, the church takes seriously that care for the sick is an essential component of carrying on the work of Jesus. People who are sick, especially those who are gravely ill, feel vulnerable and helpless. Of course, they want the best medical care possible. However, every physical crisis is also a psychological and spiritual crisis. Questions become more pressing about how we fit into the grander scheme of life, whether our frail existence has meaning, and whether there is cause for hope in the face of physical death. The sacrament of the sick includes an array of practices to help people during these difficult times.

Before Vatican Council II the sacrament was called ***extreme unction***, referring to anointing with blessed oils when someone is near death, or the ***last rites***. These designations suggested that the focus of the sacrament was preparation for death rather than healing. Since Vatican II the sacrament reflects more Jesus's ministry of healing. Even when they are not in danger of death, people who are sick benefit from the prayers and support of their local community. Prayer and anointing by a priest can offer great comfort to the dying, as can the prayers of the local Catholic community. Facing death is such a lonely, isolated affair. The sacrament represents the reality that Christ and the church accompany people on this final journey and reminds them of the message they heard and celebrated at every baptism, Eucharist, and church service they ever attended. Christ too died and was raised from the dead, leading the way for everyone else. Nothing, not even death, can separate us from the love of God in Christ Jesus.

> How can prayer, the sacraments, anointing, the message of Jesus, and other elements of the church's ministry of healing help those who are sick?

II. Sacraments of Service to the Community

Marriage, A Covenant of Love

> Keep them faithful in marriage and let them be living examples of Christian life. Give them the strength which comes from the gospel so that they may be witnesses of Christ to others.
>
> The Rite of Marriage

The concept that the Israelites used to describe their relationship with their God was *covenant*. It meant contract or agreement, but applied to their relationship with God it also included a sense of intimacy and mutuality. (See Isaiah 54:5, Jeremiah 31:32, and Hosea 2:19.) In a sense the Israelites were married to their God, just as later Christians referred to the church as the bride of Christ. Catholicism recognizes marriage as a similar covenant. It too involves intimacy, mutual give and take, creativity, and commitment. For the Roman Catholic Church marriage has a distinction among the sacraments in that the official ministers are the couple themselves. The priest or deacon who officiates at the ceremony is the official witness of the church. In Eastern churches, the priest is considered the minister as he blesses the couple in the name of the church. As a covenant, sacramental marriage is an act of faith. One of the prayers used in the Catholic ritual says, "We come before you with faith in God and faith in each other." To commit oneself to another person in marriage is a true act of faith.

People don't need the church to tell them that marriage is a special event. People were getting married well before the church became involved in overseeing the ceremony, and now couples around the world get married every day without the benefit of the church. Why marry in a church service? Although love and lifelong commitment are holy apart from the church, Catholics connect all that is important in their lives to Christ. The church designates marriage to be a sacrament because it is clearly a pivotal way that people experience God in their lives. Every sacrament is an encounter with Christ. Typically, the Reformed tradition in Protestantism only recognizes two sacraments, baptism and Eucharist, since they find only these two having a solid biblical foundation. That means that in their tradition marriage, which is clearly a blessed event in people's lives, is not explicitly connected to an encounter with Christ, as it is in the Catholic and Orthodox traditions.

As a sacrament, Catholics recognize marriage as an experience greater than just the couple pledging commitment to each other. It doesn't involve two people alone. Marriage in the church reminds everyone that more people are involved in making this commitment work than the couple themselves. They have been deeply blessed to be where they are—in love and ready to commit themselves to each other for life and to the possibility of offspring. Their commitment to each other is sacred. Catholics humbly recognize that this gift they have received comes from God and is a means for giving back. If the wedding ceremony is performed at Mass, the couple may bring up the bread and wine during the offering. They also are encouraged to make a gift to some charity as a reminder that their marriage is not for themselves alone. A Catholic wedding places all that has led up to the ceremony and all that will come of it in the context of God's ongoing love in Christ Jesus. Vatican Council II called the family the "domestic church." Parents sitting down with their children to go over homework, husbands and wives doing what they can to make life better for each other, and both sacrificing for their children—those are essential, sacramental works of the church that receive little recognition or fanfare. Marriage provides a "home base" from which families can be involved in the broader community.

Symbols and Rituals

How Christians went about getting married in the beginning centuries of the church is unclear. It appears that there was a great deal of variety in the ceremony itself, but it typically did involve a blessing from a bishop or priest at some point. As late as the sixteenth century the church acknowledged that variety was acceptable and encouraged in marriages:

> If certain locales traditionally use other praiseworthy customs and ceremonies when celebrating the sacrament of matrimony, this Sacred Synod earnestly desires that these by all means be retained.
>
> Council of Trent (1545–1563), quoted in Kenneth W. Stevenson,
> *To Join Together: The Rite of Marriage*

Today, Catholic couples are invited to provide input into the design of their ceremony, including songs and readings. Two rituals are central to the ceremony: the exchange of vows and the exchange of wedding rings. "I promise to be true to you in good times and in bad, in sickness and in health. I will love and honor you all the days of my life. ... Take this ring as a sign of my love and fidelity. In the name of the Father, and of the Son, and of the Holy Spirit" (Rite of Marriage). One problem with some popular add-ons to the rite is that they can take away from the central event, which is the exchange of marriage vows. For instance, one popular custom that some couples like to use is a lighting of a "unity candle." It makes for good photographs but can distract from the essence of the rite. Some cultures have their own customs that are incorporated into the ceremony. For instance, in Filipino culture a marriage is viewed as the joining of two families, not just the union of two people.

In a real sense, the bride and groom are the principal symbols in the sacrament. If every sacrament is a visible manifestation of the love of God in Christ, then the couple committing themselves to each other is a clear expression of that love. Couples preparing for marriage can get caught up in all the details that the ceremony and celebration involve. The real sacrament continues after the celebration and the honeymoon are over. The family is "the natural society in which husband and wife are called to give themselves in love and in the gift of life" (*Catechism*, #2207).

Questions and Controversies

What about annulments? Catholicism views marriage as a lifelong commitment, mirroring the eternal relationship that Christ has with the church. However, divorce has become commonplace in recent years. The church grants annulments. An annulment is not a divorce. Rather, it is a determination that there is an impediment that makes the marriage agreement null and void in the eyes of the church. In other words, the church does not say that a marriage is annulled. Rather, it is declaring that no true marriage in the full sense of the word exists. The flaw could be as simple as one or the other partner having no clear understanding of what marriage to this person meant, and over time they came to realize that. Even after years of marriage, a husband or wife can tell the spouse, "I realize that I never loved you," or "I realize that I never wanted to be married." More often than not, cracks in the relationship started showing up well before this heartbreaking announcement by one partner to the other. Canon Law, which spells out the regulations about matters such as sacramental marriage, says that a person may enter into marriage with his or her spouse but suffers from a "grave lack of discretion of judgment concerning essential matrimonial rights and duties which are to be mutually given and accepted" (Canon 1095.2). Sometimes the "lack of judgment" doesn't surface for years. It isn't a matter of casting blame on one party or the other. Recognition that one is living in what is not a covenantal marriage is always painful. The annulment process does not seek to add to the pain but to help the couple identify whether or not "matrimonial rights and duties" have been fulfilled and "mutual give and take" between them has or has not existed.

A marriage can be legal in civil law but not a valid sacrament. Since the late 1960s, the church began to apply a much broader determination of what constitutes entering into a marriage freely and with proper understanding. So many factors could come into play that render someone incapable of entering into sacramental marriage. Since the annulment process is subject to the official rules of the church called Canon Law, it involves a process similar to a civil court case for and against granting an annulment. Work on each case requires a number of people, such as canon lawyers and secretaries, to handle the paperwork—similar to a civil court hearing. The church does not charge a couple applying for an annulment a fee, but it does suggest making an offering if the couple can afford it. The church makes very clear that recognizing a marriage covenant annulled in no way affects the legitimacy of the children born of the couple.

What about same-sex marriage? A number of countries, including the United States, now recognize the right of same-sex couples to marry. The official position of the Catholic Church is that marriage can only be between a woman and a man. The problem remains: How does the church show "respect and sensitivity" to homosexual persons and those who enter into either a civil union or marriage while upholding its teaching that marriage is solely for heterosexual couples? In 2017 Pope Francis sent a letter of congratulations to two Brazilian men who had been married in 2011 and were getting their three adopted children baptized. The pope congratulated them for having the children baptized. The Vatican reassured Catholics that the pope's letter was a "pastoral response" and did not indicate a recognition of same-sex marriage. Nonetheless, Catholic dioceses and parishes are now faced with the dilemma of how to be loving and caring toward all people while upholding church teaching on sex and marriage. The dilemma surfaces in a number of ways, such as, should children of same-sex couples be baptized and confirmed? Should children of same-sex couples be allowed to attend Catholic schools? Should people married to a same-sex partner or living in a committed relationship with someone of the same sex be permitted to serve as teachers, coaches, or in church ministries such as choir directors and youth ministers? In Germany some priests were blessing couples who were entering into same-sex unions. In March 2021 the Vatican issued a statement that, although people in these circumstances should be treated with respect and sensitivity, nonetheless church ministers should not be involved in blessing such unions as it suggests that they are similar to marriage, which it views as only the union of a man and woman.

What does the concept of covenant add to an understanding of marriage?

Read through the Catholic Rite of Marriage, available online, and write about what strikes you about the words and rituals that bring out the meaning of the sacrament.

What manifestations of family as "domestic church" have you seen among families you know?

Read reports about church practices related to the annulment process and the families of same-sex couples. What is your understanding of Catholic teaching related to these two issues as discussed in the articles you read?

Holy Orders: Imaging the Priesthood of Christ

> It is true that God had made his entire people a royal priesthood in Christ. But our High Priest, Jesus Christ, also chose some of his followers to carry out publicly in the church a priestly ministry in his name.
>
> Rite of Ordination to the Priesthood

The second sacrament of service to the community is holy orders. For Catholics, Jesus is actually the one high priest, and all baptized members of the church share in that priesthood. However, three specific types of priestly service are singled out in the sacrament of holy orders. The root meaning of these three orders tells us something of their roles: overseers (bishops), elders (presbyters or priests), and assistants (deacons). Early in Christian history overseers led their communities in prayer and worship and organized the services required for those in need. They were assisted in their work by deacons. At the same time elders shared in governance of their communities, in presiding at liturgical services, and in caring for the needs of community members. This structure of leadership and service continues in the Catholic Church in the form of the three holy orders of bishop, priest, and deacon. When members of these three orders serve in their official duties, they wear special articles of clothing that represent the role they were ordained to perform.

Today parish priests spend much of their time preparing for and presiding at daily and in particular Sunday Masses. They are also called upon to preside at baptisms, weddings, and funerals when not performed as part of a Mass. Parish priests are usually on call all the time to visit the sick and administer the sacrament of the sick. Only priests can preside at Mass and hear confessions. In addition to caring for the spiritual needs of their parishioners, parish priests are also involved in administration of parish finances and property. And priests are called upon to maintain a rich prayer life, often by reading psalms, scripture passages, and prayers at different times of the day in what is known as the Liturgy of the Hours. In addition to priests who serve a particular geographical location known as a diocese, priests can also be members of one of the many religious communities found in the church. Communities of priests, brothers (nonordained men), and sisters or nuns commit themselves to particular kinds of work, such as education or health care and usually take vows of poverty, chastity, and obedience. Some monks and nuns are *cloistered*, meaning "behind a wall." Their "work" is contemplation, engaging in acts of devotion aimed at helping them be aware of God's presence. Other religious-order priests, brothers, and sisters are committed to particular kinds of ministry such as education, hospital ministry, or caring for people who are homeless.

For Catholics, priests stand out not only for what they do but also for what they represent. Priesthood is a sacrament, meaning that priests are one more "outward sign" of God's care for people. Priests are visible reminders of Jesus's sacrificial love. They are men who have been called by the church and affirmed by their local community to dedicate their lives to serving the people in a priestly role. All Catholics are part of a priesthood of service, and all Catholics participate in prayer and liturgy. As mentioned above, married couples are a sacramental sign of God's presence in the world. However, priests take on special significance as a unique representative of Christ and his ministry of service. The word "elder" (presbyter) is appropriate here. A priest serves as an "old one" who represents the community to God and God to the community.

For over three decades now the world has been scandalized by reports of sexual abuse by some priests. Even though the number of priests guilty of such behavior appears to be no greater than in the general population, it is particularly horrendous when done by someone considered a "man of God." In that regard, priests have been likened to "earthen vessels" or clay jars—a reference to 2 Corinthians 4:7. In that passage from St. Paul the question is asked, why is the treasure of God's grace housed in fragile, easily broken vessels of clay? The answer Paul gives is, "So that it may be made clear that the extraordinary power belongs to God and does not come from us."

Symbols and Rituals

There are three "orders" and therefore three different ordination rituals. (Someone is "ordained" into an "order" with a specific role to play.) Bishops are ordained to the fullness of priesthood. They are recognized as descendants of the apostles. At least three bishops place their hands on a new bishop, a ritual for passing on authority that goes back to the apostles themselves. In the words of the rite, "By the laying on of hands, which confers the sacrament of orders in its fullness, the apostles passed on the gift of the Holy Spirit which they themselves had received from Christ. In that way, by a succession of bishops unbroken from one generation to the next the powers conferred in the beginning were handed down, and the work of the Savior lives and grows in our time." The new bishop receives a ring as a symbol of his authority and a staff to symbolize that he is to serve and care for people as a shepherd would his sheep. For ordination to the priesthood, bishops and already-ordained priests who are present lay hands on the head of the men being ordained. A bishop then anoints the hands of the newly ordained to signify the special role they will play in presiding at the Eucharist. Then they are robed with the garb worn by priests at liturgies and given a cup and plate proper for use at Mass. Deacons receive a copy of the book of the Gospels, since with their ordination they are given the role of proclaiming the gospel at Mass, preaching, and living the message of the gospel.

> Receive the Gospel of Christ, whose herald you have become. Believe what you read, teach what you believe, and practice what you teach.
>
> Rite of Ordination for Deacons

"Laying on of hands" is a ritual used for the ordination of Catholic priests.

Questions and Controversies

Can priests be married? The short answer to that question is yes. There are married priests in Eastern Rite Catholic churches. In some cases, for instance if an Anglican/Episcopalian priest or Lutheran pastor joins the Roman Catholic Church—that man may be recognized as a validly ordained priest even if he is married. It's a matter of church regulations, which could be changed if the pope decided to allow priests to marry. Married priesthood was actually brought up for discussion at Vatican Council II, but the bishops decided not to address the issue at that time. One rationale behind what is known as celibacy for priests is that St. Augustine, a leading figure in the Western church, saw monks as models for Christian spiritual life. Monks take vows of poverty, chastity, and obedience, as do all religious-order priests, brothers, and nuns. Most parish priests do not belong to a religious order and therefore do not take vows. They do make a promise of obedience to their bishop and make a promise to live a celibate life. The discipline of celibacy became the standard for the Roman Rite of the Catholic Church. It represents the sacrifice made on the part of the priest to give his life in service of the church and its people.

After Vatican II, the church began ordaining married men as "permanent deacons." These men are ordained into one of the holy orders of the sacrament and serve in various ministries such as presiding at baptisms and weddings and preaching at Masses.

Can there be women priests? Allowing women to be ordained has had its vocal advocates for the past fifty years now. Pope St. John Paul II tried to end any discussion of the issue during his papacy at the end of the last century. He said that the issue was settled and he was powerless to change it. He said that the practice is based on scripture and not church teaching, and therefore no church leader can change it. Priests represent Jesus, who was a man. Metaphorically, Christ is the bridegroom and the church is the bride. Only male priests can be a sacramental sign of Christ the high priest and the bridegroom of the church. More importantly, Jesus appointed only men to be his apostles. Bishops and priests have always been men and have always been viewed as descendants of the apostles. Even Mary, Jesus's mother, was not afforded a priestly role.

Three observations need to be made about this issue. For one thing, church leaders insist that an exclusively male priesthood in no way indicates that women and men are not equal or that women shouldn't have important leadership roles in church governance. Pope Francis, in particular, has brought in more women to have decision-making roles at the Vatican. He has been very supportive of women religious (sisters and nuns), and he encourages bishops to involve more and more women in governance. Women already play a primary role in many church ministries, from Catholic schools to lectors at Mass to eucharistic ministers. In many hospitals, request to see a Catholic chaplain and chances are that a woman will show up at your door to pray with you and offer comfort. Even altar servers, not long ago exclusively a boys' club, are now just as likely to be girls. Secondly, despite pronouncements by a succession of popes, the issue of women priests hasn't gone away. Catholics who attend a wedding or funeral at an Episcopalian, Methodist, or Lutheran church encounter women leading services more and more. Increasingly Jewish rabbis, except for Orthodox Jews, can be women. A 2015 Pew Research poll of self-identified Catholics found that 59 percent were "comfortable" with the idea of women priests. Thirdly, a separate but related issue is that of deacons: Can women be ordained as deacons in the Catholic church? There have been some church leaders who have called for acceptance of women into this role, and some scholars claim that there is a scriptural case that can be made for women deacons.

> Catholics look upon their priests differently from how Protestants look upon their pastors and ministers. How would you explain the sacramental nature of priesthood to non-Catholics?
>
> A Catholic military chaplain noted that soldiers often sought out a Catholic priest more than other chaplains for counsel and spiritual guidance. He perceived that being celibate made him stand out more as a "man of God" than his married confreres. What do you see as the positives and negatives to the rule of celibacy for priests in the Roman rite of Catholicism?
>
> Recent studies have found that priests and nuns tend to be happier and more satisfied with their life than the general population. What do you think are the greatest challenges and rewards of being a deacon, priest, or bishop?

In 2018 there were 37,000 Catholic priests in the United States. More priests were set to retire that year than seminarians preparing to take their place. Why do you think there has been a decline in the number of men entering the priesthood since the 1970s? What possible steps could be taken to change that trend?

Jesuit Father Daniel Berrigan said, "Until women are fully integrated into this church, every time I go to the altar I feel compromised." Does Catholicism's male-only priesthood result in Catholics concerned about equal rights for women and men feeling compromised?

Let us keep the flame of faith alive through prayer and the sacraments: let us make sure we do not forget God.

Pope Francis

As Pope Francis reminds Catholics, the sacraments keep the flame of faith alive and make sure that they do not forget God. The sacraments celebrate Christ's presence in multiple ways and make his actions while on earth present realities. Each sacrament confers grace, that is, the gift of life with God. Catholics would say: In the end, is there a better gift?

Chapter Review

1. What was the formal process for reconciliation in the early church?

2. What practice did Irish monks introduce to Western Europe?

3. How did Vatican Council II change the focus of the sacrament of reconciliation?

4. Why does confessing sins to a priest illustrate the Catholic sacramental worldview?

5. What change in the understanding of the purpose of the sacrament of the sick happened after Vatican Council II?

6. What does it mean to say that marriage in the church is a covenant?

7. What are the two primary rituals in the Catholic wedding ceremony?
8. What is an annulment?
9. What is the Catholic position on same-sex marriages?
10. What are the three holy orders?
11. What does it mean to say that a priest is *sacrament*?
12. What is the official Catholic position on (a) married priests and (b) women priests?

For Further Study

Lynn Cassella-Kapusinski. *The Divorced Catholic's Guide to Parenting*. Our Sunday Visitor, 2020. Attempts have been made recently to eliminate the stigma of Catholics getting divorced without diluting Catholic teaching about the sanctity of marriage. This book, by someone involved in church ministry, addresses the challenge of parenting following divorce.

James Dallen and Joseph Favazza. *Removing the Barriers: The Practice of Reconciliation*. Liturgy Training Publications, 1991. It may be hard to get a copy, but this book gives a clear history of the development of the sacrament of reconciliation.

Pope John Paul II. *Ordinatio Sacerdotalis* ("Apostolic Letter on Reserving Priestly Ordination to Men Alone"). vatican.va, 1994. Pope John Paul declared that he is powerless to change church teaching restricting priestly ordination to men and cites the biblical basis for that teaching.

Michael G. Lawler. *Marriage and Sacrament: A Theology of Christian Marriage*. Michael Glazier, 1993. Examines the theology, history, and "disputed questions" related to marriage.

Kenneth W. Stevenson, *To Join Together: The Rite of Marriage* (Studies in the Reformed Rites of the Church). Pueblo Publishing Company, 1987. Following Vatican Council II, a new rite for Catholic marriage was introduced in 1969, replacing one that had been used since the seventeenth century. Stevenson describes the background and evolution leading up to the new rite, and discusses the rite along with that used in other Christian traditions (For example, Eastern Christians refer to marriage as a "crowning.")

Arlene Swidler and Leonard J. Swidler. *Women Priests: A Catholic Commentary on the Vatican Declaration.* Paulist Press, 1977. In 1976, in response to the Anglican church ordaining women, the Vatican issued a declaration that women could not be priests in the Catholic church. The authors make the case that there is a basis for ordination of women.

Chapter 10
Prayer and Devotions: Catholic Spiritual Practices

Catholic spirituality is more distinctive for its holy objects and gestures than its words. While the seven sacraments are the core of Catholic spiritual practice, Catholics find comfort and meaning in many other ways. Blessing themselves with the sign of the cross or showing up for work with ashes smeared on their foreheads on Ash Wednesday are dead giveaways that people are Catholics. Many spiritual practices Catholicism shares with other religions, such as the use of candles and incense or prayer beads similar to Catholic rosaries. In this chapter, we will look at some of the ways to pray that Catholics engage in. Catholic spiritual practices serve as reminders of the presence of the holy and the intimate connection to God that Catholics seek to make a constant part of their lives.

> The Lord is near. Do not worry about anything, but in everything by prayer and supplication with thanksgiving let your requests be made known to God.
>
> Philippians 4:5–6

What is your understanding of prayer?
Do you pray? If so, how, when, where, and in what words do you pray?
Do you believe it is important to have a prayer life? Why or why not?

I. Pray Always

What is Prayer?

A young American soldier, fresh out of Catholic high school, ended up patrolling through jungles during the Vietnam War. When his reconnaissance group was attacked, he was left stranded on the banks of a riverbed, his legs shattered by shrapnel. He couldn't move, and he knew no help would be coming until daylight. Not particularly religious, he spent the night reciting over and over again the Lord's Prayer he had said so mindlessly while in school. In the morning, a rescue helicopter finally spotted him and brought him to safety. He credits the prayer for sustaining him through his harrowing ordeal.

What exactly is supposed to happen when you hear the words: "Let us pray"? What do Catholics do when they pray? The *Catechism* looks to an early church father for a traditional Catholic definition of prayer: "Prayer is the *raising of one's mind and heart to God* or the requesting of good things from God" (#2559). The image of "raising" one's mind and heart can imply that God is "above" and distant from us. Prayer is more often a "deepening" of our consciousness of God. Jesuit theologian Walter Burkhardt describes prayer as "a long, loving look at the real." The sixteenth-century Spanish mystic, St. Teresa of Avila, said that prayer is simply *an intimate conversation with a friend:* " ... an intimate sharing between friends, it means taking time frequently to be alone with Him who we know loves us" (Life 8:7). She lived a monastic life, so her entire life was dedicated to prayer. Nonetheless, when they pray, all Catholics seek an intimate connection with God, spending time with the Friend. Therefore, silence—taking a long, loving look—means turning one's gaze inward to see more clearly what can otherwise be overlooked. Even in more active forms of prayer, an *attitude* of silence is important. An attitude of silence implies leaving room in one's consciousness for any glimmer of light that may fill the void. Therefore, in prayer it is best not to think too much. Many forms of Catholic prayer are criticized for being "mindless," as if more active thinking would be more meaningful. There are times when the words of the Lord's Prayer and the Hail Mary are worth studying, but those are not necessarily times of prayer. St. Teresa encouraged making prayer a habit. Catholicism has many brief prayers that can be said throughout the day and on different occasions. For Catholics, prayer is more an attitude than an action, a relationship than an intellectual exercise.

The quote from Philippians that begins this chapter suggests that there are three fundamental prayers: "Help," "Thank you," and "Guide me along the right path." (Make your request to God for help and guidance, in thanksgiving, because the Lord is near.) That being said, there is a rich array of ways that Catholics pray, all of them intended to deepen their awareness and raise their minds and hearts to God. Many types of prayer Catholics share with other religions and secular practices. Many had been adapted from what others were doing. Hindus were going on pilgrimages and holding processions long before Christianity even existed. It was common practice in some African traditional cultures to pour a drop of wine onto the ground before eating to thank God for the food before Catholics began "saying grace" before meals. We could continue on with examples of sharing, borrowing and adapting forms of prayer among cultures. Even nonreligious, secular cultures engage in practices that reflect the spirit of prayer—for instance, a bell being rung when each victim's name is read at the site of the World Trade Center in New York City in services commemorating the September 11, 2001, tragedy.

Discerning the Spirit

So far this description of what happens when Catholics pray sounds similar to what many other people, religious and otherwise, engage in—meditation. Prayer does share much in common with meditative practices, but St. Teresa reminds us that prayer is a two-way exchange. When you turn your gaze inward, how do you know you are encountering the presence of God and not simply your own inner self? According to the *Catechism,* "Prayer is *Christian* insofar as it is communion with Christ and extends throughout the Church, which is his Body. Its dimensions are those of Christ's love" (#2565). In other words, Catholics don't pray in isolation. Their prayer life is shaped by ongoing experiences of Christ filtered through Christ's loving community. It is impossible to pray without some sense of God's love. Prayer requires faith; prayer in turn strengthens faith. Someone's prayer life can be misshapen, finding in oneself a message of hatred or selfishness, but that would not be tapping into the wellspring of love that Jesus revealed as underlying who we are and who God is. A selfish prayer is not prayer at all. That does not mean that the full range of human emotions cannot be present in prayer. The Psalms, used most extensively in formal Catholic settings, express frustration, anger, hope, and rejoicing. In authentic prayer, people lay out all that they are before God.

Catholics bring their knowledge and experience of God's loving concern for them into their prayer life in whatever condition they find themselves. A simple image for prayer is this: *Imagine God, looking at you, smiling*. Catholics know that God looks lovingly upon them from all that they have learned about God from Jesus and the community around them that proclaims Jesus. If not fortified by prayer, that knowledge can be forgotten. Prayer is a reminder for Catholics of the presence of God in their lives and in the world. For devout Catholics, it makes sense to pause to pray before meals, before sleep, when calling to mind a loved one who is sick, and even before a basketball game. Catholics might pray while lighting a candle or kneeling before a statue, alone or in a communal setting, directly to God or through the intercession of a saint. In several of his letters, St. Paul admonished people to "pray always" (e.g., Romans 12:12). In addition to praying *always*, Catholics also pray *all ways*, or at least in a great variety of ways.

Aside from the sacraments, name Catholic practices you are familiar with.

What Catholic practices do you find personally appealing, or what do you think Catholics find appealing about practices you associate with Catholicism?

When talking to someone facing a difficult time, a friend might say, "I'll be thinking of you" or "I'll be praying for you." What's the difference between those two statements?

The text suggests one image to contemplate during prayer is of "God, looking at you, smiling." What words or images would you suggest as a focal point of prayer?

Prayer is essentially an attitude. We trust God, we believe in Him, we turn to Him. An attitude is something permanent. So how could prayer stop when we, as it were, stop praying? It would be as if your relationship with your parents existed only when you were in actual contact with them.

Sister Wendy Beckett, British art critic and spiritual writer

Jesus, Model of Prayer

In its discussion of prayer, the *Catechism* says that humility is the foundation of prayer (#2559). Being humble means recognizing that we could be wrong. In humility we seek to make room for God. Jesus himself modeled this attitude of humility when he prayed on the night of his arrest: "Father, if you are willing, remove this cup from me; yet, not my will but yours be done" (Luke 22:42). Catholic spiritual writer Henri Nouwen describes prayer as a transformation from having clenched fists to open hands. The traditional Christian prayer posture, the *orans* ("praying") position, is standing with arms raised and hands open, the way priests stand when praying at Mass. It physically represents calling upon God for help and being open to whatever form that help might take.

The model for Christian prayer is, of course, the Lord's Prayer, a legacy from Jesus that has sustained Christians ever since his time. Here's the wording from the gospel according to Matthew:

> Our Father in heaven,
> hallowed be your name.
> Your kingdom come.
> Your will be done,
> on earth as it is in heaven.
> Give us this day our daily bread.
> And forgive us our debts,
> as we also have forgiven our debtors.
> And do not bring us to the time of trial,
> but rescue us from the evil one.
>
> Matthew 6:9–13

Every prayer is a plea that God's will be done. Every prayer seeks a connection with God's kingdom, now present and to come. The Lord's Prayer is a series of petitions, requests for God's help. However, just before these words in the Gospel, Jesus tells his listeners that God already knows our requests. God doesn't need to hear them; we do. God doesn't need to be reminded of God's promise of forgiveness and our need for help in times of trouble; we do. Catholic Masses give concrete expression to prayer as calling upon God's help when someone reads a series of petitions called the Prayer of the Faithful. In it, the particular concerns of the community are expressed, including reading aloud the names of those who are sick or recently deceased. If prayer is a time of connection between the pray-er and God, then it involves seeking to put on the mind of Christ and to look upon all that has been requested through his eyes. As Sister Wendy reminds us in the above quote, prayer doesn't end when the words have been spoken.

Therefore, prayer is not simply passive, a matter of receiving rather than also giving. It is a call to action, just as proclaiming love for another in words calls for action. After participating in the 1965 march for civil rights from Selma to Montgomery, Alabama, Rabbi Heschel was asked if he prayed while marching. He famously replied, "I felt my legs were praying." Many Catholic dioceses have programs for young people called Prayer and Action. Pope St. John Paul II described this twofold dimension to prayer in these words: "Look to Mary to see how to respond to Jesus's call. First, she kept all things, pondering them in her heart. She also went in haste to serve her cousin Elizabeth. Both attitudes are essential parts of our response to the Lord: Prayer and Action. That is what the Church expects of her young people." To pray is to be open to change one's point of view and also one's behavior.

Reflections on Prayer

> Come with me to a solitary place where we are alone, and rest awhile.
>
> Jesus (Mark 6:31)

> God speaks in the silence of the heart. Listening is the beginning of prayer.
>
> St. Mother Teresa

> Oh God, please make my mind clear.
> Please make it clean.
>
> Flannery O'Connor, Catholic novelist

> Usually, prayer is a question of groaning rather than speaking, tears rather than words.
>
> St. Augustine, fourth-century African bishop

> My Lord God, I have no idea where I am going. I do not see the road ahead of me. I cannot know for certain where it will

end. ... But I believe that the desire to please you does in fact please you. And I hope I have that desire in all that I am doing.

Thomas Merton, American
Catholic monk

Give Our Lord the benefit of believing
that his hand is leading you,
and accept the anxiety of feeling yourself
in suspense and incomplete.

Pierre Teilhard de Chardin, Jesuit
priest and paleontologist

God, grant me the serenity to accept the things I cannot change, the courage to change the things I can, and the wisdom to know the difference.

"The Serenity Prayer," Reinhold Niebuhr,
Lutheran scholar

- How would you describe, in your own words, prayer as "lifting your mind and heart to God"? Have you experienced prayer in that sense?
- For Catholics, prayer lays out our concerns before God and also implies a response from us. Give an example of how a prayer can be a request for help from God and also a call to personal action.
- If you were to pray, what would be a brief prayer that you could recite daily?

II. Prayer and the Cycles of Life

Daily Prayer

Circadian rhythms are physical, mental, and behavioral changes that follow a daily cycle. They respond primarily to light and darkness in an organism's environment.

National Institutes of Health

> Circadian rhythm affects the physiological processes of living beings, including plants, animals, fungi, and cyanobacteria.
>
> Science Daily

> Seasonal affective disorder (SAD) is a type of depression that's related to changes in seasons.
>
> Mayo Clinic website

In its spiritual practices, Catholicism pays attention to the natural rhythms of life—the time of day; weekly work, play, rest, and prayer time; and the cycle of the seasons. Other religions also tap into daily, weekly, and yearly cycles. Both Judaism and Islam have specific times for daily prayer as well as weekly communal worship. If you don't know anyone who is living a monastic life, nuns or monks in monasteries, you may not be familiar with the daily prayer cycle in Catholicism known as the Liturgy of the Hours or the Divine Office. Seven times a day people in monasteries gather in chapel to chant psalms and listen to scripture readings. All priests are to take time out from their day to pray and reflect on these prayers of the church, and some parishes hold at least the evening prayer portion of the Liturgy of the Hours so that laypeople can participate as well. As a result, throughout the world Catholics are unceasingly praising and giving thanks to God, in unison with the rhythm of the day. In the words of the *Catechism*, "The Liturgy of the Hours is intended to become the prayer of the whole People of God" (#1175).

Another form of daily prayer available to Catholics is the *Angelus*, which was begun in the Middle Ages. Church bells in Christian Europe would ring at 6:00 a.m., noon, and 6:00 p.m. to call people to prayer wherever they would be. A surprising number of people lived in monasteries during the Middle Ages in Europe, but people who didn't would have difficulty praying the Liturgy of the Hours. For one thing, it required books and people knowing how to read, both of which were rare at the time. The Angelus was a brief, three-times-a-day prayer that could be said while working in the fields or settling down for the night. The pivotal words of the Angelus are, "And the Word was made flesh: And dwelt among us." Praying the Angelus reminded Christians of Christ's never-ending presence. Many Catholics today say morning and evening prayers as well as a brief blessing before meals. If so, that would mean that Catholics match Muslims, who regularly pray five times a day. In all of these practices, Catholicism is recognizing the importance of being mindful of the presence of God throughout the changes of the day.

Millet's famous painting of two French farm workers pausing to pray the Angelus, mid-nineteenth century.

Keeping Holy the Lord's Day

> Just as God "rested on the seventh day from all his work which he had done," human life has a rhythm of work and rest. The institution of the Lord's Day helps everyone enjoy adequate rest and leisure to cultivate their familial, cultural, social, and religious lives.
>
> *Catechism,* #2184

How do you look upon Sunday? Is it different from every other day of the week? Is it a day of rest and recreation as well as worship? Up until sixty years ago the entire ambiance of American life was different on Sundays. Only essential stores were open for business. Factories shut down. No mail was delivered. Most people attended church services. Many families gathered for a leisurely Sunday dinner. Nowadays, only a few stores close on Sundays. The majority of Americans do not attend any kind of religious service. (A 2020 poll found that 24 percent of

Americans attend services weekly.) And fewer and fewer families have special meals on Sunday.

The Bible does say, "Remember the Sabbath day, and keep it holy" (Exodus 20:8). Of course, the Sabbath day referred to in Exodus and elsewhere is Saturday. God created the world in six days and rested on the seventh day. Jews set aside the Sabbath, Saturday, to remember God and thus keep it holy. Jews today, especially Orthodox Jews, continue to practice ways to keep holy the Lord's Day. As Christianity separated itself more and more from its Jewish roots, Sunday came to be looked upon as the Sabbath.

Why and how did that happen? The most important reason is that Christians have always connected Sunday and Christ's resurrection. Every Sunday is an Easter celebration. For Christians, Sunday, not Saturday, is "the Lord's Day." Another way to understand Sunday is to look upon it not as the first day of creation but as the *eighth day*. In the creation account in Genesis, God created the world over seven days. Christ's resurrection marked a "new creation," a new beginning, a world transformed—the eighth day of creation.

As to how it happened, in 321, Emperor Constantine decreed Sunday as a day of rest throughout the Roman Empire. It's not clear whether he had in mind the pagan god of the sun or Christianity when he made this decree. (His mother was Christian, and he was on the way to becoming a Christian himself.) His decree made Sunday rest the law of the land. It was certainly a welcome gift to all those who worked hard every other day of the week. In time, the Christian church also decreed that Sunday rest and attendance at Eucharist to commemorate the Lord's Day were obligatory. It was a recognition that remembrance of the world-transforming event of Christ's resurrection was essential to keeping faith alive. The rest of the week could be taken up with *doing*; Sunday was set aside simply for *being*. Every Sunday is to be a day-long meditation, permeated with an aura of prayer, even when it includes visiting relatives or playing games with friends. It resembles the Jewish recognition that Jews must keep the Sabbath so that the Sabbath will keep the Jews as the people of God.

> If you are a Christian, describe the experience of Sunday for yourself, your family and friends, and members of your community.

How would you balance maintaining Sunday as the Lord's Day for Christians with sensitivity for people who are not Christian? In our secular nation, should there be laws based on Sunday as a day set aside for rest and worship?

What do you do to "enjoy adequate rest and leisure to cultivate your familial, cultural, social, and religious life"? Assess how successful you are with this challenge.

The Liturgical Calendar

It is difficult to be religious, impossible to be merry, at every moment of life, and festivals are as sunlit peaks, testifying above dark valleys, to the eternal radiance.

Clement A. Miles, in *Mr. Ives' Christmas* by Oscar Hijuelos

Does each season of the year affect how you feel and look upon life? Does winter wear you down after a while, and do you find springtime invigorating? The story of the life of Christ parallels the story of the seasons of the year. The church divides the year into what is called the ***liturgical calendar***. If you attended Sunday Mass regularly, you would even notice that priest-celebrants wear different vestments that reflect the different seasons of the liturgical year. It begins in the northern hemisphere as winter approaches with the four weeks of ***Advent***, anticipating Christmas, which occurs soon after the winter solstice. It makes sense that the birth of the *sun*, when daylight begins to lengthen following the winter solstice, would be an appropriate time to celebrate the birth of the *Son*, Jesus, who brings light to the world. Christmas time is followed by what is called ***ordinary time***, which runs until winter winds down and the anticipation of spring takes over. This end-of-winter season parallels what Catholics refer to as ***Lent***, a time of fasting and preparation for the new life to come. The great season of Easter follows, and then another period of ordinary time until Advent, when the cycle begins anew.

Built into the liturgical year are periods of fasting, feasting, and going about the ordinary business of life. Liturgical practices acknowledge that our spiritual life cannot be separated from our bodily existence and the spirit of the seasons. Lent offers a time for giving up certain pleasures, for fasting between meals, and for abstaining from eating certain foods on Fridays, the day of Christ's death. Lenten practices are a form of *asceticism*, meaning spiritual discipline or training. Asceticism involves self-denial for the purpose of spiritual enrichment. Recently the church has encouraged Catholics to include more active forms of asceticism for Lent. Rather than simply giving up things, get involved in charitable works, help people in need, and make positive contributions to the community. Spring cleanup would make sense as a Lenten asceticism if done in a spirit of self-giving.

Catholicism can be so strongly associated with "giving up" that the seasons of feasting get overlooked. Christmas and Easter are to be times of feasting and celebrating. In an Easter sermon, St. John Chrysostom said, "Whoever you are, come, celebrate this shining happening, this festival of light." St. Francis of Assisi, known for his extreme asceticism, told his community of brothers that Easter was no time for fasting but was to be entered into with a spirit of rejoicing. Neither Christmas nor Easter is meant to be a one-day affair. There are the twelve days of Christmas, made famous by the song; but the Christmas season lasts a few days longer than that, ending with the feast of the baptism of Jesus in January. The Easter season lasts for fifty days, until Pentecost Sunday, and is meant to be one long Easter celebration. The Jewish philosopher whose words are found in the biblical book called Ecclesiastes recognized how God speaks to us throughout the changes of the year: "For everything there is a season, and a time for every purpose under heaven" (3:1).

> O Rising Dawn, Radiance of the Light eternal and Sun of Justice; come, and enlighten those who sit in darkness and in the shadow of death.
>
> A prayer called "O Antiphon," recited during Advent season

What associations do you personally make with the seasons of the year? How well do you befriend the spirit of each season?

The liturgical calendar tells the story of Jesus unfolding throughout the year: the anticipation of his birth, his public life of helping people and proclaiming the good news of God's kingdom, events leading up to his death, and the new life that follows. Map out how those times in the life of Jesus mirror the seasons of the year.

Do you or someone you know practice an asceticism during the season of Lent? What are examples of self-denial for spiritual enrichment that people engage in? Is there benefit to such practices for enriching one's spiritual life? Explain why or why not.

What are some ways that a Christian might bring out more fully the spirit of Advent, Christmastime, ordinary time, Lent, or Eastertime?

III. Catholic Spiritual Practices

The Rosary

> Pray the rosary every day to obtain peace for the world and the end of the war.
>
> Our Lady of Fatima's message to three Portuguese children during World War I

No other prayer is so closely linked exclusively to Catholicism than the rosary. Sixty years ago, Catholic Masses throughout the world were said in Latin by the priest celebrant, who most of the time faced not the congregation but the altar. Responses were made only by one or two "altar boys" who memorized Latin responses without knowing what they meant. Members of the congregation were passive observers of the Mass taking place behind the altar rail. For that reason, many pious Catholics quietly said the rosary while attending Sunday Mass. Saying the rosary has had a long history of popularity among average Catholics. Lucia, one of the Portuguese children who witnessed to the appearance of the Blessed Mother at Fatima in 1917, became a Carmelite nun and lived until 2005. Many years after her experience in childhood, she was asked why she thought the Blessed Mother asked people to pray the rosary. Lucia replied that she never thought to ask, but she presumed it was because the rosary is simple and accessible. She told her interviewer, "To pray the rosary is something everybody can do, rich and poor, wise and ignorant, great and small." Someone can pray the rosary while riding a bus or going for a walk.

The *Catechism* points out that in the Middle Ages praying the rosary was "a popular substitute for the Liturgy of the Hours" (#2678). While monks and nuns who could read gathered in chapel to sing the psalms and prayers of the Liturgy of the Hours, those who could not read would take out their rosaries and say their Hail Marys and Our Fathers, which they knew by heart. As they counted them off with their beads, they would say three sets of rosaries—one hundred and fifty Hail Marys in all, matching the number of psalms in the Bible.

Saying the rosary is not just mindlessly repeating the same words over and over again. The repetition serves as a backdrop to what are called the ***mysteries of the rosary***: joyful, sorrowful, glorious, and luminous mysteries. Notice the use of the word "mysteries." Of the twenty mysteries, eighteen refer to events mentioned in the gospels. During the course of saying the prayers and fingering the beads, the person praying the rosary is reminded of the wonderful story of salvation manifest in the life of Christ and his mother. In fact, the *Catechism* points out that the rosary, with its focus on the various mysteries, is "the epitome of the whole Gospel" (#971).

> Look up the mysteries of the rosary along with explanations of what each mystery refers to as found on the Vatican's website (vatican.va).
>
> As in the sacraments and sacramentals, rosary beads are representative of the way Catholicism incorporates material objects into spiritual practices. Traditionally, when Catholics who regularly prayed the rosary died, they would lie in their casket clutching their rosary beads. What "holy objects" might you want to be associated with at the end of your life?
>
> Catholics often possess rosary beads, even if they never actually formally pray the words. Make a case that even having rosary beads, reminders of Christ's presence, by your bed or in the glove compartment of your car, can be a form of prayer.

Stations of the Cross

> We adore you, O Christ, and we bless you.
> Because by your holy cross you have redeemed the world.
> Traditional refrain for the stations of the cross

You can tell you are in a Catholic church if on the walls are depictions of scenes from the hours leading up to the death of Jesus. Early in church history Christians who could afford it went to Jerusalem and walked the path Jesus took on the way to the site where he was crucified. Fourteen "stations" came to be identified in this torturous journey. In the sixteenth century, Franciscan friars popularized placing stations of the cross in churches. Especially during Lent, Catholics might walk from station to station, pausing to ponder the event depicted. Many variations on the stations exist, relating them to the suffering that exists in the world today. For instance, Catholic bishops in the United States have stations of the cross programs related to racism, human trafficking, and respect for life. Some church groups even go in procession to various sites representing ways that people today are suffering as Jesus did: a homeless shelter, a drug rehab hospital, and a center for immigrants, for instance.

If you were to design a program to pray for the suffering that exists in our world, what would you include in it?

Some Catholics suggest that there should be a "fifteenth station," one depicting the resurrection. How would you defend or refute that suggestion?

Praying through Reading and Writing

Lectio Divina

St. Ignatius Loyola, founder of the Jesuits in the sixteenth century, developed an approach to reading the Gospels that involved trying to place oneself in the setting of a gospel story. He suggested picturing oneself accompanying Jesus during his encounters with people and hearing for the first time his stirring words. This Ignatian approach to the Gospels is an example of what in Latin is called *lectio divina*— "spiritual reading." It involves meditating on the Christian mysteries as you read about them. The *Catechism* views spiritual reading as a starting point whose goal is to move beyond personal reflection: "This form of prayerful reflection is of great value, but Christian prayer should go further: to the knowledge of the love of the Lord Jesus, to union with him" (#2708).

An example of a prayer from scripture that all Catholics are familiar with since it is recited at Mass is the centurion's prayer. A Roman soldier, familiar with giving orders that are obeyed, recognizes Jesus's power and requests healing for his servant who is sick. Jesus offers to come to heal his servant in person, but the centurion says instead: "Lord, I am not worthy to have you come under my roof; but only say the word, and my servant will be healed" (Matthew 8:8). Catholics recite those words before receiving communion. They may not consciously place themselves in the scene from the gospel where a representative of the great Roman Empire acknowledges the power to heal emanating from the person of Jesus, but they are conscious that their lives and well-being lie in the hands of Jesus, whom they revere as the savior of the world.

Journaling

The novelist Liz Moore says, "Every teenage girl should keep a diary." In 1888, a fifteen-year-old French girl entered her local Carmelite monastery, dedicating her life to prayer and physical separation from the rest of the world. While she was there, her mother superior asked her to keep a journal of her spiritual life. She did so, and after she died at the young age of twenty-four, her *Story of a Soul* was published and became a worldwide sensation for its insight and honesty. Therese Martin became known as the Little Flower and continues to be one of the most popular Catholic saints of all time. In her journal, she spoke of experiences both mundane and profound. For instance, she wrote about her frustration in chapel when she tried to pray and the older nun in front of her kept clicking her false teeth. How should she respond to this intrusion into her efforts to pray? She decided that she would incorporate the distracting sound into her prayer, offering it up to God.

Writing in a journal is more than keeping a diary. It can serve as an instrument to get in touch with the highs and lows, the doubts and comforts, of one's inner life. Like a diary, a journal reports on the happenings of the day, but it also seeks to understand them in light of the workings of the Spirit found within oneself and in encounters with others. If you are like most people, you carry around within yourself plenty of anxiety, sometimes without even knowing its source. Journaling offers an opportunity to express those anxieties that no one else seems to understand and hand them over to God. Over time, keeping a journal helps people recognize how God is present through all the daily hardships and joys they experience.

> I'm going to talk without restraint, without worrying about the style or the many digressions that I'm going to make.
>
> St. Therese of Lisieux, *Story of a Soul*

Popular Devotions and Good Works

> The beauty of Catholic practices is that we actually can make choices. Some of us pray a daily Rosary, but we don't have to. Some of us make Novenas, or pray for the intercession of certain saints, or attend the Mass with our favorite music, all of which can be holy choices. ... The Catholic cafeteria offers choices for all palates, and plenty of seating for all.
>
> Valerie Schultz, in *Give Us This Day*, September 2021

A large church in the Germantown section of Philadelphia, Pennsylvania, is not a parish church but the Shrine of Our Lady of the Miraculous Medal. Go there on any Monday and you will find upwards of nine hundred people who are there to attend Mass and participate in a *novena*, a series of nine days of prayer—in this case, nine consecutive Mondays. Before the novena begins, a list of specific petitions is read aloud: someone's husband is out of work and can't find a job; a son is struggling with drug addiction; a woman is having difficulty having a child. Attendees at the novena represent all nationalities and all socioeconomic levels, although the novena tends to appeal to people who are poorer than most. It is an opportunity to commit oneself to the rigors of nine days of praying with a community, one of many popular practices available in the smorgasbord of Catholic spirituality. Catholicism is not "one size fits all" when it comes to encountering the holy. Parishes make available a chapel or specific times when the body of Christ in the form of eucharistic bread is displayed in an ornate container so that Catholics can pray before this Blessed Sacrament. Every May, Catholic school children participate in a procession culminating in the crowning of a statue of the Blessed Mother. The feast days of saints offer opportunities for prayer, such as the blessing of throats on the feast of St. Blaise and of animals on the feast of St. Francis of Assisi.

In addition to popular forms of piety, Catholics also express their spirituality in good works. Some Catholics make meals to serve people who can't cook for themselves or collect food and clothing for people in need. Some community centers run by Catholics teach English to non-English-speaking immigrants. Catholics run or contribute money to organizations dedicated to helping needy people become more self-sufficient, such as Catholic Relief Services (global assistance) and the Catholic Campaign for Human Development (to support self-help programs in the United States). Catholic organizations exist to help address a wide variety of issues, from climate change to homelessness. Non-Catholics of course also engage in good works. For Catholics, all that they do is seen as an extension of reaching out to Christ in their midst and living as instruments of Christ in the world. A popular prayer for Catholics called the ***Peace Prayer***, originally written in French over one hundred years ago and later attributed to St. Francis of Assisi, expresses this active dimension of Catholic spirituality well:

> Lord, make me an instrument of your peace.
> Where there is hatred let me sow love;
> Where there is injury, pardon;
> Where there is doubt, faith;
> Where there is despair, hope;
> Where there is darkness, light;
> Where there is sadness, joy.a
> O Divine Master, grant that I may not so much seek
> To be consoled as to console;
> To be understood as to understand;
> To be loved as to love.
> For it is in giving that we receive;
> It is in pardoning that we are pardoned;
> And it is in dying that we are born to eternal life.

Explain "spiritual reading" and keeping a journal as spiritual exercises. Have you ever kept a journal? What was the experience like?

What benefit do you think people derive from devotional practices such as novenas and processions honoring Mary, one of the saints, or the Blessed Sacrament?

Do you see any benefit to praying the Peace Prayer each day? What difference might it make to recite the prayer regularly?

Modern Adaptations

> In the communion of saints, many and varied *spiritualities* have been developed throughout the history of the churches.
>
> *Catechism*, #2684

Can Catholics participate in yoga classes? Can a Catholic parish join with a neighboring Protestant church to hold a joint prayer service? Can Catholics learn something about meditation from Buddhists? Can popular songs be incorporated into Catholic prayer services? Can the Holy Family of Jesus, Mary, and Joseph be displayed as a modern immigrant family or as visual representatives of different nationalities and cultures? Can traditional African or Native American garb and forms of worship be included in Catholic liturgies? Adopting and adapting new ways to pray are nothing new to Catholicism. Early Christians combined Jewish and non-Jewish elements in their worship and even their theology. Jesus himself advocated blending the old and the new: "Every scribe who has been trained for the kingdom of heaven is like the master of a household who brings out of his treasure what is new and what is old" (Matthew 13:52).

Not every trend that comes along reflects the true spirit of Christianity; prayer is more than comfort food or a self-help program. Jesus, the scriptures, and the church remain the benchmarks for Catholic beliefs and practices. However, Catholicism recognizes that, if approached carefully and thoughtfully, a treasure trove of spiritual practices is available to help Catholics seeking to deepen their relationship with Christ. Three approaches to prayer that many Catholics are finding beneficial are the ***Ignatian examen***, ***centering prayer***, and ***Taize prayer services***.

The examen

In his book, *Learning to Pray*, Jesuit priest James Martin describes the method of prayer formulated by St. Ignatius Loyola, founder of the Jesuit order of priests and brothers. As described by Father Martin, the examen involves five steps: presence, gratitude, review, sorrow, and grace. Begin by seeking awareness of being in the *presence* of God. Start on a positive note, *giving thanks* for all God's gifts in your life. *Review* your day. Recognize all that happened that brings you *sorrow*, not wallowing in debilitating guilt but thinking about ways to make positive change. Ask for the *grace* to recognize that God is a companion, a life-giving source of comfort and help, as you journey through each day.

Centering Prayer

In the early 1970s, Trappist monk Thomas Keating and others noticed that meditation practices from Buddhism and other Eastern religions were becoming popular. As a monk himself, his life centered around meditation, and he lamented that Catholics generally were unaware that meditation had always been a major component of the Christian life, and not just for monks and nuns. He promoted a simple practice of prayer centered around silence, similar to some Eastern practices. He called it centering prayer, after a term used by an earlier American monk, Thomas Merton. He linked meditation directly to awareness of God's presence. He recommended spending about twenty minutes twice a day, following a four-step process:

1. Choose a sacred word as the symbol of your intention to consent to God's presence and action within.

2. Sitting comfortably with eyes closed, settle briefly and silently and introduce the sacred word as the symbol of your consent to God's presence and action within.

3. When you become aware of thoughts, return ever so gently to the sacred word.

4. At the end of the prayer period, remain in silence with eyes closed for a couple of minutes.

Taize Prayer

Some Catholic parishes offer prayer services based on what is known as Taize prayer, named for a French community of Catholic and Protestant monks. It uses simple chants, quiet time, and scripture readings to foster a mood of meditative prayer. It also taps into resources from a variety of religious traditions.

- Do you find any spiritual practices from various cultures meaningful? If so, give examples.
- If you are someone who prays, what different forms of prayer work best for you at different times and in different circumstances?
- Many people today advocate spending quiet time in nature as a great catalyst for prayer. How might a natural setting and contemplating the rest of creation serve as prayer?
- Look up the Ignatian examen, centering prayer, and Taize prayer services. Describe what each one entails.
- Cardinal Blase Cupich of Chicago, writing about eucharistic adoration, quotes the Jewish author Isaac Bashevis Singer: "If we don't worship God, we will worship something else, and perhaps, tragically, we will worship ourselves." Do you agree with Cardinal Cupich, and what role can prayer play in addressing his concern?

Catholic Prayer and Worship

> Hear my prayer, O Lord,
> and give ear to my cry.
>
> Psalm 39:12

Before beginning his active, public life, Jesus went out into the wilderness for forty days of prayer and reflection. He spent the hours before his arrest praying in a garden. He even prayed most earnestly as he was dying on the cross. Catholics recognize that if Jesus felt the need to set aside time for prayer before and during the travails of his life, how much more so do they. As one Catholic put it, "I'm so busy today; I'd better make sure I pause to pray. Otherwise, I get lost." Prayer is not an add-on to Catholic life. It sustains Catholics as they go about the business of their lives, especially in times of trouble, but also when giving thanks is called for. When someone they care about is undergoing surgery, Catholics find it helpful to pray. When faced with a difficult decision, devout Catholics pray for guidance. When a loved one dies, Catholics find comfort in prayer. Catholics in tune with the message of the Gospels view what they do throughout the day as prayer, and that attitude makes all the difference. St. Paul's message to "pray without ceasing" remains as true for Catholics today as it did for the first Christians.

Chapter Review

1. What is the *Catechism*'s traditional definition of prayer?
2. How did St. Teresa of Avila describe prayer?
3. Why is silence important in prayer?
4. What does the chapter suggest are the three fundamental prayers?
5. What does it mean to say that no one prays in isolation?
6. What quality of prayer did Jesus model?
7. Why is prayer also a call to action?
8. What is the Liturgy of the Hours?
9. What is the Angelus?
10. What two reasons are given for why Christians celebrate Sunday as the Lord's Day?
11. What is the liturgical calendar? When does it begin?
12. What is asceticism? Give an example of an ascetic practice.
13. Why did Sister Lucia believe the Blessed Mother asked people to pray the rosary at Fatima?
14. What are the four categories of the mysteries of the rosary?
15. What are the stations of the cross?
16. What does *lectio divina* mean?
17. Who was St. Therese of Lisieux, and what is she famous for?
18. What is a novena?
19. What is the Peace Prayer?
20. What does it mean that Catholicism has adopted and adapted new forms of prayer?

For Further Study

Sister Wendy Beckett. *Sister Wendy on Prayer*. Harmony Books, 2006. A British nun known for writing about the spiritual meaning that can be found in artworks, here she offers her suggestions for how to pray. Although she wears traditional nun's clothing, she clearly has a sense of the challenges of modern life. Her writing is elegant and insightful: Set aside a few moments of silence each day for God "to look on you, to love you, to take His holy pleasure in you."

Therese Martin Borchard. *Our Catholic Devotions: A Popular Guidebook*. A Crossroad Book, 1998. Explains traditional Catholic devotions mentioned in this chapter along with many others, such as wearing medals. Not a critical study but describes the practices along with some historical background of each.

Frederick and Mary Ann Brussat. *Spiritual Literacy: Reading the Sacred in Everyday Life*. Scribner, 1996. Over five hundred pages of brief reflections by different writers who explore what it means to be on a spiritual quest.

Michael Leach and Doris Goodnough. *A Maryknoll Book of Inspiration: Readings for Every Day of the Year*. Orbis Books, 2011. Spiritual insights from writers from different cultures, often with a focus on issues of justice and peace.

James Martin, SJ. *Learning to Pray: A Guide for Everyone*. HarperOne, 2022. A popular Catholic author who begins with his own experience to talk about his subject. His style is always personable and approachable while also offering solid information and understanding. He describes many kinds of prayer available to Catholics.

Donald Spoto. *In Silence: Why We Pray*. Penguin, 2005. An exploration into the interior life and the need for prayer. Spoto draws on insights from many sources and writes beautifully about elements of prayer.

St. Therese of the Child Jesus. *The Complete Therese of Lisieux*. Translated and edited by Robert J. Edmonson, CJ. Paraclete Press, 2009. Although she lived a short life less than one hundred and fifty years ago, this saint, known as the Little Flower, has become one of the most popular and beloved Catholic saints. Many Catholics are drawn to her spirituality of littleness, doing small acts of kindness in daily life. Her writings, especially her autobiography, earned her recognition as one of only a few women named a doctor of the church.

Words of Grace: Daily Reflections & Prayers for Catholics. AllSaintsPress. Offers reflections on the daily Mass readings, published in booklet form every three months. Includes brief passages from noted Catholic authors and suggestions for prayerful reflection for each day. Gives a sense of the richness of contemporary Catholic spirituality. Three other pamphlets that offer daily meditations are *Give Us This Day* (Liturgical Press), *Magnificat* (Magnificat Foundation), and *Word Among Us* (Word Among Us Press). All are available on a subscription basis and range from more progressive perspectives to more traditional ones. Catholics might find one or another of these pamphlets in the vestibule of their parish church.

Chapter 11
Foundations of Catholic Morality

M*orality* is about how people live their lives, the choices they make, and the actions they should or should not do. ***Christian morality*** denotes how people live their lives as followers of Jesus, asking "What would Jesus do?" (Or, more accurately, "What would Jesus want me to do?") ***Catholic morality*** is a subset of Christian morality since it seeks to understand the message of Jesus filtered through the teachings and lived experience of the two-thousand-year-old community known as the Catholic Church. Catholics look to Jesus and the church for inspiration and guidance about how to be thoughtful and caring people and act accordingly.

Teacher, what good deed must I do to have eternal life?

Matthew 19:16

What words or images immediately come to mind when you think about morality? How would you define morality based on your associations? What do your associations say about your understanding of morality?

If you were invited to speak to a group of college students about morality, what would you tell them?

Tell the story of a real-life situation, TV show, movie, or novel that involves a moral dilemma. How was it resolved?

Name some values, attitudes, or trends in our society today that do not support and encourage moral behavior. Name some elements in society that do support and encourage moral behavior.

I. Morality and the Message of Jesus

Jewish Moral Tradition

> I give you a new commandment, that you love one another. Just as I have loved you, you also should love one another.
>
> John 13:34

It is impossible to separate the message of Jesus from the compelling concept of "love." A popular misconception crept into Christian thought early in the life of the Church, that the Old Testament was all about law and judgment, while the New Testament preached a message of love. In fact, Jesus was not alone in finding love to be central to the Jewish tradition of which he was a part. The most famous Jewish scholar of the time, Hillel (died 10 CE), was asked to state the message of Torah while standing on one foot. He famously replied: "What is hateful to you, do not do to your neighbor. That is the whole Torah; the rest is the explanation of it." He told his followers: "Love peace and pursue peace; love all God's creation and bring them close to the Torah." (Hillel's wise teachings can be found in the Babylonian Talmud, a collection of writings from rabbis just before and after the time of Jesus. For a sampling of his sayings, see Hillel the Elder at AZQuotes.com.)

A story from later Jewish tradition, as told by theologian and storyteller John Shea, illustrates this teaching well. Two brothers owned adjacent farms. One brother was single, and the other was married with four children. One season, because of a drought, the grain harvest was going to be poor. The unmarried brother thought, "My brother needs grain more than I do; he has more mouths to feed." The married brother thought, "My brother needs grain more than I do; he has no one else to take care of him." For many nights, each brother loaded up his cart and in secret would take grain to his brother's barn. They discovered that, miraculously, their supply of grain never seemed to diminish. Then one night the brothers met each other halfway and immediately realized what the other was doing. They hugged each other, and on that holy ground they built an altar to God.

The story illustrates an insight that the people of Israel discovered early in their history—namely, *one's relationship with God cannot be separated from care for other people*. Worship of God is misguided and meaningless unless lived out in love. The commandments that come out of Jewish tradition list rules of conduct for the proper worship of God and for how to treat one's neighbors. The prophets constantly harangued the people of Israel about caring for widows, orphans, strangers, and others in need. The Jewish spirit of generosity and care for others did not die with Christianity. If anything, Jesus reminded his followers of the radical implications of that message. He said that not only are you to love your sisters and brothers, but you are to love your enemies as well. Don't just take care of your kinfolk; look to the needs even of strangers who are struggling.

Love as the cornerstone of the moral life can seem simplistic and too sugary sweet. It does apply to sweeping concerns that exist in the world, but it also situates morality in the commonplace and everyday experiences of life. Celeste Ng writes about how love is expressed in the greetings that take place in Chinese families. The same is true of most cultures if we pay attention to the actual words.

> In Chinese families, you greet someone by asking if they've eaten yet. It is love expressed as concern: Let me take care of you, let me tend to your most basic need. And the response—I've already eaten—is an expression of love, too. Don't worry, Mom, I'm doing fine.
>
> Celeste Ng, *New York Times*, April 8, 2021

> If I speak in the tongues of mortals and of angels, but do not have love, I am a noisy gong or a clanging cymbal. And if I have prophetic powers and understand all mysteries and all knowledge, and if I have all faith, so as to remove mountains, but do not have love, I am nothing.
>
> 1 Corinthians 13:12

What circumstances in our world today cry out for a moral response?

What opportunities to live a moral life present themselves to you?

What would you say to people who claim that "love" is too much of a warm, fuzzy term to describe the challenges that living a moral life involves?

Why Christianity's Emphasis on Sin?

Despite the clear connection Jesus made between morality and love, Catholic tradition came to place an emphasis on sin. Even the *Catechism*, written just over thirty years ago, begins its section on "Life in Christ" with an admonition to avoid sin: "Christian, recognize your dignity and, now that you share in God's own nature, do not return to your former base condition by sinning" (#1691). Morality, the Christian mandate to love, addresses how our thoughts, words, and deeds affect ourselves and others. Two sides to Christian morality are "Do good" and "Avoid evil." Christianity has a long history of focusing more on the "Avoid evil" aspect of morality. Medieval morality plays demonstrate one of the reasons for this emphasis. Sin has an allurement that virtues simply lack.

During the Middle Ages in Europe, caravans of actors would travel from town to town and stage *morality plays* in which various vices and virtues would be personified and enacted for the townspeople. No doubt the vices stole the show. Who wouldn't want to see lust, greed, gluttony, drunkenness, and laziness acted out on stage? The virtues of prudence, temperance, patience, and justice simply don't have the visual appeal of the vices. This conflating of morality and sin remains true today—would you rather hear about a politician's drunkenness and licentious behavior or her reputation for temperance and prudence?

Besides the sensual appeal of sin and vice, another factor accounts for the focus on the "Thou shalt not" message of Catholic moral teaching that has remained into the modern era: the popularity of personal *confession* of sins. Introduced to Western Europe by Irish monks seeking moral and spiritual perfection, confession became a forum for giving expression to this emphasis on the negative. Confession of sins to a priest came to be seen as the way to keep someone out of hell and open the doors to heaven, especially during times when the threat of sudden death hung over every life to a degree that we often forget about today. (Mysterious plagues ravaged Europe for centuries, often resulting in a quick and horrible death. During the bubonic plague alone, between a third and half of all Europeans died.)

Confession continues to be the place to lay out what one has done wrong. It isn't a venue for making a case for all the good deeds one has done or should be doing. Preparing for confession involves making an *examination of conscience*. Even young children are given a list such as the Ten Commandments to help them sort out ways that they have done wrong. Their examen entails identifying whether they have violated any of the rules laid out in the commandments either explicitly or implicitly. A traditional standby for children making their first confession is "I disobeyed my parents." It provides a way for them to own up to violating the commandment to honor one's father and mother, although some imaginative second-graders at times take a stab at confessing to violating the commandment "Thou shalt not commit adultery"—much to the amusement of priest-confessors.

From at least the sixth century, confession has been a venue for identifying wrongs committed and laws violated. It reminded Catholics of what they had done wrong in the past and that they should avoid doing in the future. It didn't touch on what they *should* be doing to live the life Jesus called them to live. In popular Catholic imagination, when people died and showed up at the pearly gates of heaven, they expected to be admitted if they committed no known sins; or if they did, they had confessed them to a priest and dutifully performed their penance. They would not expect to be asked, "But what good did you do? How did you make a positive difference in your community and your world? What did you do recently that God is grateful to you for?" Catholic moral life tended to be about sins, laws, and what not to do. Active engagement in addressing the problems facing the world had no place in the sacrament of penance or what Catholic moral life entailed.

- Catholics are meant to be a reflection of Christ's presence in the world,
- Preaching the gospel,
- Spreading the kingdom of God,
- Building up the community of the faithful,
- And then reaching out to those who are most in need.

Charles Chaput, *Living the Catholic Faith* (2001)

Who are some of the people you are responsible for?
What are some ways that you live out the call to live responsibly?

Catholic Morality in the Spirit of Vatican Council II

After Vatican Council II, Catholic moral teaching refocused so that it speaks more to the good that can be done in living a Christian life. The word "hell" is never used in the council documents, while "love" is used over fifty times. Attempts have been made to reconfigure an examination of conscience that moves beyond avoiding sin and breaking laws. When asked what someone should do to enter eternal life, Jesus mentioned keeping the commandments, but then he went far beyond them: "Go, sell your possessions, and give the money to the poor" (Matthew 19:21) is his challenging message. He was pushing his followers not to settle simply for avoiding sin but to consider all that love calls for. He even identifies the people who deserve particular attention—those who are poor and overlooked, the outcasts of society.

More recently, Pope Francis clearly offers a more positive approach to moral reflection beyond "Thou shalt not." From the beginning of his papacy Francis spoke about the responsibility all people have to be "protectors" and "caretakers" of one another and of all creation. In this light, an examination of conscience today goes beyond listing sins committed and commandments broken. One moral theologian, Thomas Berry, suggests that a contemporary conscientious examen would include questions along the lines of the following, which are inspired and guided by the life and teaching of Jesus:

In what specific ways do I live out my commitment to making the world a better place? What more can I do?

How can my thoughts, words, and deeds demonstrate compassion for fellow human beings and other creatures?

How can my thoughts, words, and deeds be life-giving, helping the earth and all its creatures to flourish?

How can what I say or do be a celebration of the wonder of my existence and that of all creation as gifts from God?

Such a forward-looking, action-oriented examen didn't begin with Vatican Council II or Pope Francis. It actually reflects more closely the mandate of Jesus in Matthew's Gospel, chapter 25: Feed the hungry, give drink to the thirsty, clothe the naked, visit those in prison. Those mandates from Jesus don't fit easily into the format of confession as popularly configured. It's hard to imagine a Catholic confessing to a

Chapter 11 - Foundations of Catholic Morality

priest: "I haven't served food at a homeless shelter for two weeks, and I haven't written to anyone in prison for over a month." In other words, to equate morality simply with the avoidance of wrongdoing is to miss the richness of Catholic moral teaching based on Jesus and his message. Vatican Council II included a ground-breaking document titled The Church in the Modern World. In it, the bishops of the time called for Catholics to get involved in the concerns of the world; indeed, they declared that such involvement is an essential element of the gospel message. Pope St. John XXIII, who convened the council, wrote encyclicals about pressing issues of the time that he believed the church and all Catholics should address: war and peace (*Pacem in Terris*) and the suffering brought about by economic disparity in the world (*Mater et magistra*). He spoke about "signs of the times," identifying three areas of particular concern: women seeking equal rights, poor countries seeking a greater voice in the world community, and workers who lacked a living wage.

Simply put, Catholic morality has always been about *how to put love into action*. Since Vatican Council II there has been a change in emphasis about how to view morality and moral behavior. The shift can be summarized in these terms:

- From law-centered to person-centered
- From sin as breaking a law to sin as harming another
- From an emphasis on avoiding wrongdoing to an emphasis on doing good
- From listing offenses, be they ever so minor, to examining the overall direction of one's life as manifest in daily decisions and interactions with others

Christians can strive to be "imitators of God as beloved children, and walk in love" by conforming their thoughts, words and actions to the "mind ... which is yours in Christ Jesus," and by following his example.

Catechism, #1694

Describe ways that your actions are compassionate, life-giving, and a celebration of the wonder of existence.

What suggestions would you make for someone to become more compassionate, life-giving, and grateful for the wonder of existence?

Imagination and Compassion—Hallmarks of the Christian Moral Life

Morality involves a process of discernment. Living the Christian moral life means working with Jesus to transform the world into the best it can be. It calls for creativity, or what is also called *moral imagination*. Recently, Pope Francis has been a strong advocate of employing moral imagination, thinking outside the box, especially in times of crisis. The Catholic perspective is not a "Christ against culture" one. Rather, Christ calls people to become engaged with the world around them for good. Human beings should use all of their creative forces to serve those most in need. For instance, in his 2009 encyclical *Caritas in Veritate* Pope Benedict XVI refers to the "scandal of inequality" that exists in our world today. A few possess great wealth; the vast majority of people have barely enough to survive, and many of these die before their time. From the Catholic perspective this situation is the result of human choices and actions, albeit often couched in the language of sin. People are called upon to make choices and to take actions that will eliminate this scandalous, sinful reality. The world is in God's hands, but God works through human hands. In the Catholic tradition, all areas of human endeavor should come into play when people address problems. Scientists have their role to play, as do politicians, business leaders, construction workers, entertainers, and those in the media. Everyone has multiple ways to contribute to building up God's kingdom and thus to live the moral life.

A spark that urges people on to creative, active participation in living the Christian life is *compassion*. The biblical word for compassion literally means to be moved in our bowels, our "guts." A fundamental message of Jesus is that the suffering and sorrow we see in our world must stir us up; if we see them with the eyes of Christ, they can't help but do so. Compassion goes hand in hand with another term frequently found in the modern Catholic lexicon—*solidarity*. This concept was emphasized during the papacy of Pope St. John Paul II, influenced by the Polish labor movement of that name. It's a very Catholic concept that means we are responsible for one another. Moved by compassion and realizing our responsibility, Catholics are to contribute what they can to helping others. That's the dynamic of the Christian life.

Identify a moral problem that exists in your local community or the country. Describe at least three possible creative, compassionate responses to the problem.

Give examples to illustrate how "moral imagination" can be applied to what is happening in your personal life and your community.

Let yourself be pulled along, shaken up, challenged. Maybe it'll be through something you've read in these pages; maybe through a group of people you've heard about in the news, or that you know about in your neighborhood, whose story has moved you. Perhaps it'll be a local elderly people's home or refugee hospitality center or ecological regeneration project that is calling you. Or maybe people closer to home who need you.

Pope Francis (*Let Us Dream*, p. 137)

Models of Catholic Moral Life

Catholic morality is manifest in how Catholics live their lives. History provides many examples of people who responded to God's love for them by actively loving others in specific situations. **St. Peter Claver** (1581–1654) left his native Spain to work in the Spanish colonies of Latin America. When he arrived in Cartagena, Colombia, he was appalled at the conditions of the African people brought to America and sold into slavery. He realized that he could not eliminate the slave trade happening at the time, but he determined to help those people shackled in chains, physically and psychologically worn down, and frightened of what awaited them in this strange land. As soon as they arrived in port, Claver took food to them and cared for their needs as best he could. He stood up for those who were enslaved when he saw them mistreated. He welcomed Africans into his church, even though it cost him the support of slave owners and other Spanish settlers. Over three hundred thousand Africans chose to be baptized by this man who showed them compassion in the midst of their hardships. Yes, slave traders were "Catholic," as were those who bough t slaves. Claver found in Catholicism a different message: Care for those in need. Give comfort to the sorrowing. As best as possible, relieve suffering.

Dorothy Day (1892–1980), cofounder of the Catholic Worker Movement in the United States, spent her early adult years involved in radical groups advocating social change to benefit poor people. One day she left a socialist cell meeting where a few people were discussing the plight of the poor. As she walked through her poor neighborhood in New York City, she passed a Catholic church. Poor people were streaming out of the church. She realized that most people who were poor weren't attending socialist cell meetings; they were going to church. She began to look into Catholic teaching, especially Catholic social teaching, and realized that it provided much guidance for how people should live their lives if they are truly concerned about improving society and helping those who are poor. Despite its shortcomings, Dorothy realized that the Catholic Church offered much light, and often it was people who were poor who found hope and comfort in that light.

Dorothy Day, co-founder of the Catholic Worker movement

When we think about Alcoholics Anonymous, we probably don't think about a Catholic nun who taught music. Most Americans know someone who has struggled with alcohol addiction and know that Alcoholics Anonymous is the most prominent program for addressing the problem. AA meetings are now held in church halls and community centers in practically every community in the US. Even cruise ships host meetings. The strong scent of coffee and the clatter of folding chairs serve as the backdrop for these meetings where alcoholics commit themselves to helping one another keep sober one day at a time.

What many people don't know is that AA has only been around for less than a hundred years. One of the people instrumental in the early development of AA was a nun from Ohio named ***Sister Ignatia Gavin***.

When Sister Ignatia joined the Sisters of Charity of St. Augustine, she initially pursued her passion for music through performing and teaching. In midlife she experienced a physical and emotional breakdown. She gave up her music and became the admissions director at St. Thomas Hospital in Akron, Ohio. It was there, in the mid-1930s, that Sister Ignatia became what all Catholics are called to be—a wounded healer. Sister Ignatia got into hospital work because she herself was wounded. Despite her own setbacks, or perhaps because of them, she was a person who had great compassion for people struggling with their own failings. One doctor on the hospital staff, Dr. Bob Smith, struggled with alcoholism himself. At the time alcoholism was not considered a disease but a moral failure. This attitude left alcoholics to fight their problem alone and hidden in the shadows while also dealing with the added burden of shame and guilt. Hospital policy was that beds should not be given to alcoholics but only to people who were truly sick.

As admissions director, Sister Ignatia was determined to work with Dr. Bob to get alcoholics into the hospital to start them on the road to sobriety. However, she had to work around those in charge of the hospital who didn't want care for alcoholics to interfere with the work of the staff and take up the limited space. Sister Ignatia came up with creative ways to get around hospital policy, such as admitting alcoholics after hours, so that she could get them into treatment. Eventually, she turned a little-used section of the hospital into a separate wing strictly for alcoholics. There the focus was on alcoholics supporting and helping one another—again, the wounded healer model. This section also opened onto the balcony of the hospital chapel, where Sister Ignatia encouraged the patients to seek God's help rather than carry the burden alone. Meanwhile, Dr. Bob Smith and a New York stockbroker, Bill Wilson, also an alcoholic, created the famous twelve-step program that has been associated with AA ever since. Sister Ignatia oversaw the fledgling AA program at St. Thomas Hospital and then later in Cleveland. She helped initiate three guiding principles of AA—"trust God, clean house, help others." For her pioneering work in the care and treatment of alcoholics, Sister Ignatia is known as "the angel of AA."

What do Peter Claver, Dorothy Day, and Sr. Ignatia Gavin share in common?

Tell the story of someone you believe models an exemplary moral life today.

> Let Christians follow the example of Christ, who worked as a craftsman; let them be proud of the opportunity to carry out their earthly activity in such a way as to integrate human, domestic, professional, scientific and technical enterprises with religious values.
>
> Vatican Council II, "The Church in the Modern World," #43

II. Three Foundations of Catholic Morality: Scripture, Natural Law, and Tradition

> We do not have all the answers. We are on a spiritual journey. We look to Scripture, reason and tradition to help us on our way.
>
> Words on a sign outside St. Martin's Church, the oldest church in the English-speaking world, quoted in Timothy Egan, *A Pilgrimage to Eternity*, p. 75

Catholicism has a rich tradition of addressing moral problems. From the earliest letters of St. Paul down to the latest papal encyclicals, the church has been a strong and vocal advocate for morality and justice. What do Catholic leaders and theologians look to when making pronouncements about what is right and wrong? Catholicism looks to three sources upon which it bases its moral teachings. When you hear about where the church stands on various moral issues, look for references to these foundations.

Scripture—God's Word as Moral Guidance

The primary source of Catholic moral teaching is, of course, scripture—in particular the life and teachings of Jesus. In the Gospels, Jesus addresses moral issues most often in stories and in short, one-line statements. His very life models what the moral life should be.

However, Jesus isn't a systematic moral teacher. He doesn't address every moral problem or explore every application of his teachings such as his two great commandments to love God and your neighbor as yourself. He advocates following the "golden rule" that other traditions also express: "Do to others as you would have them do to you" (Matthew 7:12). He is silent on many of the issues that we face today, such as genetic engineering, climate change, and individual rights versus the common good (discussed in chapter 13). His moral message came through more forcefully in his actions than in his words. He was the model of love. He sided with people who were hurting, with the outcasts of society, and with fellow Jews and non-Jews alike. He had a reputation for spending time with "sinners and prostitutes." His death on the cross was a final act of sacrificial love. All of these actions have implications for what a Christian moral life should be.

Moral teachings of scripture are found in often baffling sayings, stories, responses to events of the times, and interactions among specific people or groups of people. They need interpretation and analysis. (What exactly is the moral message for today in Jesus's saying: "Give to the emperor the things that are the emperor's, and to God the things that are God's" [Mark 12:17]?) For that reason, Catholic moral teaching combines scripture with two other sources of moral truth: natural law and church Tradition.

Cautions and Clarifications

No one would question that Catholic moral teaching should be based on the Bible. However, there are a few caveats when it comes to looking to the Bible as a foundation for moral teaching.

The Hebrew Bible is considered the word of God by Jews, Christians, and Muslims. Christians and Muslims also include the New Testament as God's word. However, the *Catechism* reminds us that the Bible is filtered through the words of actual human beings. In other words, biblical moral teachings reflect the perspectives of particular times and places. For instance, Exodus 22:25 condemns charging interest when lending money to a poor person. Does that mean that modern banking practices, such as charging interest for a car loan, are an abomination? Leviticus 18:22 famously says, "You shall not lie with a male as with a woman." Does that prohibition mean the same today as it did in the context of ancient Middle Eastern cultures? The ancient

Middle East was a patriarchal society in which women were considered subservient to men. In that culture, treating a fellow male as a woman would be tantamount to belittling and demeaning the man. Is it an accurate interpretation of scripture to equate the mindset and mores of a particular culture three thousand years ago with what we know today? That question applies to any number of moral issues. This dilemma points out why church leaders rely on additional foundations for Catholic moral teaching—natural law and Tradition.

Secondly, the Bible does not directly address many moral issues that we face today. For example, is driving an electric car a more morally responsible choice than driving a gas-powered one? Are certain practices used today in the treatment of farm animals immoral? Can frail, elderly persons refuse certain treatments, unimagined during biblical times, that would only delay their death by a few years? Can the Bible provide clear guidance on medical and psychological issues related to gender identity that have only surfaced in modern times?

Thirdly, the Bible at times contradicts itself. Throughout most of its history, Christianity used the Bible to justify slavery. Several passages in the Bible admonish slaves to be obedient to their masters. There are other biblical passages Christians cite to condemn slavery. Does Jesus reject any form of violence, as he does in Matthew, chapter 5, or is he an advocate of violence as portrayed in the book of Revelation?

Finally, scripture is always subject to interpretation. The Sabbath is to be a day of rest and worship. Should fast-food restaurants close on Sundays for Sabbath observance so that their workers can be home resting? Is capital punishment acceptable despite the biblical commandment often translated as "Do not kill," even if it is more accurately translated "Do not murder"? The Bible, especially the prophets, makes it clear that God expects everyone to welcome strangers. What does that mean about people from other countries entering the United States, whether or not through proper channels? Christians disagree on all of these moral questions. In other words, *scripture* and *interpretation* go hand in hand. The Gospels themselves are filled with interpretations of the scriptures that came before them. For Catholics, that reality does not diminish the power of the Bible; rather, it makes it a dynamic, living vehicle for exploring the meaning of God's word.

> This is the challenge of the "imitation" of Christ. It is not the challenge to see if we could mimic Jesus, a first-century Palestinian Jew. Rather, it is the challenge to live our human adventure as authentically as he lived his.
>
> Richard M. Gula, SS, *What Are They Saying about Moral Norms?*

The Ten Commandments

Although the same for both groups, Catholics number the Ten Commandments differently from how most Protestants number them. They are found in two places in the Bible: Exodus 20:2–17 and Deuteronomy 5:6–21. Here is the standard Catholic listing of the Commandments.

> I am the Lord your God: you shall not have strange gods before me.
> You shall not take the Lord's name in vain.
> Remember to keep holy the Lord's day.
> Honor your father and your mother.
> You shall not kill.
> You shall not commit adultery
> You shall not steal.
> You shall not bear false witness against your neighbor.
> You shall not covet your neighbor's wife.
> You shall not covet your neighbor's goods.

Jesus summarized the Commandments in this way: "You shall love the Lord your God with all your heart, and with all your soul, and with all your strength, and with all your mind; and your neighbor as yourself" (Luke 10:27).

Natural Law—Using Reason to Determine Moral Principles

> There will not be one law for Rome and another for Athens, nor will there be one law now, and another law in the future, but one everlasting and immutable law will govern all peoples at all times.
>
> Roman Statesman Cicero (106–43 BCE), quoted in Jean Porter, *Nature and Reason*, page 2

Jews, Christians, and to an extent Muslims look to the Bible for moral guidance. However, is there a way to speak to other people about what is right and what is wrong behavior besides appealing to scripture? Is there morality that is based simply on what it means to be human? As the Christian community moved away from its Jewish moorings and into the Greco-Roman world, it relied more and more on the modes of thought prevalent in that world. By the time of Christ, the great Greek philosophers had been addressing morality for centuries. The approach to morality formulated by Aristotle and others is known as **natural law**. The philosophers of old relied on one instrument as the gateway to truth, including moral truth—reason. With the help of reason, human beings can better understand the morality of their actions. What does moral reasoning investigate? It studies nature—specifically, for determining the morality of human actions, human nature. Certain behaviors flow from what it means to be human; other behaviors do not.

According to the natural law tradition, people do not create morality; rather, they discover it within the natural order itself. Human nature is universally shared. Individual people differ to some degree, of course, and each culture differs somewhat from all others; but underlying all humanity is this universally shared nature. Since human nature is common among all people, reason can identify universal moral norms ("laws") based on that nature. The traditional

ARISTOTLE AND HIS PUPIL, ALEXANDER.

Christianity adopted the philosophical approach to morality taught by Aristotle and others. In this painting, he is teaching his student, Alexander the Great.

term for this approach to addressing moral issues is natural law. *Law* here means rules or norms. According to natural law, moral behavior is human behavior. Because of free will, people can act in ways that violate what it means to be human. Horses and pigs always act according to their inbred nature. A grizzly bear who mauls someone is not violating its nature. Human beings can act in ways that are contrary to their true nature, violating the "law that is engraved on our hearts." In other words, natural law does not specify *how* human beings act but rather how human beings *should* act. Catholic tradition affirms that natural law and divine law (scripture) cannot conflict; both are grounded in principles inherent in human nature as God created it. In addition, natural law offers a means for Catholics to join with people of all faiths or of no faith to explore morality since it proclaims that to be moral is to be human.

Four elements of a natural law approach to moral decision-making:

- Use reason/logic
- Investigate human nature
- Arrive at universal moral principles
- Apply those principles to specific moral decisions

What might this process of moral reasoning look like in concrete terms? Here's an overly simplified application of it. Reason tells us that part of what it means to be human is the capacity to communicate, so communication is part of human nature. Truth-telling flows naturally from this dimension of our humanity; lying distorts communication and thus what it means to be human. A general moral norm, then, is "Tell the truth." Stated negatively: "Don't lie." Moral norms derive from the very structure of our nature—our capacity to communicate, our sexuality, our need for nourishment and other basic necessities, our right to life, our dignity as human beings, and so forth. You might hear a Catholic moral theologian or church leader say that certain actions are wrong "by their very nature." Another way to state this principle is to say that an action is "intrinsically wrong" or "objectively disordered"—that is, it violates the natural order. That's the language of natural law; and, coupled with scripture, church documents on ethical issues continue to resonate with this basis for moral reasoning.

Vatican Council II offered the following list of actions that violate fundamental moral principles:

> The varieties of crime are numerous: all offenses against life itself, such as murder, genocide, abortion, euthanasia and willful suicide; all violations of the integrity of the human person, such as mutilation, physical and mental torture, undue psychological pressures; all offenses against human dignity, such as subhuman living conditions, arbitrary imprisonment, deportation, slavery, prostitution, the selling of women and children, degrading working conditions where men are treated as mere tools for profit rather than free and responsible persons: all these and the like are criminal: they poison civilization. ("The Church in the Modern World," #27)

Cautions and Clarifications

"Reason" and "Human Nature" are useful generalizations.

It only makes sense that people should use reason to guide moral choices, and it is valuable to seek to identify universally valid moral principles. Early Christian thinkers were steeped in the Greco-Roman philosophical approach to understanding all aspects of reality, including morality. In the Middle Ages, ancient Greco-Roman culture experienced a resurgence in Europe, thanks in particular to Muslim philosophers in Spain. Natural law has been the centerpiece of Catholic moral teaching into the modern era. However, more recently Catholic theology has pointed out that "human nature" is not as static and unchanging as Cicero described it in the above quote. Vatican Council II spoke about reality itself as dynamic and developing: "The human race has passed from a rather static concept of reality to a more dynamic, evolutionary one. In consequence there has arisen a new series of problems, a series as numerous as can be, calling for efforts of analysis and synthesis" ("The Church in the Modern World," #5). Accepted values and notions of truth are being called into question (#7), and human progress need not be feared but can in fact serve as an engine for greater human happiness (#37). In this more modern worldview, "nature" is not a static reality but an unfolding story. That story began billions of years ago and has been developing ever since.

Not only is human nature—or, more accurately, our understanding of it—not a static concept, in a sense it does not exist; it is an abstraction. We can't go on a field trip in search of "human nature." We will find human beings, each one sharing characteristics in common with others but also uniquely different from every other person. We seek universally applicable truths based on a generalization (human nature) couched in specific manifestations of that nature (human beings). The same is true of "reason"; it is an abstraction. In their determinations about what is right and good, people hopefully use their intellect to the best of their ability. However, it's important to remember the caution stated in "The Church in the Modern World": "Every man remains to himself an unsolved puzzle, however obscurely he may perceive it" (#21).

The More Specific Principles Are, the More Readily They Have Exceptions

The natural law approach to identifying moral principles has served humanity well for centuries. Thoughtful people have struggled to make sense of moral dilemmas by exploring what it means to be human and come up with principles about how human beings should act based on their nature. We now possess general principles that people can appeal to when making a case for what is right and wrong behavior. If people are to disagree, they need to come up with more rational counterarguments. A caution that comes from the natural law tradition itself is that the more specific principles are, the more they are subject to exceptions. For example, "Do good; avoid evil" is hard to argue with. However, the principle that people have a right to private property leaves room for exceptions without invalidating the principle in general. Saint Thomas Aquinas, the great proponent of natural law in the Middle Ages, even gives an interesting explanation of the principle "Do not steal." He claims that the principle is universally valid. However, what about in a situation in which a person does not have enough to keep her or his family alive while another person has wealth well beyond his or her needs? Aquinas proposes that the rich person is actually the one who is stealing since all people have a right to have basic needs met whenever possible. His analysis was presented in Vatican Council II's document on "The Church in the Modern World":

"If a person is in extreme necessity, he has the right to take from the riches of others what he himself needs" (#69).

Natural law maintains that morality is not imposed from some nonreflective, extra-human source. Rather, it is to be discovered within the human realm itself. It provides a means for all seekers after truth to dialogue with one another, to seek to convince one another with well-reasoned analysis and to arrive at principles for guidance in moral decision-making.

> Application of the natural law varies greatly; it can demand reflection that takes account of various conditions of life according to places, times, and circumstances. Nevertheless, in the diversity of cultures, the natural law remains as a rule that binds men among themselves and imposes on them, beyond the inevitable differences, common principles.
>
> *Catechism*, #1957

Are there actions you believe are always and everywhere wrong, intrinsically immoral?

Name some universal moral principles. Discuss whether you find possible exceptions to any of them.

Tradition—Wisdom of the Ages

Catholicism has always had great respect for reason. In Catholic moral teachings, scripture and reason—Jerusalem and Athens—go hand in hand. A third foundation in the pursuit of moral truth is ***Tradition***. Tradition means that which is handed down. Spelled with a capital "T" it refers to the great collection of teachings produced within the church over the past two thousand years. Jesus told his apostles to teach in his name. Church leaders have taken and continue to take that responsibility seriously. A Latin word for the church's teaching authority today is ***magisterium***, meaning "teacher." Catholics look to church leaders for guidance in shedding light on a variety of moral issues. For example, for hundreds of years now popes have issued special letters called ***encyclicals***. These letters often contain teaching on matters from justice and peace to care for the environment. Bishops, either individually or as a group, write pastoral letters. Since the late

1980s when it was written, the *Catechism of the Catholic Church* provides a summary of moral teachings based on the Ten Commandments. Thus, Catholic moral teaching is unique in that it is based on the interplay of scripture, reason, and Tradition—think symbolically "Jerusalem, Athens, and Rome."

Tradition as a source of moral guidance came under attack during the Protestant Reformation. As already mentioned, Protestants rejected much of what was going on in the church of the time and therefore advocated that the Bible alone is the source of moral teaching. The Council of Trent rejected this *"sola scriptura"* view of truth-seeking and spoke of the "two sources of revelation": scripture and Tradition—similar to what Judaism calls the "written law" (the Bible) and the "oral law" (commentaries on scripture by rabbis). The Catholic emphasis on Tradition is a reminder to learn from the past and to realize that our understanding of moral truth is ongoing.

Catholic tradition holds that Jesus appointed Peter to lead the church.

> It is logical to conclude, at least on the part of those who believe in the word of God, that today's "development" is to be seen as a moment in the story which began at creation.
>
> Pope St. John Paul II, *On Social Concern*, #30

Cautions and Clarifications

Can traditional teachings change?

> For the deposit of faith or revealed truths are one thing; the manner in which they are formulated without violence to their meaning and significance is another.
>
> Vatican Council II, "The Church in the Modern World," #62

Tradition, by definition, has a history. Always with an eye toward scripture and natural law, magisterial teachings percolate and then take hold. An example is Catholic teaching on capital punishment. The *Catechism* acknowledges that the death penalty was accepted by the church for most of its history. The 1917 *Catholic Encyclopedia* states explicitly, "The infliction of capital punishment is not contrary to the teaching of the Catholic Church." The *Catechism* of the 1980s, however, says that the only justification for capital punishment is self-defense; and circumstances when the death penalty is justified today "are very rare, if not practically non-existent" (#2267). During his papacy, whenever someone was scheduled for execution in the United States, Pope St. John Paul II would write to the governor of the state asking for clemency. The United States remains alone among nations of Western civilization where capital punishment continues to be practiced.

Pronouncements from the magisterium can spark discussion in Catholic communities and beyond. When in 1987 Pope St. John Paul II wrote an encyclical about economic matters, many economists voiced their support for or opposition to his point of view, especially when he was critical of capitalism. When Pope Francis wrote an encyclical about the environment, many Catholic organizations sprang up to apply the teachings in his encyclical to environmental problems. Inspired by this pronouncement, many Catholic parishes now consider ways that they can make their buildings and practices more environmentally friendly. When Pope St. Paul VI wrote the encyclical

Humanae vitae in 1968, it continued to maintain condemnation of artificial birth control as official church teaching, contrary to the position of most all other religious groups and many Catholic married couples themselves. This position has been closely associated with Catholicism ever since. Catholic leaders look to scripture, natural law, time-honored insights from past church teaching, and contemporary sources of knowledge to continue creating Catholic Tradition as it addresses current moral problems.

A challenge that Catholic leaders currently face in regard to Tradition is whether they disagree with earlier magisterial positions. Tradition is a growing, evolving phenomenon. Even in families, saying, "We do it this way because this is the way we've always done it" is not a sufficient argument for holding onto a traditional practice. ("On July Fourth we *always* have a cookout at Grandma's house and then go to the fireworks display.") Circumstances change. New insights arise. Pope Francis, for one, points out that we now face crises that never existed before, such as environmental degradation on a massive scale and the global challenge of dealing with previously unknown viruses such as COVID-19. Church leaders hesitate to say that earlier church pronouncements were wrong. For one thing, they proclaim that "the Church has always been guided by the Holy Spirit." To overturn earlier teachings is akin to denying that the church has borne the light of Christ in the world for the past two thousand years. Dismissing earlier church teachings might lead to having their own pronouncements dismissed as temporary, subject to rejection in the future, and a reflection of their own limited point of view—relativism. Pope Francis warns against a too-narrow understanding of Tradition: "Tradition is not a museum, true religion is not a freezer, and doctrine is not static but grows and develops, like a tree that remains the same yet which gets bigger and bears ever more fruit" (*Let Us Dream*, p. 57).

Moral Relativism

One of the great evils for many Catholic moral theologians is **moral relativism**. It implies that there are no universal truths; everything is relative. A relativist believes that truth claims of one culture or society are not valid for all cultures. Are there instances when cultural differences might be accepted without succumbing to relativism? Church leaders rely on the combination of scripture, reason, and

Tradition to avoid relativism and to discern what is right and good in their moral decision-making.

Pastoral Considerations

The Catholic Church considers itself both "teacher" and "mother." Church leaders point out that ***pastoral considerations*** come into play when they deal with people who face actual moral dilemmas. (***Pastor*** means "shepherd.") An example of the interplay between the church as moral teacher and its pastoral, motherly response is the heartbreaking question of suicide. As teacher, the Catholic Church teaches that taking one's own life is wrong. However, the *Catechism* recognizes that "grave psychological disturbances, anguish, or grave fear of hardship, suffering, or torture can diminish the responsibility of the one committing suicide" (#2282). In the case of suicide, church leaders are clear that judgment lies in the hands of God, the God of compassion and mercy.

Some Catholics who have had a loved one commit suicide fear that they cannot approach the church for solace because they understand that, in the eyes of the church, taking one's life is wrong. However, certainly in recent times church leaders are very clear that the local church's role in this most painful of circumstances is to represent the love of God. Members of the church community are to reach out to the grieving family and embody the unconditional love of Christ and dispel the notion of God or church as an unforgiving judge. (A helpful resource for looking at this particular issue from multiple perspectives is *Responding to Suicide: A Pastoral Handbook for Catholic Leaders*, edited by Deacon Ed Shoener and Bishop John P. Dolan.)

Name a moral issue that you have a strong position on. What is the basis for your position? How would you explain or defend it?

How might each of the three foundations of Catholic morality contribute to your own understanding of right and wrong?

Read Deuteronomy 22:28–29 for an example of moral teaching reflective of a patriarchal society. What is the role of the woman in this decree versus the roles of men?

Look up "moral relativism." Explain the term and discuss implications of it for moral reasoning.

III. Conscience: Making Moral Judgments

> Man's dignity therefore requires him to act out of conscious and free choice, as moved and drawn in a personal way from within, and not by blind impulses in himself or by mere external constraint.
>
> "The Church in the Modern World," #17

Three Dimensions of Conscience, or Conscientious Decision-Making

According to the *Catechism*, **conscience** refers to making a reasonable judgment about moral decisions (#1778). If we read through the *Catechism*'s discussion of conscience (#1776–1794), we can identify three dimensions to conscientious moral decision-making. To begin with, conscience requires a basic *awareness* that there is right and wrong and that to be human means to be drawn to doing right. To the degree that someone lacks such a basic awareness, that person cannot be said to possess conscience. (For instance, psychology labels someone with no sense of right or wrong a *psychopath* or *sociopath*.) Many factors, such as drunkenness, addiction, mental illness, or cultural influences, can diminish someone's ability to make judgments based on reason. True narcissists lack the ability to see beyond what is in their own interest. An inveterate liar cannot distinguish between truth and falsehood.

Second, conscience refers to taking steps to inform, educate, and develop our capacity to know right from wrong. Here's where, for Catholics, scripture, reason, and Tradition come into play. When it comes to conscientious decision-making, ignorance is not bliss. It involves a process of *discernment* to determine, to the best of our ability, what is the right course of action in a particular situation. Pope Francis says of this process, "Discernment means to think through our decisions and actions, not just by rational calculation but by listening for His Spirit, recognizing in prayer God's motives, invitations, and will" (*Let Us Dream*, p. 54). He also warns against what he calls an *isolating conscience*: In moral decision-making, people should seek guidance from knowledgeable sources and engage with others in seeking to know what is right. That is, avoid deciding important matters in isolation from a community. That is an important component of discernment.

Finally, conscience means *judgment*, moral decision-making itself. Thus, conscience is like the "good spirit" that "appeals to my desire to do good, to help and serve, and gives me strength to go forward on the right path" (Pope Francis, *Let Us Dream*, p. 62).

As this three-dimensional description of conscience makes clear, conscience is not a "thing" separate from who we are. It refers to a process that human beings should go through when faced with moral decisions. It's important to keep that in mind since the word "conscience" has many popular understandings that are inadequate in describing the process of conscientious moral judgment. For instance, conscience is often defined as that "little voice inside us"—Walt Disney's Jiminy Cricket. It is often described as coming into play after we do something, such as "feeling guilty" or "suffering from a guilty conscience" when we've done something that in hindsight we believe was wrong. Or we might think of conscience as the sum total of moral messages we have received during our upbringing—our "internal parent" or what Freud would call our superego. And, of course, conscience has nothing to do with what we *want* to do but rather with what we believe we *should* do. None of these popular associations with conscience is adequate to describe the reasoned decision-making that the church says moral decision-making requires.

Popular but Inadequate Understandings of Conscience

Especially in light of Vatican Council II, Catholic teaching is that people are called upon to act in accordance with a thoughtful and informed conscience—by definition, conscientious decision-making *is* thoughtful decision-making. It is neither "doing what you are told" from an external authority nor unreflectively following the "little voice" inside you. The Council recognized that conscience is necessary for the dignity of the human person. Most bishops at the Council knew the affront to human dignity that was the totalitarian mindset found in fascism, Nazism, and communism. They had heard the excuses Nazi leaders made following World War II: "I am not responsible. I only did what I was told." The bishops advocated freedom and personal responsibility as hallmarks of human dignity and thus called upon people to develop and use their conscience. To say that people should not always follow their conscience, doing what they honestly believe is the right thing to do, is an affront to their dignity as persons endowed with intellect and will.

Saint Thomas More served as Chancellor of England during the turbulent reign of King Henry VIII. You may already know about King Henry and his many wives. It was the early sixteenth century, the period of the Reformation in Europe. King Henry was married to a Spanish noblewoman named Catherine of Aragon, who also happened to be the aunt of the Holy Roman Emperor at the time. King Henry desperately wanted a son; he believed that the sovereignty of England depended on it. If he had no male heir, England could appear vulnerable, or a nobleman from the continent could claim the English crown, and England's independence would end. Henry lost faith that his wife Catherine would bear him a son, so he petitioned the pope to have his marriage to her annulled so that he could marry his mistress, Anne Boleyn. The pope refused to grant Henry the annulment. Henry then declared himself head of the church in England and granted himself the annulment. He also required that all of his leading subjects sign an oath recognizing him as head of the English church.

That's when Thomas More came face to face with the dictates of his conscience. Thomas believed that the pope was head of the universal church, including in England. This belief placed him in a precarious position. Most of the other leading men of England, including cardinals and bishops, signed the Oath of Supremacy. Thomas enjoyed life and his freedom; he had a wife and children. He was also known as a man of wisdom and integrity. If he didn't sign the oath, it called into question its legitimacy. Thomas realized that his life was in danger. Perhaps the right thing to do in the circumstances would have been to sign the oath even though he disagreed with it. No doubt other prominent men of the time did. He was imprisoned but still refused to sign. He was placed on trial, but even threatened with the death penalty he declared that in conscience he could not sign the oath proclaiming the king head of the church. For remaining true to his conscience—placing his understanding of God's law above all other concerns—Thomas was beheaded.

During Nuremberg trials following World War II, Nazi leaders claimed they were not responsible; they were just following orders.

The Question of Conscience

St. Thomas More put conscience above his personal wellbeing, making him a model for conscientious decision-making for Catholics.

Conscience is an important concept in Catholic moral teaching, but it raises many questions. Should people always follow their conscience? Ponder that question even for a few moments and a whole host of other questions arise. Not everyone is as noble as Thomas More. Do we really want all people to do what they think is right? According to the *Catechism*, conscience is the "secret core and sanctuary" of a person; but it also makes clear that people can be wrong in their judgments of conscience, what is called an ***erroneous conscience***. Conscience is a judgment of reason, but isn't reasoning swayed by a person's upbringing and culture so that people's consciences tend to differ from culture to culture? Actually, at times conscience means going against what the surrounding culture views as right and wrong. Think about other models of conscience, such as Rosa Parks, who went against the laws of her community and refused to move to the back of a bus as she, a black woman, was supposed to do by law. Or the Berrigan brothers, both Catholic priests, who broke into a draft office and destroyed draft records in protest against the Vietnam War.

Obviously, conscience doesn't mean simply doing what "feels" right. In the case of Thomas More we discover that in difficult situations it frequently doesn't mean doing what we want to do. In light of these cautions and concerns, the question remains: Should people follow their conscience? Church teaching is clear: rightly understood, people should follow their conscience. When we are following conscience, we recognize the moral quality of our actions, and we are obliged to follow faithfully what we believe to be just and right (*Catechism*, #1778).

> Return to your conscience, question it. ... Turn inward, brethren, and in everything you do, see God as your witness.
>
> Saint Augustine, in *Catechism*, #1779

Implications of Catholic teaching on conscience:

- Conscientious decision-making represents our dignity as free, rational, responsible persons.
- Conscience is a process; it is not a thing, a feeling, or a voice inside us separate from who we are. However, feelings and "that little voice" should factor into decision-making.
- Conscience is subjective; that is, people can disagree in good conscience. (One person could join the military in good conscience while for another person this would be a violation of his or her conscience. One store owner could consider it a violation of conscience to open on Sunday while another would not.)

- People can follow a stringent process of conscience and arrive at wrong conclusions—erroneous conscience. (Most people today would say that owning slaves is wrong, but surely there were people in America two hundred years ago who believed in good conscience that slavery is acceptable.)
- People can lack conscience to varying degrees, either willfully ignoring it or being incapable of thoughtful decision-making. (If you're going out drinking, make sure you make arrangements for getting home that doesn't involve driving. After a few drinks your judgment is likely to be impaired.)
- People do not always follow their conscience, instead deliberately going against what they believe is the right thing to do.
- Being conscientious can mean going against the laws and norms of one's family or community.

Use specific examples to discuss the following questions:

What are common misconceptions about conscience?

What does "follow your conscience" mean?

Should people always follow their conscience in moral decision-making?

Is there a viable alternative to following conscience as a basic moral principle? That is, are there instances when people should not do what they believe is the right thing to do (follow their conscience) and instead should do what they think is wrong?

What cautions and clarifications would you include about people following their conscience?

Morality and Our Lives

But a life of true significance has unlimited impact. It is measured in how well we've loved those around us, how much we've given away, how many seeds we've sown along our path.

Cicely Tyson, actress

Morality doesn't happen in a book or in a gathering of people discussing issues in isolation from the real world. Morality happens in our day-to-day encounters with other people and in the specific situations in which we find ourselves. Along with objective moral principles, it's important to remember that there is also a subjective dimension to morality. The Catholic tradition emphasizes that we don't exist merely as separate individuals. We exist as persons in communion with other people and in communion with God. Recognizing the personal dimension of our life, especially our moral life, doesn't take away from the importance of scripture, reason, and Tradition. Rather, these foundations for morality need to be applied to our here-and-now reality. Morality happens in Amazon rainforests, in African countries threatened by expanding deserts, in the boardrooms of multinational corporations, at the border between the US and Mexico, in the voting booth, and in our homes, hospitals, and movie theatres. Every facet of our coexistence has moral implications. For Catholics, every encounter is an opportunity to live out the loving message of Jesus. Two months before he died, Martin Luther King Jr. said: "Everybody can be great, because anybody can serve. ... You only need a heart full of grace, a soul generated by love."

Look back on the associations you made with morality when you began this chapter. How would you explain Catholic morality to a friend now after reading about and discussing it?

What insights about morality have you gained from your study of this topic?

Chapter Review

1. What is the central moral message found in the teachings of Jesus and the Jewish tradition leading up to him?

2. How did the introduction of personal confession impact Catholic morality?

3. Describe the change in emphasis about morality ushered in by Vatican Council II.

4. Explain the role of creativity and compassion in Catholic morality.

5. What are the three foundations for Catholic moral teaching? Explain how each one functions. What limitations and clarifications need to be considered when appealing to each of these in determining right and wrong?

6. Define "moral relativism" and "pastoral considerations."

7. What are the three dimensions of a Catholic understanding of conscience?

8. What are popular but inadequate descriptions of conscience?

9. How did the experience leading up to and during World War II in Europe influence the strong position about the importance of conscience found in the documents of Vatican Council II?

10. What does Catholic teaching mean by an erroneous conscience?

11. According to Catholic teaching, can people disagree "in good conscience"? Give an example.

12. What possible factors could diminish a person's capacity for conscientious decision-making?

For Further Study

Charles E. Curran. *Sixty Years of Moral Theology: Readings in Moral Theology*. Paulist Press, 2020. A leading Catholic moral theologian in the post–Vatican Council II church, Curran writes about topics related to morality such as conscience and natural law. Curran has written several books on morality, especially about social ethics. This book is a compilation of articles from books he has written since just after the council.

Dignitatis Humanae ("Declaration on Religious Liberty"). vatican.va. A document from Vatican Council II that recognizes that respect for the dignity of the human person calls for the recognition that people are free to make choices, specifically in the area of religion. This linking of human dignity and freedom of choice led to discussion of the role of personal conscience in moral decision-making as well as engagement with other religions.

Pope John Paul II. *Veritatis Splendor* ("On the Splendor of Truth"). St. Paul Books & Media, 1993. The encyclical by Pope John Paul that explains most fully his understanding of Catholic morality. Emphasizes the role of the magisterium (church leadership) and warns against "a radically subjectivistic conception of moral judgment."

John Mahoney. *The Making of Moral Theology: A Study of the Roman Catholic Tradition.* Clarendon Press, 1990. Traces the historical development of Catholic moral theology.

John T. Noonan Jr. *A Church That Can and Cannot Change: The Development of Catholic Moral Teaching.* University of Notre Dame Press, 2005. Examines how Catholic teaching on several moral issues has changed over time, such as on the practices of slavery and usury.

Timothy E. O'Connell. *Principles for a Catholic Morality*, Revised edition. Harper & Row Publishers, 1990. After Vatican Council II, many theologians explored the implications of its teachings for moral theology. This book was one of the first to explain Catholic teaching on conscience, highlighting three dimensions to conscientious moral decision-making: awareness, discernment, and judgment.

Jean Porter. *Nature as Reason: A Thomistic Theory of the Natural Law.* William B. Eerdmans Publishing, 2005. A scholarly analysis of the nuance and subtlety of St. Thomas Aquinas's understanding of natural law and how it is interpreted by scholars today.

Budd Schulberg, screenwriter. "On the Waterfront." Film, 1954. A classic portrayal of a young man's journey from self-centeredness to concern for others and the hardship and challenges that come with it. In the words of the main character: "Conscience ... that stuff can drive you nuts!"

Ed Shoener and Bishop John P. Dolan, editors. *Responding to Suicide: A Pastoral Handbook for Catholic Leaders.* Ave Maria Press, 2020. A collection of essays addressing suicide from multiple perspectives.

Anne Thurston. *Because of Her Testimony: The Word in Female Experience*. Crossroad Publishing Company, 1995. Reflects on her own experience to make the case that moral reasoning from a woman's perspective differs from that of the male theologians she encountered during her studies in Ireland.

Chapter 12
Personal and Social Dimensions of Morality

Catholic morality is based on the belief that Jesus invited people to live lives in line with his vision of what God intended for them. Catholic moral teaching, therefore, looks at all aspects of personal moral behavior—what people should do and what people are doing but shouldn't. Moreover, for over a century now the church has recognized that morality is more than just personal behavior. Good and evil can be found in the very fabric of society. The way institutions function in a society can foster Jesus's vision or be hurtful to people. In other words, morality has both personal and societal dimensions.

> What do you think is the Catholic Church's message about sin?
> What do you think the church should teach about sin?
> How would you describe the root cause of sinfulness?

I. Morality as Right and Wrong Behavior

The Sin that Underlies All Sins

> The root of sin is in the heart of man, in his free will. ... But in the heart also resides charity, the source of the good and pure works, which sin wounds.
>
> *Catechism*, #1853

The New Testament and Christian theology throughout the ages make frequent reference to the word *sin*. The concept is confusing. At times it refers to all that is wrong with the world (***sin***), and at other times it refers to specific hurtful actions that people do (***sins***). The dynamic is something like this: God is good, and God's creation is good. We don't even need to read history books to know that all in the world is not as it should be; we only need to look around us and within ourselves to see that we humans do not always measure up. All that is misguided, destructive, and contrary to God's will is sin. When individual people act out of sinfulness and not God's will, they commit sins. That is, sins (bad acts) are participating in sin, the state of the world that is not what God intended.

One example of the relationship between sin and sins is the list of **seven deadly sins** formulated early in Christian history: pride, greed, wrath, envy, lust, gluttony, and sloth. These deadly sins are not actions at all but rather inclinations that can lead to harmful acts. For example, anger is not bad. Wrath is anger out of control in such a way that it causes harm. People should feel good about themselves (pride as positive); but when they start to act like they are separate from and better than other people and look down on others, they have succumbed to the sin of pride. (In Dante's *Divine Comedy*, people guilty of sinful pride go around hell with a heavy stone attached to their neck to pay the price for their haughtiness while on earth.) St. Thomas Aquinas called these seven deadly sins "perversions of love." It is good to enjoy the food we eat—after all, they are a gift from God, as Catholics acknowledge when they say grace before meals. However, overdoing eating (gluttony) is a perversion of God's gift of food.

In his letter to the Romans, St. Paul equates sin with slavery and death. He contrasts the state of sin with the state of grace, which is Christ's offer of freedom and life. How can Paul say that the state of grace is freeing and life-giving? The presumption underlying the Christian message is that to be loving as Jesus loved is to be free. We might think, "If I'm free I can do whatever I want to do. Who cares about anyone else?" St. Paul is saying that this is a misguided understanding of freedom. Think about the seven deadly sins again. If we are greedy and envious, we are not free to enjoy what we have. There is always a better cell phone we'd love to have or a finer house in a nicer neighborhood. We don't have a perfect body; someone always looks better on the beach. Instead of looking at what we have and freely enjoying our life, we are always looking over our shoulder at what other people have that we don't. St. Paul says that the wages of such an attitude is death (Romans 6:23). On the other hand, to be selfless and concerned about others makes us free to forget about our shortcomings and share what we have with others. A free life is a shared life, give and take without the constant worry of who has more and what's in it for me.

Seven deadly sins represented by different animals.
We still associate the peacock with pride and pigs with gluttony.

What is the relationship between *sin* and *sins*?
What does St. Paul mean when he says that sin is a form of slavery and death? Do you agree with him? Give examples that show why this is true or false.
Is loving an expression of freedom? Give examples to support your answer.

Anger is like a hot coal you hold in your hand to hurl at another, but you are the one who gets burnt.

Buddha

Biblical Terms for Sin: Missing the Mark and Hardness of Heart

The *Catechism* begins its definition of sin with these words: "Sin is an offense against reason, truth, and right conscience" (#1849). It is a conscious and free choice to do wrong. The Bible uses a number of terms and images to describe sin. "***Missing the mark***" and "***hardness of heart***" are two of them. The first term implies that human beings have a mark or a goal that they are made for. Sin is missing the mark. The same word is used in archery—missing the mark, being "off center." Catholic moral teaching calls for examining how both our underlying inclinations as well as our specific actions miss their intended mark.

The church in Western Europe came to look upon sin in legalistic terms, but the Eastern churches employed medical imagery to describe sin and morality. In their view, sinning is not healthy, and people who sin are in need of healing so they can return to the state of being they are designed for. The Letter to the Hebrews uses this medical imagery for sin when it speaks about what is "out of joint" in us being in need of healing (12:12–13). Sin as hard-heartedness is the exact opposite of the compassion that Jesus called for. The prophets spoke about God's healing touch as replacing a heart of stone with a heart of flesh: "A new heart I will give you, and a new spirit I will put within you; and I will remove from your body the heart of stone and give you a heart of flesh" (Ezekiel 36:26). As hard-heartedness, sin has as much to do with our attitudes as with our actions, with our being as with our behavior.

> Give examples of "missing the mark" and "hardness of heart" that have had negative consequences either in your personal experience or in broader world affairs.

Confession and the Catholic Emphasis on Personal Sin

Protestants generally speak of overall human sinfulness; it is the reality of our human condition that cries out to be "saved." Besides this recognition of human sinfulness, Catholics also speak of specific sins. As mentioned in the last chapter, one reason why Catholics emphasize individual sins is the practice of personal confession. Accompanying the historical popularity of confession, manuals were written for priest-confessors to help them identify the seriousness of sins and appropriate penances for people who commit them. Catholic teaching distinguishes the most serious (mortal) sins and less serious (venial) sins. Underlying the Catholic practice of confession and the focus on sinful behaviors is the belief that the human condition is essentially good and the church serves as an instrument of Christ by which people can be restored to sharing in divine life with Christ. Confession offers Catholics a forum by which they can commit themselves to battling the destructive forces that got them in trouble in the first place.

In 1973, psychiatrist Karl Menninger wrote *Whatever Became of Sin?* He believed that at the time Americans were minimizing talk of personal sin and that this trend was actually having negative consequences, especially when it comes to people taking personal responsibility for their actions. One place where the debate over personal responsibility has been taking place is within African-American communities. For instance, does talk about racism's impact on young black men diminish their taking personal responsibility for their actions? Or does emphasizing their personal responsibility dismiss the harmful, pervasive effects of racism they must deal with? It's fair to say that in the Catholic community itself, as Dr. Menninger pointed out, personal sin has been less emphasized since the late 1960s than it was before then. Is this a good or bad thing? Has it led to people taking less responsibility for their actions?

In popular imagination there is still something known as "Catholic guilt," as if Catholics have a greater sense of debilitating guilt than other people. That might partially account for the de-emphasis on sin among Catholics in recent decades. The Redemptorist order of priests even has a website, "Scrupulous Anonymous," to help Catholics deal with excessive guilt feelings. St. Paul reminds us to keep sin in proper perspective: sin abounds, so don't ignore it; but grace abounds even more. Don't overlook the pervasive power of sin, but recognize that Christ's sacrificial love is greater.

Do you believe that Dr. Menninger's thesis is true today, that we Americans don't emphasize sin enough, which leads to people not taking personal responsibility for their lives? Should schools avoid discussion of sinfulness in society because it might upset children and ban books such as *To Kill a*

Mockingbird that might make them upset about the history of race relations in the United States?

In 1997 a book titled *The Race Card* declared that black people should stop blaming racism for their problems ("playing the race card") and instead emphasize personal responsibility. What do you understand that to mean? Do you agree? Is there a danger to emphasizing personal responsibility over socially-embedded evils, such as racism, and vice versa? Explain.

Is emphasizing personal responsibility and downplaying the harmful effects of racism "blaming the victim"? Read Rev. Michael Eric Dyson's suggestions about addressing racism directed to white people in his 2017 book *Tears We Cannot Stop.*

If you had children, how would you address sin and personal responsibility?

What about the Devil?

In the Gospels, when Jesus talks about sin it is almost always in terms of forgiveness. "Go, your sins are forgiven" is the constant refrain from Jesus in his encounters with people in need of healing. However, Jesus also had many confrontations with demons. Whether people of his time understood them to be persons or personifications, the crux of the message is that Jesus conquered the powers of darkness: "Victory over the 'prince of this world' was won once for all at the Hour when Jesus freely gave himself up to death to give us his life" (*Catechism*, #2853). Catholic Tradition reminds us that the power of evil in the world must not be minimized—watch any evening news broadcast if you need a reminder of that. However, the Christian message is "good news" because Christ's total self-giving won a resounding victory over evil in whatever form.

The Hebrew word for Satan means "adversary." **Satan** is against us, our adversary; Christ is for us, our advocate. Who wins that battle? The Christian message is clear about where victory lies. If you want an account of the battle between Christ and the forces of evil filled with fantastic imagery, read the last book of the Bible, the book of Revelation. If you have a tendency to let such stories filter into your dream life, don't read it. You will start counting days (Have we reached "a thousand years" yet?) and imagining multiheaded beasts and dragons. A story from the life of Saint Anthony of Egypt (third and fourth centuries CE) illustrates the Christian message well. Anthony spent most of his long life alone in the desert, so he had few distractions from dealing with harsh realities, including evil, face to face. One day Satan came knocking at Anthony's door. Satan asked Anthony why people feared him so much. Didn't they know that he, Satan, had become weak because of Christ? Satan had no sooner spoken Christ's name than he vanished. The mere mention of Christ's name—even spoken by Satan himself!—caused Satan to vanish. The encounter with Satan that day led Anthony to realize that his focus should be on the selfless sacrifice of Christ; Satan himself knows that he is powerless against it.

Another biblical image of the powers of evil is "the prince of lies" or "the deceiver." When Jesus alerts his followers that he will go down to Jerusalem, where he will suffer and die, his friend Peter takes Jesus aside and says, "This must never happen." Jesus replies, "Get behind me, Satan! You are a stumbling-block to me; for you are setting your mind not on divine things but on human things" (Matthew 16:22–23). Jesus did not mean that Peter was literally Satan at that moment, but that when we miss viewing things from a divine perspective, we are deceiving ourselves. Even today we can get so caught up in deceptions that we miss underlying truth. For instance, we can miss the truth that we are one, fragile community on earth and deceive ourselves into believing that we should look out only for our narrow self-interest.

> There is no fear in love, but perfect love casts out fear.
>
> 1 John 4:18

What examples of evil today come to mind? How do you think someone steeped in the message of Jesus and Catholic teaching would look upon the evil present in the world?

Name some ways Christians might deceive themselves and miss the fundamental Christian message.

Edmond Burke famously said, "The only thing necessary for evil to triumph is for good people to do nothing." What does he mean? Give examples to illustrate this maxim.

Joseph Conrad wrote, "The belief in a supernatural source of evil is not necessary; men alone are quite capable of every wickedness." What does he mean? Do you agree or disagree with his observation?

Buddhists talk about encountering demons and "hungry ghosts" when we turn our gaze inward in pursuit of enlightenment. What might demons and hungry ghosts be like in your own internal struggles? Might the Catholic practice of confession help?

> Silence in the face of evil is itself evil. ... Not to speak is to speak. Not to act is to act.
>
> Dietrich Bonhoeffer

II. Virtue and Character

Developing Good Character: The Seven Principal Christian Virtues

> Who can be wise, amaz'd, temperate and furious,
> Loyal and neutral, in a moment? No man.
>
> William Shakespeare, "Macbeth"

How we respond when faced with a moral decision is greatly influenced by values and character traits that have been nurtured within us our entire lives. If we notice that a store clerk gave us five dollars too much change, what we do in that split-second decision is largely influenced by what we bring to the situation beforehand. In Catholic Tradition, good qualities ingrained within us are known as *virtues*. The *Catechism* calls virtue a firm disposition and tendency to do what is good (#1803). We don't face moral dilemmas that come our way as if for the first time. We bring to them a whole history of thinking about consequences, making choices, deciding right from wrong, and being concerned about more than ourselves. Thomas Groome describes the dynamic of virtue formation in these simple terms: "We become truthful by telling and living the truth; we become kind and loving by doing acts of kindness and love; and so on" (*What Makes Education Catholic*, p. 75). Who we are is shaped at least in part by what we do;

what we do is largely determined by who we are. The decisions we make today reveal our character and also shape it.

Virtues are habitual—good habits developed through our own efforts, but actually gifts from God. (Talk to an alcoholic struggling to remain sober. It takes great effort, but that person also recognizes that a Higher Power is behind the effort.) The Latin root of the word virtue means strength, power, and courage. The composite of our virtues makes up our *character*. Virtues are character strengths that come into play as we engage with others in our daily lives.

Despite the constant presence of evil, fourteen-year-old Anne Frank wrote: "Human goodness does not lie in wealth or power, but in character and goodness."

The Seven Principal Virtues

Catholic Tradition identifies seven principal virtues: the three theological virtues, faith, hope, and love; and four cardinal virtues: prudence, justice, fortitude, and temperance.

    Three Theological Virtues
        Faith
        Hope
        Love/Charity

Four Cardinal Virtues
- Prudence
- Justice
- Fortitude
- Temperance

Virtues are intertwined and together shape good character in a person. Love stirs someone to make a positive difference in other people's lives, which would make no sense unless that person had hope that what they did would make a difference. That truly takes an act of faith, but it is grounded in a belief that God is working through them. Aquinas views prudence as the most important of the cardinal virtues. It refers to practical wisdom, being capable of making thoughtful decisions as they arise. In its discussion of prudence, the *Catechism* quotes the biblical proverb: "The prudent man looks where he is going" (#1806). The goal of the cardinal virtues is justice, a right ordering of society that promotes the common good (discussed in chapter 13)—that is, working to make the world what God intended it to be. That calls for self-control (temperance) plus courage and constant effort (fortitude).

> You aspire to great things? Begin with little ones.
>
> Saint Augustine

- Explain and give an example to illustrate this quote: "Responsible behavior at one moment in life will prove crucial many years later."
- The virtue of prudence is the ability to "think on our feet," the habit of making good and thoughtful decisions as they arise. Give an example of someone from a book, TV show, or movie who exhibits this character trait.
- What would you include in a list of seven vices and seven virtues for today's world?
- In 2008 the Vatican published a new list of seven deadly sins. Look them up. Make a case that the "sins" listed are or are not relevant today.

III. Modern Catholic Social Teaching

> Action on behalf of justice and participation in the transformation of the world fully appear to us as a constitutive dimension of the preaching of the Gospel, or, in other words, of the Church's mission for the redemption of the human race and its liberation.
>
> *Justice in the World*, World Synod of Catholic Bishops, 1971, #6

Something happened to the Catholic conversation about morality toward the end of the nineteenth century that gave rise to what is known as modern Catholic social teaching. A backdrop to the change is what was happening in Europe and America at the time, specifically the transformation from a predominantly agricultural society to an industrial one. Men with money (capitalists) owned the factories and amassed great fortunes while the proletariat (workers) did all the work and received very little of the rewards. Who worked, in what conditions they worked, how much they would be paid, and what happened when they could no longer work, were all determined by factory owners. In the middle of the century Karl Marx famously criticized this arrangement and made his clarion call: "Workers of the world, unite!" He proposed communal ownership of factories so that everyone would benefit equally, creating a "workers' paradise." In America, the majority of factory workers were Catholic, part of the great influx of poor immigrants from Catholic countries in Europe. Voices arose among Catholic leaders to address the problem.

In 1891, Pope Leo XIII wrote a groundbreaking encyclical called *Rerum Novarum*, "On the Condition of Labor." In it he decried poor conditions in factories and declared that workers have a right to join together to form associations, unions. At the time this position was not universally accepted. For one thing, it diminished the ability of owners to "do the right thing" on their own and take care of their workers. More importantly, it changed the focus of Catholic moral teaching. As Catholic teaching had always asserted, morality has to do with "Do good; avoid evil." Pope Leo was pointing out that factory conditions were often evil and harmful; workers were getting hurt in so many ways beyond their control. Who was to blame for this evil, and what would "doing good" mean in this situation? A realization arose that people were hurting not simply because of the actions of individuals.

Factory owners were often "good people." With industrialization, people were hurting because of the way the system was structured. Sin was not just personal wrongdoing but social sin. In the words of the *Catechism*, "Sins give rise to social situations and institutions that are contrary to the divine goodness" (#1869). The 1891 encyclical opened up a whole new arena of moral inquiry. Ever since then popes have written about social conditions that are sinful and need to be addressed as part of the church's mission.

> God intended the earth and all that it contains for the use of every human being and people.
>
> Vatican Council II, "Constitution on the Church in the Modern World," #69

Social Conditions Can Change

"How are people hurting?" as a starting point for moral discussion did not begin in 1891. It runs throughout the Hebrew scriptures and is a focal point of the teachings of Jesus. Read again the Beatitudes in Matthew, chapter 5, and the Last Judgment scene in Matthew, chapter 25, for examples. Modern Catholic social teaching recognizes that people are hurting not just because of the actions of individuals but also because of the way institutions of a society operate. For instance, individuals can be racist; but now there is also discussion of institutional racism. When the United States Conference of Catholic Bishops declared that "racism is a sin," they didn't simply mean that individual persons with racist attitudes are sinners; they meant that racism in a society and its institutions and policies is sinful. The fact that schools in poorer neighborhoods, often populated by particular minority groups, are in worse conditions than those in neighborhoods where wealthier people live is not caused by one or two mean-spirited people. It's also not something about which we should say, "Well, that's just the way it is. Nothing we can do about it." Inequality in educational opportunities has to do with a society's values, priorities, worldview, tax system, historical developments, and so much more. The quality of education children receive depends largely on where they are born and on the wealth of their parents. The current world economic system relies on people working for wages that do not, or at best just barely, provide for their family's needs. Poorly nourished children don't learn as well as well-fed children. Children who live in neighborhoods where drug use and violence are commonplace do not begin their lives on an equal footing with children who don't.

Modern Catholic social teaching says that such destructive conditions are made by the people of a society, and people can take steps to change those conditions. In other words, morality and the Christian message are "political" in the broad sense of the term. It is not a matter of some people being "less fortunate" and other people being "more fortunate." ("I am so fortunate to have grown up in my wealthy neighborhood with the best-equipped schools and stores nearby filled with healthy food choices. It's a shame that there are children who grow up in rat-infested, crime-filled neighborhoods and go to school without breakfast where textbooks are out of date.") Differences in social conditions are not a matter of luck. Maxims such as "That's just the way it is" and "Everything happens for a reason" can be understood as dangerously fatalistic if they diminish personal responsibility on the part of everyone involved in deciding what society should be. A major concern of Catholic social teaching has always been the common good. Catholic teaching proposes that everyone can and should take steps to ensure that the vast majority of people in a society are surviving and thriving. Praying for "those who are less fortunate" is not enough if it is divorced from working to make societal changes. For example, Ibram X. Kendi points out that it is not enough to say, "I am not a racist." Rather, if we are serious about creating a more equitable society we need to say, "I am antiracist" and actively work against racism in policies and practices. Pope St. John Paul II described modern society's falling short of serving the common good and the need to be active in bringing about change in terms of inequality:

> We are therefore faced with a serious problem of *unequal distribution* of the means of subsistence originally meant for everybody, and thus also an unequal distribution of the benefits deriving from them. And this happens not through the *fault* of the needy people, and even less through a sort of *inevitability* dependent on natural conditions or circumstances as a whole.
>
> *On Social Concern*, #9

In other words, as the world's bishops said in 1971, "Action on behalf of justice is a constitutive dimension of preaching the gospel." Christianity is hollow without it.

> Pope St. John Paul II pointed out that social conditions, for good or ill, don't just happen; they reflect choices people make. One issue where the categories "choice" or "inevitability" regularly surface as part of the conversation is that of gun violence. The United States has by far the greatest number of gun deaths in the world. Whenever a mass shooting occurs, some people call for making changes to gun laws, while others say that we are powerless to do anything about it. ("Guns don't kill people; people do. Bad people will do bad things, and there's not much we can do to stop them other than to get guns in the hands of more people, such as kindergarten teachers.") Name some social ills that are often viewed as inevitable and out of our control. Are there creative responses to them that you would suggest?
>
> Pope St. John Paul II cautioned against seeing inequality as the fault of needy people. He is condemning what is known as blaming the victim, which is expressed in language such as "Rich people work hard and deserve what they have. If poor people don't have what they need, it's their own fault." Do you agree with the pope? Why or why not?
>
> What does it mean to say that Catholic moral teaching is political? Give examples to illustrate what that means.

The Two Feet of Love in Action

The realization that people are hurting or being helped because of societal factors has led to new ways of addressing problems. The charity approach, "haves" helping "have nots," has been called into question as inadequate by Catholic leaders. The operative word for an alternative approach to charity is social justice. The United States Conference of Catholic Bishops talks about "the two feet of love in action." On their website, they describe social justice with a quote from the Compendium of the Social Doctrine of the Church: "Social justice concerns the social, political, and economic aspects and, above all, the structural dimension of problems and their respective solutions" (#201).

According to the United States Conference of Catholic Bishops, charitable works seek to meet the basic needs of individuals. On the other hand, social justice seeks to root out the causes of problems and improve the way society is structured so that people's basic needs are met. These "two feet," or two approaches to dealing with social problems, need explanation.

- Charity concerns itself with addressing the immediate symptoms of problems, while justice looks to identify and address the underlying causes of problems. For example, serving food at a homeless shelter is an act of charity. There are people who are homeless and under bridges who need immediate help. However, feeding them today is like a band-aid that does not address what causes people to end up homeless and unable to provide food for themselves in the first place.

- Charity focuses on individual needs, while justice looks at social structures. In certain settings, a disabled person who uses a wheelchair to get around may need help getting in and out of buildings, bathrooms, and vehicles. On the other hand, structural changes can make buildings, bathrooms, and vehicles more wheelchair accessible. Such change would call for financial investment, thoughtful planning, and new laws to make it possible for people with disabilities to be less dependent on others. It would call for political action.

- Charity provides direct service to bring about temporary results, while justice seeks long-term and if possible permanent change. After-school tutoring of children in poor schools is a wonderful act of charity. Some children in need would benefit, but unfortunately others would be left out. Lobbying government officials to provide more funding so that all children in such schools receive better services during the school day itself is aimed at creating a more long-term solution.

- Charity means "haves" helping "have nots." Justice seeks to create a society in which "haves" and "have nots" work together. In other words, justice aims to bring about empowerment. The transformation from a "power over" to a "power with" model was behind what Pope Leo had in mind when he said factory workers had a right to form associations independent of control by factory owners. He believed that workers had a right to have input into working conditions. More recently, Pope John Paul described this move toward empowerment in terms of what he called "solidarity."

- Charity does not aim to bring about a change in the way a society is structured, while justice seeks to bring about changes to social structures and institutions.

Since the advent of modern Catholic social teaching, the church has advocated a role for both of these approaches. Catholic-affiliated organizations have been at the forefront of providing charitable help to people who have immediate needs, such as running homeless shelters and soup kitchens, getting Catholic school children involved in tutoring programs, making used furniture and clothing available for low-income shoppers at thrift stores and parish centers, and having schools and parishes run food and clothing drives. The church also sponsors organizations dedicated to social justice. However, some Catholics have questioned the charity approach to addressing social ills. For instance, a leading voice for social justice in the early twentieth century, the American Father John Ryan, wrote that charity was a "poison" if it distracted from social-justice reforms. In other words, people can feel good about helping "those poor people" by donating some old clothing they no longer want or contributing to a Thanksgiving food drive. Such charitable works don't get to the root of a problem and don't lead to long-term solutions. They may temporarily help people in need, but they don't empower them. Modern Catholic social teaching reminds us that putting all of our efforts into charitable works can distract us from working to bring about changes in the ways society is structured. Without social justice, unequal power distribution within society remains the same, even though "haves" might feel good about themselves for helping others, and "have nots" would feel some relief from having one more meal in them and a warmer blanket for sleeping outdoors in the cold.

The standard Catholic position on helping people has been the combination of charity and justice. Some situations call for charity. If a neighbor gets sick and can't work for a period of time, it would certainly be a good idea for neighbors to get together and bring meals to tide the family over. However, charity is not the solution to instituting a living wage for all people who work. That's where the intense work of helping people gets political. The hope expressed at Vatican Council II was that people would be "inspired by charity" to engage in the work of justice. That is, a spirit of charity is not meant to take the place of working for social change but to be a starting point for addressing why people are in need of charity in the first place.

Which social problems do you think are best addressed by a charity approach? Which by a social justice approach? What problems can be addressed through a combination of both?

Name three ways that people are hurting in the world today. Identify possible underlying causes for these problems, ones rooted in the way our society functions.

Explain what Michael E. Lee means by the following statement (*National Catholic Reporter*, Jan. 7–20, 2022): "If there is one thing we have learned in the last few years, it is that the great problems that we face, such as racism, poverty and the climate crisis, are structural in nature. They have long histories and are embedded socially in ways that are often masked in day-to-day life." Do you agree with his assessment?

How can social systems (for example, health care, education, and criminal justice systems) help or hurt people because of the way they function?

What are some "social sins" that exist today? Besides changing individual behaviors, what are societal changes that could make a difference in alleviating these "sins" ingrained in society?

The term "institutional racism" is used today to name ways people of certain races are hurting because of policies and structures in our society. Make a case that institutional racism, sexism, and classism does or does not exist in our society.

Key Themes in Catholic Social Teaching

> The living God, the Lord whom we worship, is the God of the poor.
>
> Catholic Bishops of Appalachia,
> "This Land Is Home to Me," Part II

In 1998, the United States Conference of Catholic Bishops identified seven principles and themes in Catholic social teaching. The principles are meant to serve as guideposts for Catholic action in the world today.

1. Life and dignity of the human person
2. Call to family, community, and participation
3. Rights and responsibilities
4. Option for the poor and vulnerable
5. The dignity of work and the rights of workers
6. Solidarity
7. Care for God's creation

The bishops consider these principles to be interconnected. For example, people lack dignity if they are not participating responsibly on an equal footing with other people. An important source of human dignity is engaging in work and being recognized as an important member in solidarity with all other people in society. Because the life and dignity of all people are essential, it follows that the poorest and most vulnerable members of society should be of special concern since their life and dignity are most precarious. Concern for nonhuman creation is also important because of its vulnerability and our solidarity with it.

> Since the late 1800s, the Catholic Church has been a strong advocate for recognizing the dignity of work. Pope St. John Paul II in particular expressed strongly that creation is ongoing and that one important way human beings continue the work of creation is through their own work. Think about people you have encountered in the past week in their capacity as workers. Did you sense that they had a feeling of

personal dignity and of contributing to society in the work they were doing? Did you have a sense of your solidarity with them in the work they were doing? Did you express your appreciation for the work they were doing? If you work, do you experience it as contributing to the common good in some way? Discuss your observations.

Access the website for the following two Catholic Church–sponsored organizations and describe the approach they take to addressing helping people in need: Catholic Campaign for Human Development and Catholic Relief Services.

Personal and Social Morality in Our Lives

Catholic morality brings Christ and his vision into the heart of human life. It looks at both the individual and societal dimensions of human life. In both, the church and its members seek to determine how to live his message and to transform the world into the image of the body of Christ. Certain themes recur throughout Catholic moral teaching, which resonate with the message of Jesus himself—human solidarity, special concern for people who are poor or suffering, and the dignity of all people. The dynamic of Catholic morality is that, when people are found hurting, they pray to God seeking divine help but also ask themselves, *What can I do to help? What is my responsibility?* That is, Catholic morality involves not just avoiding evil but also replacing it with good on both personal and social levels.

Chapter Review

1. What is the difference between *sin* as a general term and *sins* as specific actions or inactions?
2. Describe two images of sin found in scripture.
3. Protestants tend to emphasize the overall sinfulness of the human condition while Catholics also talk about specific sins. Why?
4. What do the life story of Jesus and his message say about the power of evil?
5. What qualities are associated with Satan in scripture?

6. What is the role of virtue in Catholic morality?
7. What are the three theological virtues and the four cardinal virtues?
8. What transformation in European society led to the origins of modern Catholic social teaching?
9. What is *Rerum Novarum*? How did it transform the Catholic perspectives on morality?
10. What is *social sin*? How is it different from personal sin?
11. What are the differences between the "two feet of love in action" proposed by the United States Conference of Catholic Bishops?
12. What are the seven key themes of Catholic social teaching?

For Further Study

Athanasius. *The Life of Antony of Egypt* (A Paraphrase by Albert Haase, OFM). IVP Books, 2012. St. Athanasius wrote a biography of the saint who lived in the Egyptian desert during most of his long life. He tells the story of Antony's encounter with Satan, in which "the very sound of the name of the Savior inflicted upon Satan such a severe sting that he immediately vanished."

Herman E. Daly and John B. Cobb Jr. *For the Common Good: Redirecting the Economy Toward Community, the Environment, and a Sustainable Future*. Beacon Press, 1989. What does a barrel of oil or plastic bag use cost? The authors explore questions such as these to call for recognizing the true human cost of economic decision-making, for example, using oil costs increased air pollution leading to worsening asthma attacks among children.

Edward P. DeBerri and James E. Hug, with Peter J. Henriot and Michael I. Schultheis. *Catholic Social Teaching: Our Best Kept Secret*. Orbis Books, 2004. Outlines major official church documents on justice and peace followed by an explanation of the key contributions to Catholic social thought in each document.

Michael Eric Dyson, *Tears We Cannot Stop*. St. Martin's Press, 2017. Lays out his thesis in the first sentence: "America is in trouble, and a lot of that trouble—perhaps most of it—has to do with race." Explores what the US Catholic Bishops have called the social sin of racism and offers suggestions specifically to white Americans about what they can do about it.

Pope Francis. *Laudato Si'* ("On Care for Our Common Home"). Our Sunday Visitor, 2015. Addresses a key concern expressed by Pope Francis from the beginning of his papacy. He urges people to see themselves as members of one world and to come up with a common plan to address environmental problems.

Joe Holland and Peter Henriot, SJ. *Social Analysis: Linking Faith and Justice,* Revised and enlarged edition. Dove Communications and Orbis Books, 1984. Represents an early examination of a social analysis approach to addressing how people are hurting in a society, identifying root causes and long-term solutions to problems.

Ibram X. Kendi. *How to Be an Antiracist.* One World, 2019. Points out that not engaging in racist behavior is not sufficient for addressing racism. To be against racism means to take action to overcome racism in social policies and practices.

Jacqueline Novogratz. *The Blue Sweater: Bridging the Gap Between Rich and Poor in an Interconnected World.* Rodale Books, 2009. A Catholic high-school girl donates her blue sweater to Goodwill. Years later, working in Africa for a major banking firm, she finds a woman wearing the very same sweater. She decides to start an organization that addresses global poverty through a middle way between venture capitalism and traditional charity.

Pontifical Council for Justice and Peace. *Compendium on the Social Doctrine of the Church.* USCCB Publishing, 2005. A comprehensive resource that combines pertinent passages from church documents on topics related to justice and peace.

Brandon Vogt. *Saints and Social Justice: A Guide to Changing the World.* Our Sunday Visitor Publishing, 2014. A study of fourteen Catholic saints and how their life and work represented Catholic social teaching.

Chapter 13
Catholicism Today

Catholicism today is an anomaly. It continues to speak of angels and miracles at a time when those notions are viewed more as science fiction than reality. It has a system of governance and a liturgical style that would be more at home in the Middle Ages than in the modern world. Many of its churches, such as St. Patrick's Cathedral in New York City, look antique next to modern skyscrapers and office complexes. It tells people they have a moral responsibility to care for strangers in need when the modern spirit so often makes looking out for one's own benefit, and even "greed is good," priorities over the common good. It advocates measuring the value of persons and other living things based not on their monetary worth but on their God-given dignity. It proclaims itself as home to the holy but must address egregious sinfulness among its own members. This chapter looks at some trends taking place in Catholicism today, especially as manifest in the words and actions of Pope Francis. He has dedicated his papacy to modeling the church as a vital presence in the world, a church with a beating heart and not just an intriguing past. The Catholic worldview is both the same and ever developing, holding fast to Jesus and the gospel while applying its message to today.

What stories or images come to mind when you think about Catholicism today?

What do you know about the current pope and his message to the world?

I. Pope Francis, Model of Catholicism Today

The Church is called to come out from itself and to go to the peripheries, not just the geographical but also the existential peripheries: those of the mystery of sin, of suffering, of injustice, of ignorance and lack of religion, those of thought and those of every kind of misery.

Jorge Bergolio, Address to fellow cardinals
prior to his election as Pope Francis

In 2013, one hundred and fifteen men were called upon to elect a new pope because the previous one, Pope Benedict XVI, surprisingly resigned from the position. These men, the cardinals of the church, elected one of their own from Argentina, Cardinal Jorge Bergoglio. As it became clear that he was going to be elected, a cardinal from Brazil sitting next to him whispered in his ear, "Don't forget the poor." When asked what name he would take as pope, he replied: "I take the name Francis, in honor of St. Francis of Assisi." No saint is more closely associated with those who are poor than St. Francis, whose nickname was Il Poverello, "little poor man." Bergoglio, Pope Francis, was well aware of both his poverty and his littleness. He is the first non-European pope in almost thirteen hundred years. He comes from the Southern Hemisphere and an area of the world not known to be at the center of wealth or power. When he addressed the crowd gathered to greet him after being named pope, he jokingly told them, "My brother cardinals have gone to the end of the earth" to "give Rome a bishop." (The pope is the Bishop of Rome.) Francis was also the first member of the Jesuit order to be pope. Before beginning his training for the priesthood, he had worked as a bouncer and a janitor. The cardinals that day clearly understood that their decision to elect this outsider from the periphery was a recognition that Catholicism needed to expand its worldview, as Vatican Council II had called for a half-century earlier. As the future Pope Francis himself said, "I sometimes think that Jesus is knocking from the inside, for us to let him out."

Pope Francis came from the margins, geographically and in many ways theologically as well. All popes—indeed, all Christians—are at least nominally concerned about those who are poor. However, Pope Francis has made concern for people on the margins of society the hallmark of his papacy. In his encyclical *The Joy of the Gospel*, he says, "Each individual Christian and every community is called to be an instrument of God for the liberation and promotion of the poor, and for enabling them to be fully a part of society. This demands that we be docile and attentive to the cry of the poor and to come to their aid" (#187).

As a model of those who have traditionally been on the periphery of power and privilege, Pope Francis represents trends that exist in the church itself, both globally and in the United States. Latin America has the largest share of the world's Catholics, and the continent of Africa has seen much growth in the number of Catholics who live there. In the United States, people from Hispanic backgrounds are a growing percentage of the population overall, and Catholics are more likely to be Hispanic than other Americans are. Over one in four Catholics in the US are foreign-born, most of those from Latin American countries. The Catholic Church today is increasingly a church of those people who are on the periphery, so it is reasonable that its pope should be from the periphery as well. Since becoming pope, Francis has named an unusually large number of cardinals, men responsible for advising the pope and electing the next pope, from poor and marginal countries. He says, "I've always thought that the world looks clearer from the periphery. ... You have to make for the margins to find a new future. ... To embrace the margins is to expand our horizons, for we see more clearly and broadly from the edges of society" (*Let Us Dream*, 2020, pp. 11, 126).

Pope Francis is from Argentina and the first pope from South America.

A look back reveals that for much of American history, Catholics were unwelcome and looked down upon by nativists who wanted to preserve American identity; from a nativist perspective, Catholics and most other immigrants came from the social, economic, and religious periphery and were viewed as a threat. (According to dictionary.com, ***nativism*** is "the policy of protecting the interests of native inhabitants against those of immigrants.") That dislike of Catholics largely changed in the middle of the last century, following World War II. However, more recently some Americans are fearful of and even feel threatened by the influx of immigrants, most of whom are from Latin America and Catholic. The thinking behind this new version of nativism is that Western civilization, and by extension Christianity, is under threat. In this view, American culture is the child of European Protestant Christianity, and that culture is being undermined from the outside by non-European immigrants and from the inside by secular humanism. Untainted America is white, Anglo-Saxon, and Protestant (WASP). Any additions to this national identity are unwanted dilutions. Renowned historian W. E. B. DuBois countered this understanding of the American identity in his 1920s book commissioned by the Catholic organization the Knights of Columbus:

> It is high time that this course of our thinking should be changed. America is conglomerate. This is at once her problem and her glory—perhaps her sole and greatest reason for being. Her physical foundation is not English, and while it is primarily it is not exclusively European. It represents peculiarly a coming together of the peoples of the world. (*The Gift of Black Folk*, 1924, page vii)

A worldwide phenomenon that shares the same sentiments as nativism is what is called ***populism***, which Pope Francis views as a distortion of Christianity. He sees it as built on fear and hatred, which in turn leads to an increase in fear and hatred. In *Let Us Dream* he writes:

> The heart of Christianity is God's love for all peoples and our love for our neighbors, especially those in need. To reject a struggling migrant, whatever his or her religious belief, out of fear of diluting "Christian" culture is grotesquely to misrepresent both Christianity and culture. Migration is not a threat to Christianity except in the minds of those who benefit from claiming it is. (p. 119)

Pope Francis's first pastoral visit outside of Rome was to the island of Lampedusa, a major entry point of migrants fleeing the poverty of Africa in hopes of finding work in Europe. The pope placed a garland of flowers into the sea to commemorate all those who had died in their attempt to find a better life. He decried indifference to the plight of migrants throughout the world. Catholicism today is more and more a church of the periphery, and Pope Francis embodies that realization.

Were the teachings of Jesus radically different from the dominant worldview of the time? What would be his attitude toward the dominant worldview of today and of people and ideas from the periphery?

Research the state of migrants in the world today. What are the causes of recent increases in migration in the world today?

Look up articles on "nativism today" and "Catholicism and nativism." Discuss the state of nativism today and the experience of Catholics vis-à-vis nativism today and during American history.

Read about "populism" in the world today. Is populism a defense of Christianity or a distortion of it?

Discuss: The recent influx of non-Christians into predominantly Christian countries is a threat to Christianity and the values of "Western culture."

When a pope visits a country, he often participates in events that have symbolic significance. When visiting the United States, the pope went to a prison and spoke to the men who were imprisoned there. What other people and places might a pope visit who wanted to represent the message of Jesus? Find out if there is a Catholic presence of some kind already in these places.

Pope Francis and Science

Pope Francis did not enter his training for the priesthood immediately upon entering adulthood. For a period of time, he studied chemistry and worked as a lab technician. Later, as a Jesuit, he taught psychology. In other words, he has a background in both science and theology. His first public Mass as pope took place on March 19, 2013, the feast of St. Joseph. In his homily he spoke about St. Joseph as the protector of the Holy Family. He reminded Christians that they too are called upon to be protectors of the most vulnerable. Who are the most vulnerable today? For one, people who are poor—again, those on the margins. However, he extends the circle of concern to include not only members of the human community but of the broader family of nature. Human beings are called by God to be protectors of all the vulnerable family members who make up the natural world. He later wrote an encyclical on the environment, *Laudato Si'*, that blends scientific analysis with theological insights. At the time, some commentators said that the pope should "leave science to the scientists" and not talk about such worldly concerns, as if the supernatural and the natural, the seen and the unseen, are somehow unrelated. However, the pope was following in a long Catholic tradition of applying the teachings of Jesus to problems facing people, even though those problems might be "scientific," "economic," or "political." The church has a number of organizations that address issues where science and religion intersect, such as the Pontifical Academy of Life and the Pontifical Academy of Science. There is even a papal astronomer, director of the Vatican Observatory.

One recent issue that the church has been called upon to address is the COVID-19 crisis. In the midst of the crisis, Pope Francis referred to vaccines against the virus as both a grace from God and the result of human ingenuity. On the plane returning to Rome following a trip to Slovakia and Hungary in September 2021, he told reporters that getting vaccinated was an "act of love" and that "humanity has a history of friendship with vaccines." At the time, some people even within the church were against receiving the vaccine.

In its incarnational and sacramental worldview, Catholicism proclaims the human as holy and the rest of nature as a manifestation of divine presence that deserves our care and respect. Although science is not the only lens by which to understand humanity, scientific discoveries should not be divorced from the work of the church, which is in constant search of the holy. Catholicism points out that science can help us address questions such as when human life begins that are not answered solely by science or even philosophy. (See the 1974 "Vatican Declaration on Procured Abortion.") What about the question of human cloning? If it were scientifically possible, would it be morally acceptable? In 1987, a Vatican Instruction called *Donum Vitae* addressed developments in reproductive technologies taking place at the time. It makes the case that something being scientifically possible does not make it a good thing to do. Catholic theology is not antiscience; rather, it enters into the questions and challenges facing humanity and seeks to bring the light of Christ and the wisdom of Catholic Tradition to the problems of the day. At the same time, it learns from the ever-expanding knowledge provided by science. As Vatican Council II said, "The joys and the hopes, the griefs and the anxieties of the men of this age, especially those who are poor or in any way afflicted, these are the joys and hopes, the griefs and anxieties of the followers of Christ. Indeed, nothing genuinely human fails to raise an echo in their hearts" (*Gaudium et Spes*, #1). From the time of Christ, Catholicism has set course to be a voice for all humanity; and following the leadership of Pope Francis, the church continues in that mission.

What would a church look like if it were faithful to the message of Jesus and addressed the human problems of today? What problems should Catholicism be particularly concerned about?

Pope Benedict XVI, who was pope before Pope Francis, took steps to make the Vatican the "greenest nation on earth" by installing solar panels and making other changes that reduce carbon emissions. Read about Catholic organizations for the environment. What kind of work do they do? How do they blend scientific and spiritual perspectives?

Do you believe that insights from science, such as from evolutionary biology and Einstein's theory of relativity, can help people in their spiritual quest? If so, how?

"There Is No Catholic God."

> I believe in God—not in a Catholic God; there is no Catholic God. There is God, and I believe in Jesus Christ, his incarnation. Jesus is my teacher and my pastor, but God, the Father, Abba, is the light and the Creator.
>
> Pope Francis, in a 2013 interview with
Italian journalist Eugenio Scalfari

Pope Francis has gained a reputation for making statements that turn heads, such as saying that "there is no Catholic God." Upon closer examination, his "controversial" statements actually reflect Catholic tradition and common sense. God is the God of all people. The Bible itself makes that case in the book of Jonah; in the actions of Jesus, who praised the faith of a non-Jewish Roman centurion and a Samaritan woman; and in the message of St. Paul to the people of Athens who worshiped "the unknown god." Vatican Council II addressed this question in particular in its "Declaration on the Relation of the Church to Non-Christian Religions." At the very beginning the document declares, "One is the community of all peoples" and that today more than ever people are being drawn together. People who practice other religions are not the enemy, as they had at times been perceived throughout history. "The Catholic Church rejects nothing that is true and holy in these religions. She regards with sincere reverence those ways of conduct and life, those precepts and teachings which, though differing in many aspects from the ones she holds and sets forth, nevertheless often reflect a ray of that Truth which enlightens all men" (#2).

Decades ago, Pope St. John Paul II embodied this message when he became the first pope in centuries to visit a Muslim mosque and a Jewish synagogue. He met with the Dalai Lama, head of Tibetan Buddhists, and Rev. Billy Graham, a leader of American Evangelicals. He even referred to himself and Graham as "kindred spirits." In his 2008 visit to the United States, Pope Benedict XVI included a meeting with members of other religions. He said approvingly, "Today, in classrooms throughout the country, young Christians, Jews, Muslims, Hindus, Buddhists, and indeed children of all religions sit side-by-side, learning with one another and from one another." Catholics attending prayer services where representatives of different religions preside has become commonplace, and Catholic organizations join together with other organizations working to promote peace and to assist people in need.

Louis Massignon's Incarnational Theology

When Vatican Council II and later popes spoke of other religions in a positive light, it did not represent a radical departure from sentiments that were brewing in the church before them. One person who influenced Vatican Council II and Pope St. Paul VI, the pope who oversaw most of the council proceedings, was **Louis Massignon** (1883–1962), a French Catholic layman who lived most of his life focused on the suffering of both Christians and Muslims in Muslim-dominant lands. He found in traditional Catholic theology and imagery the basis for an appreciation of Islam and compassion for Muslims who during his lifetime often suffered at the hands of non-Muslim Europeans. (At the time, most areas of Northern Africa and the Middle East were colonies of European nations, especially England and France.) With a friend he formed a group, the ***Badaliya Movement***, blessed by Pope Pius XI in 1934, whose purpose was to explore how to live as Christians alongside Muslims in a fruitful, compassionate way—what he would consider a Christlike way. Massignon was a Third Order Franciscan, meaning that he was a layperson dedicated to the ideals of St. Francis of Assisi, who himself had met with a Muslim leader during the time of the Crusades. Massignon wrote annual letters to the members of the group encouraging them in this work. In those letters we find how popular Catholic piety about Jesus and Mary, especially the concept of Incarnation, inspires Christians to find the proper approach to the tensions existing between Muslims and the Western world that claims affiliation with Christianity.

For Christians, Incarnation refers to the doctrine that Jesus was the human embodiment of God. But should that central belief of Christianity be expressed solely in the past tense, as if relegated to the vaults of history and not relevant to our own lives or the contemporary world? Louis Massignon spoke of Incarnation in vibrant, dynamic terms. For him, the mystery of the Incarnation was embodied in the concrete circumstances in which he and other Christians found themselves from the 1930s through the early 1960s when he died. Massignon explored what the Incarnation meant in the lands where the majority populations were Muslim but were often oppressed or lacked power equivalent to their numbers. To complicate matters even further, small groups of Christians lived in communities surrounded by a Muslim majority, and they often suffered at the hands of Muslims. If Incarnation was in fact a living reality, then what exactly did it mean in the circumstances in which Massignon chose to live? How were Christians to live a Christlike life in mid-twentieth century Egypt or Algeria or Arabia? Massignon pointed out that if Christ is present in the poor among us, as Jesus says in the Gospel of Matthew, then Christ is surely present in oppressed Muslims who at the time lived under European colonialism. This radical understanding of Incarnation led

Massignon to form a community of Christians, the Badaliya Movement, some of whom willingly substituted themselves as an Incarnate presence within Muslim communities. (The future Pope St. Paul VI was a member of Massignon's group and received his mailings.)

Massignon didn't limit his understanding of Incarnation to refer to Christians alone. His understanding of Christianity led him to realize that Muslims, who were often oppressed, lacking basic human rights, and enduring hardships, were also an embodiment of Christ's presence. The poor Christ is present in the poor, not just the Catholic poor. Although he died as Vatican Council II was just beginning, Massignon's theology influenced the perspective on other religions expressed at the council and later espoused by popes ever since.

Discuss: Openness to the "rays of truth" in other religions can strengthen one's own faith or lead to a watering down of one's faith. How might someone maintain a balance between learning from other religions and remaining faithful to one's own?

Watch the 2011 film, *Of Gods and Men*, about a group of Catholic monks who lived among poor Muslims in Algeria and were killed rather than leave this place where they found God's presence.

Make a case that it would or would not be acceptable for a Catholic to attend a Jewish Seder meal on Passover, practice Hindu yoga or Buddhist meditation, or join friends at a nondenominational Christian service.

II. Clergy Abuse and Misuse of Power

Clergy Sexual Abuse

Sin is an abuse of our God-given powers to do good.

St. Basil, in John Portmann, *A History of Sin*

A few years ago, a man called his local parish priest and said, "Did you read the paper today? A priest in New England was just arrested for stealing thousands of dollars from his parish to buy a condominium in

Florida that he shares with his partner with whom he spends lengthy vacations. What do you think of that?" His parish priest replied without pausing, "Sometimes it is embarrassing to call yourself Catholic, isn't it?" If you kept up with the news over the past few decades, stories about some Catholic priests and bishops have been more than embarrassing; they have been maddening. The trail of sin, deceit, and harm has been a long one. What could be worse than abusing children? Accounts of Catholic clergy sexually abusing young boys and, at times, young girls, have been too numerous to ignore. Yet, making matters worse, for decades some bishops at times ignored the problem or tried to cover it up. The most innocent interpretation of their inaction is that they wanted to avoid any public recognition of such hurtful realities for fear that "the church" would be blamed and its image as a holy institution would be tarnished. They intended to prevent scandal, upsetting and confusing Catholics who put their faith in the church, that publicly airing the abuse would cause. Therefore, in some cases, ostrich-like, they stuck their heads in the sand, hoping the problem would magically go away. However, a more insidious motive was also at work. Some bishops dismissed the accusations of the victims, further victimizing them, and instead tried to protect their fellow priests. They admonished priest-abusers to stop doing what they were doing and then transferred them to a new setting where they often continued their abusive patterns.

Over the past thirty years, extensive reports of sexual abuse of minors by priests and church workers came from one diocese after another, one country after another. For example, the *New York Times* reported on what an independent commission found in France, that over 200,000 minors there were sexually abused during the previous seventy years. The actual number is almost certainly higher. The report also described how church leaders kept victims from publicly telling their stories and did not report abusing clergy to civil authorities or discipline them for their offenses. The report found that 2,900 members of the French Catholic clergy abused minors, and an additional thousand nonordained church workers also perpetrated abuse ("Over 200,000 Minors Abused by Clergy in France Since 1950, Report Estimates," *New York Times*, October 5, 2021). A year earlier, the *Times* also reported that over twenty dioceses in the United States sued for bankruptcy after paying out large settlements to victims of abuse.

It would be an insult and a disservice to victims of sexual abuse if this horrendous reality were overlooked or dismissed in any discussion of Catholicism today. The stories of victims of abuse by priests and other church workers are heart-wrenching. It is a wound that they will carry with them throughout their lives. It colors their sense of self and affects every relationship they attempt to enter into. Far too many victims engage in self-destructive behavior and battle constantly to maintain some semblance of a happy and fruitful life. The term PTSD has been applied to what many victims must deal with heroically. So many questions surround the church today in relationship to the horrors of this part of its reality. How effective and appropriate has the response of church leaders been? Are there root causes within the very structure of the church that contributed to the problem? What would effective and appropriate change look like? Finally, why have the majority of Catholics not left the church because of it?

A 2019 Pew Research Center survey found that "one-quarter of US Catholics say they have scaled back Mass attendance (27 percent) or reduced the amount of money they donate to their parish (26 percent) in response to the recent reports of sexual abuse and misconduct. Fewer (18 percent) say they have expressed support to the priests at their parish." That means that, while many Catholics walked away from the church and stated that clergy sexual abuse is what caused their departure, most Catholics did not leave. A Pontifical Commission for the Protection of Minors now exists at the Vatican. In September 2021, Pope Francis addressed church leaders and the commission, stating:

> The wellbeing of victims [must] not be sidelined in favor of the misguided concern for the reputation of the institutional Church. Rather, only by facing the truth of these evil practices and of humbly seeking pardon from victims and survivors will the Church find its way to a place where it can be relied upon once again as a place of welcome and safety for those in need. Our expressions of sorrow must be converted into concrete pathways of reform to both prevent further abuse and to give confidence to others that our efforts will bring about real and reliable change.

Pope Francis and other leaders of the institutional church continue to struggle to come to grips with the realization that one way the suffering Christ is present in the world today is in the victims of abuse who are members of the church. In the Beatitudes, Jesus called "blessed" those who are mistreated, the "little ones" suffering at the hands of any who would take advantage of their powerlessness. Those members of the church—that is, victims of abuse, who continue to suffer because of the actions of others in the church, face a great challenge along with all those who seek meaning and hope in Catholicism today.

Watch the TED talk by Gerard J. McGlone, "Finding the Words ... Transforming Trauma," which emphasizes putting victims first in any discussion about abuse. His presentation ends with these words: "There is no greater agony than an untold story within you." What suggestions does McGlone make for addressing sexual abuse within the church?

Much discussion is taking place in the Catholic Church about what the root causes of sexual abuse in the church are and what can be done about it. After the release of a report on clergy abuse in Germany, Catholic leaders there identified four areas that need to be examined if serious reforms are to take place: distribution of power, the place of women in the church, the priesthood today, and sexual morality. (See "As German Synodal Assembly begins, lay Catholics express anger at Vatican," [National Catholic Reporter, October 1, 2021]). Read reports about the causes of and solutions to the problem and discuss how church leaders and all Catholics might address it.

Read Matthew 18:2–6, where Jesus has strong words calling for the protection of children. How would you describe the message of Jesus about children?

An October 2022 study of US Catholic priests found that, while they overwhelmingly supported measures to combat sex abuse, the vast majority also feared being falsely accused and not supported by their bishop against such accusations. What measures would you recommend to balance this "guilty until proven innocent" mentality with concern for child safety?

Clericalism

> Clericalism ... gradually extinguishes the prophetic flame to which the entire Church is called to bear witness in the heart of her peoples.
>
> Pope Francis, 2016

A devout Catholic mother had a son named Joe. She called him Joe up until the day he was ordained a priest. From then on, she always called him "Father," or "Father Joe," as if with ordination he had been transformed into another entity altogether, not one of the ordinary faithful but extraordinary, separate and above them. The church's teaching about priesthood does talk about the sacrament of holy orders bringing about an indelible mark that sets a man apart forever. That creates quite a bit of pressure on flawed, flesh-and-blood persons who become priests. "Be perfect as your heavenly Father is perfect" is a message from Jesus for all who believe in him, but that command has particular implications for priests. For one, priests in the Western church make a promise to be celibate, abstaining from marriage and having sexual relations. That could imply that any sexual attraction a priest might have for a woman or another man can be viewed as an imperfection. Shouldn't priests be asexual? Catholic laypeople often believe that priests have renounced not only the possibility of marriage but also their sexuality, and often priests expect the same of themselves.

In Catholicism, priests are men set apart. At least in formal settings, they wear distinctive garb that identifies them not as just another person but as someone special. They bear the title "Father" or "Reverend." They are not expected to have office hours but are expected to be available at all times. They may have friends who are not priests, but only a few break through the barrier that keeps them from being "just one of the guys." People seek them out and expect them to have wise and consoling words for any occasion. It would be a great honor to have a priest visit a family for dinner or show up in a hospital room to pray for a sick parishioner. Just as this "set apart" existence is a challenge for priests themselves, so it is for laypeople who are often unsure about how to relate to them. Meanwhile, parish priests now often live alone, apart from other Catholics in their neighborhood. Their training for the priesthood typically takes place in a setting in which only other men who share the same aspirations live and study, making it a seedbed for a sense of separateness.

Pope Francis has named clericalism one of the great problems facing Catholicism today. In an August 23, 2018, article in the online magazine *Aleteia*, Kathleen N. Hattrup describes the problem: "Clericalism could be defined as a false or sycophantic respect and esteem for clergy. It lends to the persons of priests, in view of their clerical office, an excessive deference and acquiescence. In a clericalist culture, the clergy often stand above and aloof to their flocks, to which distance the faithful can respond in a childish spirit of obedience and false reverence." Vatican Council II referred to the church as "the people of God." All Catholics are called upon to be active participants in the work of the church. Pope Francis would point out that he is no more Catholic than the hairdresser who volunteers her time giving free hair care to women in a homeless shelter. For Francis, the opposite of clericalism is co-responsibility; all Catholics are called to advance the mission of the church. St. Paul's analogy of the church as a body made up of many different parts attests to that vision. Prior to Vatican Council II, the dominant attitude in Catholicism was that the real work of the church was to be done by priests and men and women in religious orders. Laypeople were to "pay, pray, and obey." That is, they were to support the work of ordained and vowed religious through their monetary contributions and prayers and then obey whatever their bishops and priests told them to do.

Pope Francis and other church leaders are not calling for an end to the priesthood. He calls clericalism a distortion of the priesthood. Therefore, he admonishes seminarians (training for the priesthood), priests, and laypeople to look upon the role of both priests and laypeople in a different light. In 2012 he recommended to seminarians that they travel by bike and that "it hurts me every time I see a priest or sister riding in a new car." He himself took the subway to work when he was an archbishop in Argentina. One practical step he has taken to counter clericalism at the highest level in the church is appointing a number of women to be consultants in the various departments (called ***dicasteries***) that oversee church governance at the Vatican. Now women will even be involved in selecting bishops. There are not that many priests in the world; there are a lot of lay Catholics. The church would have little impact if laypeople did not take it upon themselves to bear Christ in the world. Pope Francis has said, "From the beginning, the Christian community was characterized by many different forms of ministry." He has continued the message of Vatican Council II that all Catholics are to carry on the work of the church.

Following Vatican Council II, a group of Italian Catholic young people, inspired by the council and St. Francis of Assisi (who refused ordination to the priesthood for himself), formed the Community of Sant'Igidio, named after the church in Rome where they met. They committed themselves to work as laypeople in various endeavors aimed at making the world a better place. They worked for peace and interreligious dialogue as well as programs that help people who are poor or sick. In January 2020 they even brought leaders of warring factions in South Sudan to their church in Rome and helped to broker a peace treaty between them. The Catholic Worker Movement, begun by a laywoman and man, has been a model for service to people in need in the United States.

Many individual lay Catholics have found comfort and courage in their Catholic faith. For instance, a young Catholic poet named Amanda Gorman read a stirring poem at the presidential inauguration in January 2021. Catholic gymnast Simone Biles transfixed the world with gymnastic performances that no one else had ever achieved. Two basketball greats, Michael Jordan and Kobe Bryant, came from Catholic backgrounds, and the morning before Bryant and his daughter died in a helicopter crash in 2020, they attended Mass at his local church. Lebron James attended a Catholic high school before going on to a stellar NBA career, and the great Bill Russell attended the Catholic University of San Francisco when other colleges offered him no scholarship despite his obvious talent. In 2021, six of nine Supreme Court justices were Catholic.

The Catholic faith has given birth to organizations specifically designed to meet basic human needs. The Kensington section of Philadelphia is rife with illegal drug use, poverty, and homelessness, but three safe havens can be found on one street: St. Francis Inn, founded by Franciscan priests and brothers, offers meals to people who are homeless. House of Grace, a Catholic Worker house, provides free medical care and showers. Marie's closet, a thrift store, makes available clothing items for free. All of these places are run primarily by women volunteers, and the college students who volunteer to help out are practically all women. Except for the Franciscan friars and brothers who sponsor St. Francis Inn, none of the volunteers are ordained or represent the church officially, and yet all of them are inspired by their Catholic faith to engage in this good work.

In a 2018 "Letter to the People of God," Pope Francis wrote, "To say no to abuse is to say an emphatic no to all forms of clericalism." Read more about clericalism in the Catholic Church. Discuss how the priestly function can be carried out in the church without the negatives associated with clericalism.

How are priests portrayed on television, in films, and in other media? Do such portrayals support clericalism? Give examples.

Read about and report on Catholics in the world today who are inspired by their faith to make a difference in the world.

Amanda Gorman's inaugural poem, "The Hill We Climb," expresses a message that can apply to Catholicism today as well as to the United States:

So let us leave a country better than the one we were left.
With every breath from our bronze-pounded chest,
We will raise this bruised world into a wondrous one.

Read about other contemporary Catholic writers and artists and discuss how Catholicism influenced their art. (For instance, the writer Toni Morrison, who converted to Catholicism at age twelve and took her name from St. Anthony of Padua, described Christ's crucifixion as the lynching of an innocent man and did not shy away from writing about cruelty experienced by characters in her novels.)

It is not the Church's role to organize every action of the people but rather to encourage, walk with, and support those who carry out these roles.

Pope Francis (*Let Us Dream*, p. 122)

III. What Does Catholicism Offer Today?

Roots and Wings

> A living faith draws strength from remembering the past while continuing to grow in love of God and service to others. ... Go to the roots, get nourishment there and move forward.
>
> Pope Francis, General Audience, September 22, 2021

A tree without a strong root system may show flashes of life, but it soon withers and dies. Roots that do not receive fresh water and nutrients do not flourish. As Pope Francis observes, a living faith draws strength from the past while continuing to grow in love to God and service to others. The rapid pace of change in today's world can leave people feeling displaced and alienated; the familiar dissolves without our even noticing it. Catholicism is based on memory, which contains within it a message for today and hope for the future. Jesus's words "Do this in memory of me" refer to more than just the breaking of bread in the Eucharist but to his life, death, and resurrection as well. Catholicism offers a connection to this past so that people can have a sense of place rather than feeling displaced, an experience of family when so much is becoming more and more unfamiliar, a taste of home now and in the future.

When discussing the unsettling changes taking place today, British Dominican priest Timothy Radcliffe cites a sociologist who uses the term *root shock*. (See his 2005 *What is the Point of Being a Christian?*) Signs of root shock are all around us. What was a cornfield not too long ago is now a big box store surrounded by a large parking lot that looks exactly like every other such store throughout the country. Once thriving commercial centers of small towns are now home to second-hand stores, take-out pizzerias, and tattoo parlors. Too often the only people who gather in these downtowns are young people hanging out and turning to dangerous drugs to dull the pain of their restlessness and lack of connection to a grander story or deeper meaning to life. Catholicism is not immune from the uprooting taking place in the culture at large. As far back as 1949, E. B. White wrote about the dangers of creeping materialism associated with Christmas in America: "To perceive Christmas through its wrappings becomes more difficult with every year." He reminded his readers at the time that it is more and more challenging "to hear the incredibly distant sound of Christmas in these times, through the material woods that surround it." And he was writing before Elf on the Shelf and the endless lineup of syrupy Christmas movies shown each year. What could be more inspiring and hopeful than the birth of Christ? But its meaning is becoming a distant sound, muffled in the clatter surrounding Christmas that is more and more overpowering with each passing year.

Along with material changes has come what philosopher Thomas Kuhn calls a *paradigm shift*, a fundamental change in one's assumptions and perspectives. Even when people engage in time-honored celebrations and practices, those practices don't have the power and meaning they once had. Christmas and Easter are still on the calendar; priests and nuns continue to serve the church, although in decreasing numbers; churches still dot the landscape. However, in less than half a century there has been a shift in how people perceive these elements of Catholicism. That's part of a paradigm shift that Catholics, and all people today, must grapple with. There is talk in the church of the need for a "new evangelization," new ways to spread the good news. Schools and parishes run retreat programs for young people, offering them an opportunity to experience Christ in a personal way that they've never had before. Parishes are also trying different programs to renew and revitalize Catholic life. Dioceses run "theology on tap" programs, where people gather in an informal setting away from a church to discuss religious questions.

Pope Francis lays out a model of Catholicism that gets nourishment from its roots and goes forward from there, incorporating new insights and responding to new challenges. He recognizes that we live in a time of crisis when "your categories and ways of thinking get shaken up; your priorities and lifestyles are challenged. ... The basic rule of a crisis is that you don't come out of it the same. If you get through it, you come out better or worse, but never the same" (*Let Us Dream*, p. 1). In the face of the crises we face, he decries indifference, what he calls "so-whatism," that excuses people from taking the steps necessary to help make the world come out better. In our understanding of ourselves, our world, and our God, we need to leave room for surprises.

If you were to design a program that blended Catholic roots and wings, what would it look like?

In the October 2021 issue of *America* magazine, its editor wrote, "We should always heed the words of the Lord and 'be not afraid' to talk about challenging questions and how they affect our faith lives" (p. 3). What challenging questions do you have about Catholicism at this time?

A Bulwark against Secularism

Today, in Europe, it is more important than ever to emphasize the spiritual and religious dimension of human life. In a society increasingly marked by secularism and threatened by atheism, we run the risk of living as if God did not exist. ... It is so important to remember, however, that our life is a gift from God, and that we must depend on him, confide in him, and turn towards him always. ... God is holy, and the life he has given is holy and inviolable.

Pope Francis, meeting with a delegation from the
Conference of European Rabbis, 2015

Have you ever seen the face of a child who has made you a special gift and looks on excitedly as you open it, hoping that you will love it as much as he or she does? That is the state of Catholicism today. It sees itself as being a herald of a great gift, the love of God in Christ Jesus, but it finds that most people are indifferent to the gift. Part of that indifference lies in the spirit of the age, secularism—a concept addressed at the beginning of this book. A trend that accompanied the changes in the mindset at the time of the Reformation and later the Enlightenment was *iconoclasm*. The word means "smashing icons/images." It refers to tearing down beliefs, persons, institutions, and things once held sacred. An American flag, even one that is threadbare, is not supposed to be thrown in the trash. The flag is something of a sacred icon for Americans. Jews have rushed into burning synagogues to save their Torah scroll, and Catholics consume all remaining eucharistic bread when churches are under threat of attack.

Some icons become idols and deserve to be taken down from their pedestal, whether they are objects, persons, or beliefs. Secularism dismisses everything and everyone holy, creating a completely desacralized world. Catholicism, on the other hand, proclaims that holiness surrounds us. Pope Francis ends his 2020 encyclical *Fratelli Tutti* with "An Ecumenical Christian Prayer" that calls Catholics to hold fast to a recognition of the sacredness of the world and its people:

> Grant that we Christians may live the Gospel,
> discovering Christ in each human being,
> recognizing him crucified
> in the sufferings of the abandoned
> and forgotten of our world,
> and risen in each brother or sister
> who makes a new start.
>
> Come, Holy Spirit, show us your beauty,
> reflected in all the peoples of the earth,
> so that we may discover anew
> that all are important and all are necessary,
> different faces of the one humanity
> that God so loves. Amen.

Assess the impact of a secular worldview on your own worldview.

Discuss signs of secularism present in the world today.

Read the lyrics of Bob Dylan's 1979 song, "Gotta Serve Somebody." What is its message? Do you agree with its message? Add a stanza of your own to the song.

The Common Good

> The US repeatedly ranks as the most individualistic country in the world.
>
> University of Virginia Researchers, 2020

Being at the same time Catholic and American understandably would leave someone torn. America prizes individualism; people should succeed or fail through their own efforts. Meanwhile, income inequality in the United States is the worst of any similar nation, and indications are that it has been getting steadily worse. At least part of the blame for the rampant poverty in the United States and the world is the result of systems that favor the rich over the poor. It's not that rich people work harder or better than poor people. The price of America's emphasis on individualism is that most people are left behind, and a sense of social cohesiveness gets lost. An overemphasis on individualism results in a spirit of "us against them." Pope Francis refers to this attitude of individualism as "the myth of self-sufficiency, that whispering in our ears that the earth exists to be plundered; that others exist to meet our needs; that what we have earned or what we lack is what we deserve; that my reward is riches, even if that means that the fate of others will be poverty" (*Let Us Dream*, p. 14).

Catholicism has a longstanding tradition of another point of view— the ***common good***; we are all in this together, and we should all work together. In 1986, the United States Conference of Catholic Bishops wrote that a society is judged by how the least among us are doing (*Economic Justice for All*). As a community and an institution, the Catholic Church is not confined to one nation or culture. Universality lies at the heart of what the word *catholic* means. Catholics are called upon to care for family members, the one human family, people in need in all parts of the globe. In the midst of the COVID-19 crisis and the environmental crisis, Pope Francis described how important a common good perspective is: "For a long time we carried on thinking we could be healthy in a world that was sick. But the crisis has brought home how important it is to work for a healthy world" (*Let Us Dream*, p. 30). It is a tragedy that so many people at home and abroad do not have the resources or the opportunity to contribute to the great human adventure of sustaining the world as our common home and caring for one another. Here again, Pope Francis calls for people on the margins of wealth and power to gain power and take on a central role in transforming the world: "When I speak of change I don't just mean that we have to take better care of this or that group of people. I mean that those people who are now on the edges become the protagonists of social change" (*Let Us Dream*, p. 18).

Concern for the common good is not communism or socialism, although Catholic statements about economic issues have been labeled that for over one hundred years. On the other hand, it is a far cry from an individualistic mindset. Pope Francis describes the Catholic dream that appears to be at odds with the American dream. He uses the word *fraternity* to describe the common good. His entire encyclical *Fratelli Tutti* is an examination of this most Catholic of concepts:

> Here we have a splendid secret that shows us how to dream and to turn our life into a wonderful adventure. No one can face life in isolation. ... We need a community that supports and helps us, in which we can help one another to keep looking ahead. How important it is to dream together. ... By ourselves, we risk seeing mirages, things that are not there. Dreams, on the other hand, are built together. Let us dream, then, as a single human family, as fellow travelers sharing the same flesh, as children of the same earth which is our common home, each of us bringing the richness of his or her beliefs and convictions, each of us with his or her own voice, brothers and sisters all. (#8)

Do you find that Americans value individual freedoms and initiatives over interdependence? Explain.

Read about individualism. Discuss whether an individualistic mindset is detrimental or helpful to a society. Which is the more hopeful and more realistic mindset: an emphasis on individualism or the common good? Is a balance possible?

Research the state of income inequality in the United States today. Discuss the following questions: What are the causes of the inequality? Does a large income gap lead to increases in poverty?

Is Catholicism's emphasis on the common good at odds with dominant American values? Is the "dream" that Pope Francis talks about different from the American dream? Explain.

Read through the encyclical *Fratelli Tutti*, available on the Vatican website (www.vatican.va). Discuss how certain passages can be applied to social, economic, and governmental programs and community life in general.

The Good News of Jesus Christ

Who made us?

God made us.

Who is God?

> God is the Supreme Being, infinitely perfect, who made all things and keeps them in existence.

Why did God make us?

> God made us to show forth His goodness and to share with us His everlasting happiness in heaven.

What must we do to gain the happiness of heaven?

> To gain the happiness of heaven we must know, love, and serve God in this world.

From whom do we learn to know, love, and serve God?

> We learn to know, love, and serve God from Jesus Christ, the Son of God, who teaches us through the Catholic Church.

> *The New Baltimore Catechism Number 2,*
> Official Revised Edition, 1953

In 1885 a priest was given the task of creating a standard summary of Catholic teachings for American Catholics in a simple question-and-answer format. He used existing catechisms as the basis for his, and it became known as the Baltimore Catechism. This catechism became the standard instrument for teaching the basics of Catholicism in the United States up until the 1960s.

The first five questions, listed above from a 1953 edition, state the core Catholic teaching that human beings were made for happiness. Human beings are meant to spread happiness throughout the world and can look forward to eternal happiness that transcends death. The basis of human happiness lies in the life, death, and resurrection of Jesus, who is proclaimed through the Catholic Church. Serving God through serving others is the way to happiness and the way to make God present in the world. The Catholic Church exists to spread this good news. That basic message found in the Baltimore Catechism continues to be expressed by church leaders today. In his General Audience of September 22, 2021, Pope Francis said, "Our life should be like this: to worship, to pray, to journey, to be a pilgrim, to do penance. ... The healing answer comes from prayer, witness and humble love. The humble love that serves. Let us reiterate this idea: the Christian is to serve." Catholics hear that message every time they attend Mass, which usually ends with the words "Go in peace, to love and serve the Lord." In other words, the question Catholicism answers is not "Who are you?" but "Whose are you?" Catholics belong to the Lord who became flesh; to serve the Lord in his many embodied manifestations leads to ultimate joy.

The happiness that comes from the Christian call to serve is not all sweetness and light. The world is a dangerous place; the needs of the planet are so great. Many Catholics who have given their lives to serve have undergone great suffering. For instance, during the Korean War, a priest raised on a Kansas farm decided to serve as a military chaplain. Father Emil Kapaun received a bronze star for his selfless service to wounded soldiers, and late in 1950 he ended up in a North Korean prisoner of war camp. There he continued to serve both the physical and spiritual needs of the other prisoners, caring for the sick and lifting everyone's spirits with his humor and prayers. After seven months in the camp, he developed pneumonia and a blood clot. His captors used the occasion to take him to the "hospital," which everyone knew was simply a place where the sick were left to die. When his fellow prisoners were released, they kept alive his story of bravery and compassion. In 2013, President Barack Obama, who also has family ties to Kansas, signed legislation so that Fr. Kapaun could receive a posthumous Medal of Honor. In 2021, his remains were identified and brought back to Kansas. He has been officially named a Servant of God, a step on the way to sainthood.

Another American being considered for canonization as an official saint is Julia Greeley, known as Denver's Angel of Charity. Born into slavery, her right eye was destroyed by an overseer's whip while he was beating her mother. After emancipation, Julia made her way to Denver, where she worked as a servant in the homes of wealthy white people. She spent her free time helping poor families in the area, often doing so at night to avoid embarrassing the people she helped. She joined the Catholic Church in 1880 and used her parish as the home base for her charitable work, as well as for spreading the message of the Sacred Heart of Jesus, until her death in 1918. Devotion to the Sacred Heart became popular in Catholicism beginning in the late 1600s. The image is of the heart of Jesus, surrounded by a crown of thorns, with rays spreading out from it. The image illustrates the great love Jesus has for all humanity and the rays of grace that emanate from his sacrifice on the cross. Julia Greeley was one embodiment of that grace.

Discuss: The world would be better off without Catholicism.

If you were to replace Catholicism with something else, what would that "something else" be?

Look back through this book. Write about a few concepts, persons, or passages you encountered that can help you in your own spiritual quest. Explain why.

A Cloud of Witnesses

Therefore, since we are surrounded by so great a cloud of witnesses, let us also lay aside every weight and the sin that clings so closely, and let us run with perseverance the race that is set before us, looking to Jesus the pioneer and perfecter of our faith.

Hebrews 12:1–2

The world today can be a confusing and discomforting place. Preconceived notions are being shaken at their foundations. Do I refer to individual persons as "he," "she," or "they"? Can doctors, scientists, priests, and the police be trusted? Are we close to the doomsday scenario climate scientists are warning us about? Can the results of nationwide elections ever be fair, and is democracy a sham? Should we celebrate Columbus Day and wish strangers "Merry Christmas"? With the pressures they face, are families too often stressful and even toxic environments? Are we in charge of the technology that inundates our lives, or is technology transforming us in ways we are unaware of? Is the United States still a shining city on a hill, a melting pot of people from many cultures who share common ideals and purpose? Is a religion such as Catholicism the source of more harm than good?

What does a Catholic worldview offer in the face of all the daunting questions and uncertainties that accompany life today? Catholics see themselves as part of the "cloud of witnesses," people who espouse faith, hope, and love as hallmarks of the human enterprise. At times, they carry on in the face of despair and in the realization of their seeming helplessness—some of the greatest saints have done so. (St. Teresa of Calcutta, who set as her life's work ministering to people dying in gutters, nonetheless endured personal doubts and questions.) The hope of Catholics lies ultimately in Jesus, "who for the sake of the joy that was set before him endured the cross, disregarding its shame, and has taken his seat at the right hand of the throne of God" (Hebrews 12:2). Catholicism sees in Jesus the perfect articulation that the human and all creation are holy. Despite personal anxieties and global challenges, God is as close to us as our breath, as intimate as our heartbeat. Catholicism proclaims Jesus as the "bright morning star" who beckons, "Let everyone who is thirsty come. Let anyone who wishes take the water of life as a gift" (Revelation 22:17).

Chapter Review

1. Give examples to illustrate why Pope Francis is called a pope from the periphery.
2. What is *nativism*? How was it manifest in American history?
3. What was the message of Pope Francis about nature in the homily of his first public Mass as pope and in his encyclical on the environment?
4. What is the Catholic attitude toward science?
5. What was the attitude toward other religions expressed at Vatican Council II?
6. Give examples of how recent popes modeled this attitude toward other religions.
7. Who was Louis Massignon, and how did he apply Incarnation to the world of his day?
8. Why were bishops criticized early on for their handling of clerical sexual abuse?
9. What was the message of Pope Francis to church leaders about victims of abuse by priests and other church workers?
10. What is *clericalism*?

11. What is Pope Francis' message about clericalism?
12. What are the origins and purpose of the Community of Sant'Igidio?
13. What does it mean to say that Catholicism must cultivate roots and wings?
14. To what does the term *root shock* refer?
15. Define the term *paradigm shift*.
16. What is the attitude of secularism toward people and the world?
17. Define *iconoclasm*.
18. Explain the difference between individualism and an emphasis on the common good.
19. What is the Baltimore Catechism?
20. What is the source of happiness in Catholicism?
21. Who were Father Emil Kapaun and Julia Greeley?
22. What does it mean to say that Catholics are part of a "cloud of witnesses"?

For Further Study

Matthew Bowman. *Christian: The Politics of a Word in America* (Harvard University Press, 2018). Traces how some people have come to identify Christianity exclusively with the Protestant Reformation, Western civilization, and especially socially conservative Americans. Such people fight against non-Western immigrants, minority groups, secularists, and others they see as threatening "Christianity" and "Western civilization."

Pierre Teilhard de Chardin and Ursula King. *Pierre Teilhard De Chardin: Writings* (Modern Spiritual Masters Series). Orbis Books, 1991. A Jesuit priest and paleontologist combines his Catholic faith with scientific knowledge to offer new insights into Christ's presence in the universe. Teilhard is the leading voice recognizing the spiritual underlying scientific discoveries and calling for religions such as Catholicism to take modern science seriously.

W. E. B. Du Bois. *The Gift of Black Folk: The Negroes in the Making of America*. Martino Fine Books, 2021. Concerned about nativist sentiments in the 1920s that looked down on members of minority groups, many of whom were Catholic, a prominent Catholic lay organization sponsored a series of books that extolled the contributions of various minority groups to America. The first in the series was this book by the most distinguished African-American scholar of the time.

Pope Francis and Austen Ivereigh. *Let Us Dream: The Path to a Better Future*. Simon & Schuster, 2020. A journalist interviews Pope Francis amid the COVID and climate crises facing the world. Pope Francis identifies actions and attitudes that bring hope when facing crisis.

Pope Francis. *Fratelli Tutti* ("On Fraternity and Social Friendship"). Our Sunday Visitor Publishing, 2020. An encyclical letter from Pope Francis in which he addresses social and political problems in the world today. Calls for openness, dialogue, and friendship among all people to save the world.

Joe Holland. *Roman Catholic Clericalism: Three Historical Stages in the Legislation of a Non-Evangelical, Now Dysfunctional, and Sometimes Pathological Institution*. Pacem in Terris Press, 2018. A short book, sixty-seven pages, that points out that the clerical state was constructed by legislation, first by Emperor Constantine, and is not the same as the servant leadership of priesthood called for by Jesus. Holland suggests that clericalism must be eliminated if the Catholic Church is to survive and thrive but that changes must take place cautiously and slowly.

Thomas G. Plante and Kathleen McChesney, eds. *Sexual Abuse in the Catholic Church: A Decade of Crisis, 2002–2012*. Praeger, 2011. A collection of essays by leading experts on the topic of priestly sexual abuse of minors. Represents multiple points of view, from professionals to members of the clergy to victims.

Timothy Radcliffe, OP. *What Is the Point of Being a Christian?* Burns & Oates, 2006. A British Dominican priest explores what it means to be Christian in today's world.

Leonard Swidler. *Authentic Humanity: The Human Quest for Reality and Truth* (Big Little Books). iPub Cloud International, 2020. Affirms the need for dialogue among people from different cultures and backgrounds as an essential component of making a better future. Describes elements of authentic dialogue.

Acknowledgements

I would like to thank my wife, Mary, John Bohrer, and Frank Champine, who constantly offered suggestions and feedback during the writing of this book. Fr. James MacNew, OSFS, former campus minister at Holy Family University, saw a need for this book and read portions of it with enthusiasm.

Thank you to my daughter-in-law Shannon Fitzgerald for the photo of her nephew, Aidan, greeting the sunrise in Cape May, NJ.

Thank you to Ann Marie Bahr, Ph. D., for her close read of the text and for identifying some needed clarifications and to Philip Cunningham, Ph. D., Director of the Institute for Catholic-Jewish Relations at St. Joseph's University, for sharing his knowledge of developments in early Christian history. I am grateful to those who read the manuscript and offered reviews for the book.

Finally, I wish to thank all those at iPub Cloud International who were always supportive and encouraging. I am grateful to Sandi Billingslea for her probing questions about this project, to Sandy Mayer, publishing director, for guiding me in setting up a website, JosephStoutzenberger.com, where I can post journal entries related to themes in the book, and to Elyse Draper, marketing manager, who designed and continues to oversee the website. I'd also like to thank the editorial team, especially Henry Whitney, editor, who worked diligently to bring the book to print, and Jessica DiDonato and Jennifer Wyman, production coordinators, for guiding the book to completion. They indulged me by allowing personal touches to be included in the text.

About the Author

Joseph Stoutzenberger, Ph.D., is Professor Emeritus of Religious Studies at Holy Family University, Philadelphia, PA. Most recently, he has written on St. Francis of Assisi, including *Looking to St. Francis: The Man from Assisi and His Message of Hope for Today* (coauthor) and *Singing with Crickets: Meditations on Francis of Assisi and Nature*. He is the author of *Celebrating Sacraments*, a text for high school students, and *The Human Quest for God: An Overview of World Religions*.

Meet iPub Cloud International

At iPub Cloud International, our mission is steadfast: to be a beacon for brilliant minds seeking to share their journeys towards a brighter tomorrow. We believe in the transformative power of storytelling and the profound impact it can have on inspiring social change and contributing to the betterment of society.

Our goal is to foster a culture of enlightenment and progress, where voices advocating for positive change can be heard and amplified. We are more than a publishing company; we are a community of thinkers, dreamers, and change-makers, united in our quest to create a world enriched by knowledge, understanding, and compassion.

Join us as we continue to champion the stories that need to be told, the ideas that provoke thought, and the visions that pave the way for a better future.

iPub Cloud International, LLC
www.iPubCloud.org
Poughkeepsie, NY 12603
info@iPubCloud.org

Come and visit our website to stay up to date on your favorite writers and subscribe for news on new releases, events, and promotions. www.iPubCloud.org. Join the conversation at Facebook.com/iPub-Cloud.org.

Join our community at iPubForum.com.

Publisher's Acknowledgements

This book was published with special thanks to:
- Ann Marie Bahr
- Frank Champine
- Vincent O'Malley
- Rob Robinson
- Esther Elizabeth Suson
- Henry Whitney

We are grateful for your contributions.

You may share your support for this book by publishing a review and sharing with your friends and family:

www.iPubCloud.org.

For a free copy of *The Dialogue Decalogue* by Professor Leonard Swidler, please scan the QR code below.

www.ingramcontent.com/pod-product-compliance
Lightning Source LLC
Chambersburg PA
CBHW011949150426
43194CB00019B/2851